The Consolations of Economics

Gerard Lyons is an expert on the world economy, macro-economic policy and financial markets. He is widely credited with accurate forecasts before the financial crisis, and has regularly topped forecasting polls. He has testified to the US Senate and to US Congress, spoken at the EU–China Summit in Beijing, and at the IMF and other global meetings. He has been a regular on international TV and written press columns across the globe. He is married with three children and lives in Kent.

Further praise for *The Consolations of Economics*:

'Gerard Lyons is a wise and thoughtful observer, and analyst of the world economy. He has worked through five financial crises. His assessment of where the world may go is of great value . . . This is a very important book.'
Professor Lord Nicholas Stern, President of the British Academy

'Gerard Lyons's solid and convincingly optimistic perspective is a welcome counterpoint to the narrow concerns about the overall decline of the West.'
Hamish McRae, *Independent*

'Gerard Lyons is an unusual character: a serious economist who can explain the world in language that the rest of us can understand, and who is more interested in public policy than he is in abstract theory. He is also an optimist, which is especially attractive at a moment when the fashion is for gloom.'
Sir Richard Lambert, former Director-General

'His assessment of the economic state of affairs is more considered and less visceral than is typically found in books on this subject. It is refreshing to encounter a book from such a respected authority that takes a more upbeat view.'
Iain Morris, *Observer*

'As an economist, Gerard Lyons has two trump cards: he allies careful and deep analysis with a first-hand understanding of how the world works. His world view is more rounded and realistic than most others on offer.'
Sir Howard Davies, former director of the LSE

'A significant book for both the general reader and the professional economist . . . Gerard Lyons is unusual in that he is a first-rate theorist, and also has vast knowledge of the real economic world. He is the ideal author for such a volume, and has succeeded admirably.'
Professor Lord Maurice Peston, Emeritus Professor of Economics, Queen Mary, University of London

'An economist that the financial world has listened to for his evidence-based analysis, his sound judgement and great understanding.'
William R. Rhodes, author of *Banker to the World*

'Gerard Lyons has a great ability to combine rigorous economics with wide-ranging knowledge of how business works and a truly global perspective. He uses his skills and understanding well to weave an optimistic but thought-provoking overview of a changing world.'
Lord Adair Turner, Former Chairman, Financial Services Authority

'Gerard Lyons is one of the very few that has truly tried to understand the complex evolving world – this adds to the importance of people reading his book.'
Jim O'Neill, Former Chairman of Goldman Sachs Asset Management

'Gerard offers us a tantalising, upbeat tale of how the world economy's most vibrant days are ahead. The four growth drivers he cites are compelling, but portend dramatic shifts in the current geopolitical landscape.'
Tim Adams, Managing Director of the Institute for International Affairs and former Under Secretary of the US Treasury for International Affairs

The Consolations of Economics

Good News in the Wake
of the Financial Crisis

GERARD LYONS

FABER & FABER

First published in 2014
by Faber and Faber Limited
Bloomsbury House
74–77 Great Russell Street
London WC1B 3DA
This paperback edition published in 2015

Typeset by Agnesi Text
Printed in the UK by CPI Group (UK) Ltd, Croydon, CR0 4YY

A CIP record for this book
is available from the British Library

ISBN 978–0–571–30779–1

FSC
www.fsc.org
MIX
Paper from
responsible sources
FSC® C101712

2 4 6 8 10 9 7 5 3 1

To my wife Annette
and to my three children,
Emily-Anne ('Elf')
Marie-Louise Kezia ('Lulu')
and
Gerard Benedict Alfred Francis

Contents

Introduction

You are driving a car through beautiful countryside. There are trees and hills around you and the road ahead is straight. The weather is great; the car has an open top; the sun is shining. You are feeling good about the world. You put your foot down. The road dips and there are a few bumps but you don't take your foot off the accelerator. Why should you? After all, you're a great driver. The road starts to bend, gradually at first, then more sharply. What was a straight road is now a zigzag.

It looks dangerous but it seems easy to you as you swing round the hairpin bends. You relax a little too much, gazing in the rearview mirror, admiring the scenery behind you, letting your mind wander, oblivious to what lies ahead. You are not concentrating. Still you don't slow down. Now it is getting really dangerous.

More by luck than judgement you manage to keep the car on the road. The trouble is, you are not half the driver you think you are and the more you ask of the car the less it seems to respond. A crash is inevitable. The only question is when.

The 2008 financial crisis was like this. Beforehand, traders and investors were behaving like this driver. Some were behaving even more recklessly, as if they were driving blindfolded, buying and selling things such as collateralised debt obligations that they knew next to nothing about.

The 2008 financial crash left a big mess. The survivors sat by the side of the road waiting for someone to come along to sort it out. At the time, some observers thought they should be left there as a lesson to others, but the authorities decided to help them, fearing the consequences for everyone else if they didn't.

The survivors then saw something that they hadn't expected. Coming along the same stretch of road were a lot of new cars, from other parts of the world. They had to slow down sharply as a result of the crash but once they had safely navigated the scene they moved on, at a controlled speed, with some cars going faster and being driven more skilfully than the others.

The year 2008 was pivotal for the world economy and it is the starting point for the argument of this book. It was pivotal because it cast doubt on the economic model in the West and exposed deep flaws within our financial system. Much has been done since to make everything safer and more secure, although the fear of another financial crash remains. The year 2008 also highlighted the changing shape of the world economy and the emergence of new economic engines and motors of growth. It is the combination of these new ways of achieving global growth and the right economic lessons being learned by the West that should imbue us with confidence.

The years since the financial crisis of 2008 have revealed a divided and disconnected world economy that faces major policy dilemmas. The divisions are evident in the different growth rates between the East and West and between the periphery and the core of Europe. The imbalance is evident in high rates of youth unemployment in many Western economies and across large parts of Africa. It is also apparent in a squeeze in living standards in a number of countries, while, at the same time, a global elite is flourishing. In Western economies, dilemmas have included how to use policy to restore growth without triggering widespread panic because of high levels of debt and the unintended consequences of record-low interest rates.

Success has also brought challenges, such as how to channel global savings into financing future investment, or how to ensure that the many economies that have done well proceed with economic reform rather than take recent growth for granted. Even in the aftermath of the 2008 crash, the world economy has continued to grow. How can it be that a world economy so divided and disconnected and facing such dilemmas is still growing?

Policy plays an important role, as some of the post-crisis growth has been boosted by a combination of higher debt and increased leverage across the globe and ultra loose monetary policy in Western economies. This requires a focus on future exit strategies from low interest rates in the West and the correct approach globally for future economic policy. But it is not just policy. The outlook in any economy depends on the interaction between the fundamentals, policy and confidence, and the fundamentals are improving globally and confidence is recovering.

Reasons to be positive

There are many reasons to be positive about what lies ahead and how things are likely to play out. Hence this book's title: *The Consolations of Economics*. Once we come to grips with what is driving the world economy, we might begin to see solutions to our economic challenges – and great opportunities.

I wanted to write this book to challenge some misconceptions: that the West would suffer in the new world economy; that the East, or the new growth or emerging economies would always do well, and that we should be cautious about the global outlook. I felt this was far from the truth.

It is often suggested that the West will lose out in the future. But here it is vital to differentiate between relative and absolute. In relative terms, many Western economies might lose out, but in absolute terms they will still do well. This means that in terms of the global economic cake, the slice that goes to the West might be smaller, but there will be much more cake than before.

Here I outline that the trend for emerging economies is up, but that they will have setbacks along the way. In many respects the financial market volatility of mid-2013 and early 2014 reflected this, as many emerging economies were at the stage of the economic cycle where a pause for breath was needed, to prevent inflation or trade challenges from re-emerging, or to address credit growth. The business cycle exists in the East, as it does in the West, and it is important that inevitable setbacks do not divert attention from the strong, positive, underlying upward trend across many emerging economies.

The key message is that the world might be set to enjoy one of its most exciting periods of growth ever in coming decades. The size of the global economic cake will increase.

If so, there will be an explosion of activity across the emerging world and an economic renaissance in the US. It is hard to be pessimistic about the US, given its innovation and ability to reinvent itself. This outlook implies a strong but more sustainable pace of growth in China, and regions such as Africa and India realising some, but not all, of their potential for growth. Even Europe will blossom in this success – provided it continues to make tough choices. It might seem surprising that this could be possible but, for all the challenges, there are also some extremely strong and positive economic developments in the offing. Many countries will continue to innovate and grow, and globally the economies that will succeed will have the cash, commodities or creativity.

Perspiration and inspiration

The key drivers of growth can be thought of as perspiration and inspiration: 'perspiration' as populations and workforces grow; 'inspiration' as investment and innovation occur, boosting productivity in the process. There is already evidence of new trade corridors, as more goods, commodities and people move around the world. There are more financial flows, as people working away from their own countries send money back home or people invest in markets overseas. These links will grow and flourish in a cat's cradle of mutually supportive transactions and pathways.

We are witnessing the growth of a wider and wealthier middle class across the globe, despite the squeeze on living standards in many Western economies during the recent recession. More people across the world are in a position to spend, to improve their homes, lives and leisure. The opportunities are boundless for businesses wanting to sell: more customers; more markets. Over the next few decades the middle class could swell to 5 billion people,* a staggering proportion of the world's population. Definitions of the 'middle class' vary considerably, as the numbers needed to fit into this category vary from country to country, but for our purposes it is people who can now exercise the choice to purchase discretionary items. A growing middle class is a motor of domestic consumption and can often be a trigger for policies that promote inclusive growth.

Increased urbanisation is already bringing more people out of poverty and leading to attractive cities that are cleaner, safer and more exciting to live in. Greater innovation and technical change mean increased opportunities for people of all ages across all continents. An infrastructure boom the likes of which has never been seen before has already begun.

Change can trigger uncertainty. However, this economic transformation should be relished, not feared. Yet, if the current economic climate sounds so good, why aren't more economists shouting about it from the rooftops? Perhaps because there was too much optimism before the crisis there might be a bias to too much caution now.

It would be wrong to dismiss the problems. There are risks. Many Western economies are coming out of the crisis in a fragile state, dependent for now on loose monetary policies and still high levels of debt, and financial markets are displaying the same characteristics seen before the crisis of not pricing properly for risk. It will take

---

* Research from the Brookings Institute shows the global middle class rising from 1.8 billion in 2009 to 3.2 billion in 2020 and 4.9 billion by 2030.

some time to return to health. Across the emerging world, meanwhile, policies need to evolve and reform agendas need to be pursued. Despite this, there is a danger of overlooking the pace and scale of current change and the potential for many economies across much of the globe to catch up in terms of economic size.

There are challenges, but they can trigger solutions. One challenge facing many Western economies is a lack of demand as those countries, firms and people with the ability to spend lack the confidence or desire to do so. There is pressure on those countries and individuals with debt to cut their coat according to their cloth. Meanwhile, across many emerging economies, there is a different set of challenges, not least the need for reform in order to address inflation, trade or potential asset bubbles in real estate and stock markets. Rising demand for food and resources is already leading to increased investment across the commodity-producing world.

The US, the UK and Europe have many lessons to learn as a result of the financial crisis, not least in terms of the financial sector, monetary and fiscal policy. These include the need to improve governance and to avoid economic policies that encourage and exaggerate the cycle of boom and bust. Such pro-cyclical policies make the current situation worse, not better.

This book sets out to answer some of the key economic questions of our time. What is happening to the world economy and driving its future? What does this mean for different parts of the world? What policies should governments put in place; what strategies should business focus on, and what does this mean for our individual daily lives? Should our personal outlook be positive or negative?

Four areas

I focus on four key areas that are vital for understanding the changing world economy: economic and financial power; soft power, which is effectively the power of persuasion; hard power, which is based on military strength and the ability to coerce; and political institutions and policy. When there is a shift in the balance of power, it would normally result in all these four areas changing in unison. This is not the case now – what is happening is far more complex.

The following chapters will deal with each in turn, since these four areas shift at different speeds. We can take encouragement from the fact that the complex interaction between the four indicates a growing global economy, with rising living standards, favouring multiple regions of the world and many different countries. The next century will not be China's. Nor will it be Africa's. It will be a global century, where many different parts of the world will do well. This new world order should offer more economic comfort and hope across the globe.

The outcome is likely to be win-win for the West and for the East: a multipolar world with a number of key economic players, and the end result being a bigger global economic cake.

1

Stopped clocks don't help you tell the time

It's often been said that everyone who was alive at the time could remember where they were when President Kennedy was shot, or when man first walked on the moon. Over the decades since there have been other momentous events, such as the fall of the Soviet Union, the opening up of China, and the Arab Spring. Who can forget where they were when the Berlin Wall was brought down or when the horrific terrorist events of 9/11 occurred? There have been other occasions that have caught media attention, such as the release of Nelson Mandela, or Live Aid in the mid-1980s, when huge concerts in London and Philadelphia focused attention on hunger in Africa, or the Boxing Day tsunami of 2004. And there have been moments that promised change, such as the election of Margaret Thatcher in Britain in May 1979 or President Obama's first presidential election victory in 2008.

In economics, such earth-shattering events are not so common. But they do occur. September 2008 is one example. A badly run investment bank, Lehman Brothers, went bust, and there was a meltdown across parts of the financial sector. It was *the* financial crisis and it led to pain and panic as the world economy virtually ground to a halt. In years to come, people might well recall how the 2008 crisis started to unfold.

The 2008 financial crisis is pivotal in many ways. It raised questions about the role of the financial sector, about economic policy, and also inequality and future growth prospects in Western economies. Is strong future growth sustainable? It might also be seen in years to come as the turning point in the shift in economic power from the West to the East. To understand this shift, we need to examine the way in which we look at the world economy. One way has been to compare countries, for instance the performance of the US compared with that of Japan, or Indonesia's against Brazil's. Increasingly, though, individual economies are being grouped together – but what these groupings are, or should be, is far from straightforward.

The Western economies are often called the 'advanced' or 'industrial' countries. These include North America, Western Europe, Japan and Australia. Countries in other parts of the world are split into emerging economies, which are moving away from rural growth and are industrialising, and the poorer, least-developed countries or LDCs, which struggle to mobilise the resources for industrialisation or higher sustained growth to take place.

The term 'emerging economy' has been around since the early 1980s and for a while it worked well as a description. But now, to many, it seems out of date and misleading. Who can seriously call Singapore an emerging economy, when it has one of the highest living standards in the world? Or even Chile? Santiago feels much like Geneva: it is clean, safe and efficient. The problem is that the term 'emerging market' is not applied only to those economies that fit the definition but too often is used haphazardly for any or all countries outside Western Europe, North America and Japan. There is a tendency, for simplicity, to continue to differentiate between countries in terms of West versus East.

The classifications of countries are far from clear. The term 'BRIC' or 'BRICS' has become more common, coined by the economist Jim O'Neill to mean Brazil, Russia, India and China, the four largest emerging economies, with South Africa now sometimes added. There are different variations on this, with other acronyms, or talk of the 'growth economies'.

One alternative is to refer to countries simply by region, especially as there might be a trend towards addressing issues on a regional basis. Geographical division is less likely to cause offence and it is easier for most people to understand. Flexibility is needed in the way countries are referred to. This is borne out by the way different countries across the globe view and have responded to the crisis. In New York, London and Berlin there is talk of *the* financial crisis. In Dubai, Mumbai and Shanghai it is referred to as a *Western* financial crisis, not a global one. The difference is not just in language, but also in action and performance.

Democracy brings accountability, not responsibility

One of the exciting aspects of the coming decades will be how economic systems across the world change. The combination of new social media, improved communication and technology, and an increasingly knowledge-driven economy should make us aware of best economic practice throughout the world, raising questions as to why some countries perform better than others. The post-war era saw extreme contrasts between repressive and open political regimes, pursuing vastly different economic models. The West's free-market system won out, but 2008 and the political reaction to it has raised legitimate questions about how that system operates. Does democracy bring accountability but not responsibility as vested-interest groups protect their domains, and as politicians take short-term approaches to seek re-election?

Increasing inequality of income in many Western economies, both before the crisis and since, has sparked concern about social cohesion. Often it can take a long time for economic problems to be addressed, and even when the right economic policies are in place it can take some time for positive results to be seen. Unfortunately both the public and politicians tend to be impatient for immediate solutions, but tackling the underlying economic issue, rather than finding a short-term answer, will always produce the best outcome.

In economic terms, the market mechanism usually works best. However, the public sector has a vital role to play in creating the right enabling environment, giving people and firms the opportunity to succeed. A number of successful economies are showing the role the state can play, both in strategic planning and in longer-term investment and infrastructure decisions. Singapore is a good example. At a global level, countries will not only be competing against one another, but will also find room for co-operation in their economic approaches, as many of them will be facing similar challenges.

Modern economics

Before we can understand the financial crisis and the new path it has led us down, we need to understand something of our economic history. To get a feel for now, it is necessary to look back. Modern economic history began towards the end of the eighteenth century. Its founding father, Adam Smith (1723–1790), lived in Scotland during the Scottish Enlightenment, and there is a statue of him today on the Royal Mile in Edinburgh. His two seminal works were *The Theory of Moral Sentiments* (published in 1759) and *The Wealth of Nations* (1776), the first modern economics book. Although one of the greatest thinkers of the time and the founder of economics, he was not eligible to vote in British elections as he did not own enough land.

It is hard to imagine that Smith, influential thinker as he was, in what was seen as enlightened times, did not have the right to vote. In the UK it was not until 1918 that the Representation of the People Act allowed men over twenty-one and women over thirty to vote, and women to become members of parliament. By 1928 anyone over twenty-one could vote, and the age was lowered to eighteen only in 1969. This should remind us how many of the things we take for granted in the West are quite recent and that it might be premature for us to pass judgement on other economies that are going through change now. Many economic activities, particularly those facilitated by now familiar technology, are likewise relatively new developments.

The end of the eighteenth century saw continuous change. It was the early stages of an industrial revolution that transformed Britain into the economic power of the day. It was also a period of great turmoil across Europe and elsewhere. Indeed, 1789 saw the French Revolution and George Washington elected as the first US president.

The opening lines of *A Tale of Two Cities* by Charles Dickens, written in 1859 and describing London and Paris in the wake of the French Revolution, also captures, to my mind, the mood not only of then but of the years following the recent financial crisis:

> It was the best of times, it was the worst of times, it was the age of wisdom, it was the age of foolishness, it was the epoch of belief, it was the epoch of incredulity, it was the season of Light, it was the season of Darkness, it was the spring of hope, it was the winter of despair, we had everything before us, we had nothing before us, we were all going direct to Heaven, we were all going direct the other way.

There are many such contrasts now, reminding us that what might appear new and unprecedented may have been experienced before.

Three major periods of modern history are relevant to our current situation. The first is the era described in *A Tale of Two Cities*: that of the first industrial revolution, usually referred to as *the* industrial revolution. It is relevant now not just because of the contrasts of that time but also because current technological advance might be a prelude to a new industrial revolution. I shall also consider the second industrial revolution at the end of the nineteenth century and the beginning of the twentieth, and the post-war 'golden era' of the mid- and late twentieth century.

The first industrial revolution

The first industrial revolution began in the UK around 1780 and lasted about seventy years until the middle of the nineteenth century. As now, it was a period of huge change: the pace of development seemed far in excess of expectation, and it triggered other changes, both in Britain and overseas. It ushered in many transformational developments, across a multitude of areas: new ideas, new innovation and new technology. A new way of living and of doing things. Britain led this revolution, benefiting from ample cheap energy in the form of coal and, just as importantly, from an age of reason in which ideas were freely exchanged.

Communication was also key in the transformations seen in the nineteenth century and has always played a vital role in economic development. The 1830s and 1840s saw what was called 'accelerated connection', with a great reduction in the speed and cost of transportation. The electric telegraph was invented in the 1830s, and by the 1850s there were attempts to connect the US and the UK, which after a few setbacks eventually led, in 1865, to Brunel's steamship SS *Great Eastern* laying the cable along the ocean bed, from Valentia in the west of Ireland to Heart's Content in Newfoundland. The first transatlantic phone call was made between Queen Victoria and President Buchanan in August 1858. In the foreign-exchange markets, the sterling–dollar exchange rate is still referred to by traders as 'cable' in reference to this Atlantic line. With communication today better than ever before, the future now looks bright in terms of the exchange of ideas and knowledge, and the speed of doing business.

The decline in transport costs also helped usher in mass migration, as Europe provided cheap labour for the new world of the Americas. Then transport was important for trade and migration; now it is both the speed and openness of communication that matter for trade and ideas. Information is exchanged and accessed more widely and quickly than ever before. Globalisation has also now increased the available labour force, of both skilled and unskilled (and therefore cheap) labour.

When the current problems with debt levels are considered, it is interesting to note that in Victorian Britain, as it was benefiting from economic growth, the idea was to keep politics out of economics in order to avoid short-term solutions that could lead to longer-term difficulties. From the 1840s to the 1860s the British political leaders Robert Peel and William Gladstone had the idea of an impartial state kept above competing economic interests. They implemented the balanced-budget convention that spending had to be matched by tax increases. They established the gold standard, which allowed the Bank of England operational independence, as sterling was fixed to a specific price in gold. Another idea was free trade, so that no group of producers could argue for political favour. While we might not want to adopt each of these policies in precisely the same form now, the underlying aim was a sensible one. I tend to the view that good economics is good politics, not the other way round, and solid economic rules mattered in the nineteenth century, as they should today. The lesson for today is to pursue sensible policies in the good times to provide both stability and the flexibility to cope with shocks in the bad times, and at the same time to ensure that the right institutions are in place.

The combination of the gold standard and free trade was seen as necessary to keep the UK competitive both at home and in international markets. When one also considers the philanthropy that was common at the time and the investment in infrastructure that was led by the private sector, it is clear that there is much that many countries, not just the present-day UK, could learn from the Victorians. Success breeds success, and others copied nineteenth-century Britain. It is important to bear that in mind now, particularly given the extent and speed of communication and transport links.

Perhaps we should think nowadays about having technocrats and experts, rather than politicians, running fiscal, infrastructure and trade policy, as they are able to think long-term. After all, much of monetary policy is already in the hands of specialists, although it is important for institutions to be accountable in a way that does not undermine their independence. There is a benefit in having experts in charge of specialised areas; politicians can lack expertise and be too focused on the short term.

This whole period in Europe was still a tough one. Again this is a lesson for today, as it should remind us that not all economies need to do well at the same time, as those with a competitive edge can gain an advantage over others, before they catch up. A slump in 1841–2 was followed by the 'Hungry Forties' in Europe, which foreshadowed the writing of the *Communist Manifesto* in 1848 by Karl Marx and Friedrich Engels, and there was continuing upheaval elsewhere. However, the strong growth that was to follow later in the nineteenth century, linked to the rise of America, Germany and Russia, could also hold lessons for us now.

The second industrial revolution

The second relevant period is 1870–1914: the second industrial revolution. This was the time when economic leadership started to pass from the UK to the US. The main driving force for the world economy then was the emergence of the US as an economic super-power. It went from being the fourth-largest to the largest economy in the world, and from accounting for 9 per cent of the global economy to 19 per cent.

Industrialisation and urbanisation were two of the key features of the US then, just as they are in China now. The US accounted for over a quarter of global growth during that time. That period also saw the adaptation and wider use of technologies from the original industrial revolution. As previously, there were other drivers, including technological innovation and improved communication. The world economy grew by an average 2.8 per cent per annum in real terms, adjusted for inflation – a significant pick-up from 1.8 per cent in the early part of the nineteenth century. But it is worth noting that industrialisation was also accompanied by protectionism for domestic industries against established industrial powers, something evident in China and East Asia at the present time.

It wasn't just America that did well. Other economies saw strong growth too. Russia was one; Germany another. Electrification benefited both the Russian and German economies, just as steam had powered the UK's rise a century earlier.

Roger Owen's analysis of how the eastern Mediterranean was affected at this time demonstrates how communication allowed economic progress to spread to many new regions:

> One index is the coming of telegraph lines to Salonika, Istanbul, Beirut and Alexandria, which not only further increased the speed of communication, but also permitted the eastern Mediterranean to participate in the real-time commodity markets for cottons, cereals and other primary products in Liverpool, Hamburg, London and New York.

Communication brought many benefits and increased trade; for instance, Egypt's trade increased in value by 200 per cent during this period. When growth happens and trade flourishes, many regions can benefit, as was seen then, and as will be evident now and in coming decades.

When it comes to periods of rapid growth, the challenge is how to sustain them. 'The trend is my friend' is a common belief in financial markets: those early to a trend can profit from it. Yet it can be seen to be a trend only after it has gone on for a while. Trends can reverse, and also they can trigger overconfidence. This was seen in the later part of the nineteenth century and is a salutary lesson for today.

Although growth was high in the second half of the nineteenth century, it was not a case of growth only ever moving upward. There was volatility, linked to credit cycles, bank failures and overinvestment. There was also excessive exuberance in many places, including London and Latin America.

America was not the only country seen as an attractive investment at the end of the nineteenth century. Surprising as it seems, one of the many debates in the City of London, then the centre of global finance, was which emerging country – Argentina or America – offered the better potential? Nowadays, when one considers the debate that sets the potential of India against the potential of China, one might ask which is the modern-day version of Argentina, and which America? If both economies learn the lessons of the past, it will be possible for both to prosper and succeed as America has done. If anywhere today is the modern-day version of the Argentina of the nineteenth century, it is the continent of Africa, with its agriculture and raw materials. Yet Africa, too, can learn from the past and avoid the mistakes Argentina made.

Argentina suffered a major financial crisis towards the end of the nineteenth century and has suffered repeated crises since. Initially, it was the result of the overexuberance that can arise when international investors become enthusiastic about a country and demand a slice of the action straight away. It was this that was to lead to the near-collapse of the City of London's oldest merchant bank, Barings. (This was the first Barings crisis; the second, 105 years later in 1995, saw the bank collapse as a result of the 'rogue trader' Nick Leeson.)

Latin America suffered in the world debt crisis of 1873, which marked a year of panic in financial markets across the globe. The trigger was the collapse of the Vienna stock market in May that year. That ushered in a period of economic difficulty for the global economy and even a short depression in the US. As for Argentina, by the early 1880s its recovery under president and war hero Julio Roca led to Buenos Aires being described as the 'Paris of South America', and investors bought into the Argentine story. Visiting Buenos Aires today still inspires a certain awe; how it must have felt then can only be imagined.

However, Argentina was borrowing too much and in foreign currency – an important lesson for countries today to take to heart and avoid. Foreign-currency borrowing is always a risk. Argentina had a current-account deficit of 20 per cent of its gross domestic product (GDP), an unsustainable situation reflecting the need for an unprecedented scale of capital inflows into the country to fund it. New debt was issued, inflation soared, the currency fell, and international investors dumped the bonds. Argentina defaulted on £48 million, representing 60 per cent of the world's defaulted debt at that time. By November 1890 the Bank of England was pooling its resources with those of the Russian central bank and British financial institutions in order to save Barings, one of the biggest names in the City of London. Even then, events on one side of the world could have a global fallout.

Argentina was endowed with great natural resources, but to succeed countries need more than raw materials. That is as important a lesson for nowadays and for the future as it has been in the past. Governance was Argentina's downfall. It did not make the right policy decisions. While Argentina failed, the US succeeded. Alan Beattie, in his book *False Economy*, points out that the US was democratic, with smaller family-farm holdings, whereas Argentina had a powerful landowning class. The US also saw larger, more skilled and earlier immigrant inflows from Europe.

The danger of running large current-account deficits – in which a country has to borrow from foreigners to fund itself – is also an important one for today. Countries with large deficits are more vulnerable to changes in both sentiment and economic conditions, being dependent on foreign-capital inflows. Such large deficits are often a good early-warning sign of problems to come, unless the deficit is corrected.

Because the US has been such a gas-guzzling economy in recent years, how rich it is in natural resources is often overlooked. Back in the nineteenth century, strong US growth was helped by its abundance in resources, and this played a major part in helping it overtake the UK, which was not so fortunate. Today, America's move back towards energy self-sufficiency because of shale gas is an encouraging sign – as long as it can be sustained. It will lower America's import bill and could allow it access to cheaper energy.

Countries need to play not only to their strengths – during this period America had plenty of land, cheap energy and lots of cheap workers – but they need to take advantage of other areas too. The railroad and transport services also had a big influence on the opening up of the US. New firms, new industry, a construction boom and the need for finance encouraged financial innovation. The economic thinker Anthony Seldon has pointed out that it was the refinement of property rights in the nineteenth century that was probably more important than technological advances in helping capitalism realise its full potential. Although it is hard to quantify each of the contributing factors, the combined positive effect was all too evident. When an economy takes off there are many contributing causes; it is never driven by just one factor.

The post-war golden era

The next period relevant to an understanding of the present situation is the three decades following the devastation of the Second World War. The years 1945–73 saw the strongest pace of global growth the world has ever seen. Its initial phase was slow and might not have seemed golden to those living through it, but it gathered momentum and culminated in a two-year boom in 1972–3, before the onset of the energy crisis.

During this time, the world economy averaged growth of around 5 per cent per annum in real terms, over and above inflation. There was also the emergence of a new economic power. Like the US economy at the end of the nineteenth century and China today,

Japan's economy saw vast change, growing elevenfold in real terms, reaching 9 per cent of the world economy.

It was not just Japan; West Germany boomed too. The Asian Tigers – Singapore, Hong Kong, South Korea and Taiwan – also enjoyed an economic emergence during this period. They were helped by the industrial policies of their governments. The story of South Korea is particularly impressive. During the 1950s South Korea's economy was on a par with that of a mid-sized African economy. It enjoyed an economic transformation based on increased investment and growth that saw it become the world's twelfth-largest economy a few years ago, although it has slipped slightly since.

Just as we saw multiple factors at the end of the nineteenth century, there were many influences at work in the 1945–73 period. One factor was the growth of consumer-durable markets in the West, as the baby-boom generation emerged in the US. There was also a post-Second World War rebound. The best example of this was the *Wirtschaftswunder*, the economic miracle in Germany in the 1950s that saw the emergence of West Germany, which for a while even became the world's second-largest economy, until it was overtaken by Japan in the late 1960s. The post-war Marshall Plan played a major part, with the US providing loans and assistance. This included the replacement of the Reichsmark with the Deutsche Mark in 1948, which helped curb inflation. Germany also benefited from the combination of cheap and skilled labour. However, during this halcyon period, the seeds were already being sown for some of today's challenges as Europe granted itself a welfare system that is already unsustainable in its present form.

Japan also has a remarkable story in the post-war period. It had no Marshall Plan to benefit from. Instead it suffered under the Dodge Plan, a stabilisation scheme that squeezed the economy hard. Whereas the Americans feared communism in Europe and wanted to help West Germany, they had no such political interest in Japan. Fate dealt Japan a good hand when, on 25 June 1950, North Korea crossed the 38th parallel. The ensuing Korean War revitalised Japan and set it on the road to recovery. But there was a long way to go. By 1955, with a population half that of the US, its economy was around only one-twentieth the size. Yet by 1968 Japan was displacing West Germany as the world's second-biggest economy. In some years Japanese savings reached around 40 per cent, and the virtuous cycle was apparent: the more you save, the faster your income can grow. It was a high-savings, high-investment model, focused on manufacturing and export success. Economies that are not rich in natural resources need investment, innovation or creativity in order to grow.

The golden period ended with the first oil shock. Following the Yom Kippur War of October 1973, oil prices soared, and for most of January, February and March 1974 Britain had a three-day week. Factories were guaranteed energy for only three consecutive days each week and so shut for the rest of the time. It is ironic that they produced as much in three days as they used to in five. I remember this time well, with the power cuts that were then common, and as one of our two school buildings depended on coal it had to shut and we went to school only one day a week for about seven weeks. That period illustrated both the importance of energy and of economies being able to withstand shocks.

So, what can we learn today from the economic lessons of the last two hundred years? What stands out is the fundamental need to create an enabling environment in which ideas and trade will flow and business will invest. For this to happen, we must embrace change, and be prepared for it.

Some say we are about to live through the fifth industrial revolution. Although not everyone agrees on the other four, I would say they were: first, the birth of industry followed by the age of steam and railways in Britain; second, the electrification, along with steel and heavy engineering, seen in the US and parts of Europe in the late nineteenth century; third, the period of mass consumption in the twentieth century, embracing oil, autos, and also the emergence of petrochemicals and plastics; and, fourth, the technology and telecommunication revolution of the last quarter-century.

Professor Nick Stern claims we are about to have a fifth industrial revolution centred on green technology – the clean-tech and biotech revolution – while Peter Marsh writes of a fifth revolution based on the ability to carry out high-quality manufacturing in smaller units across the globe. 3D printing is a reflection of this. Advances are being made in other areas, such as genomics, artificial intelligence, robotics, nanotechnology, connectivity and even in addressing problems such as how we deal with waste. What we have seen in the past should give us confidence about the future.

Divided and disconnected: policy dilemmas

In recent years, economic divisions have become apparent. Some economies have grown strongly. Among the major economies, it is China that has been the star performer, overcoming the hit it suffered to exports and confidence following the financial crisis. In contrast, some major Western economies have seen little or no growth. The US economy was already slowing down before the crisis, and then suffered its longest and deepest recession since the 1930s depression, with house prices falling, unemployment rising and deleveraging as debt was repaid, until policy stimulus contributed to a modest rebound, which now looks set to gather momentum. Europe has suffered worse, particularly at the periphery of the eurozone – Portugal, Ireland, Italy, Greece and Spain – as well the UK. All had high debt, but the periphery had little room for policy response. The UK also suffered from having a financial sector that was one of the biggest in the world in relation to the size of the domestic economy. Ireland, Switzerland, Cyprus and Luxembourg also had financial sectors that were huge in relation to their economic size, and hence found it difficult to cope with the fallout.

Finance is a global industry; many of the large national financial sectors were established ahead of the competition and found it easier to grow, often helped by a combination of low tax and light regulation. The crisis showed the downside of having a poorly regulated global industry based in your country. In the words of the Bank of England governor Mervyn King, banks were 'international in life but national in death', with clearing up the mess having to be paid for by domestic taxpayers.

Although the 2008 crisis was financial, much of the post-crisis focus has been on debt, particularly in the West. While high public debt is a concern, the problems are far from insurmountable. The UK is a useful example, as its national data is reliable and goes back a long way. The UK's national debt began in 1692 and has had some big highs – usually associated with the financing of wars. Measured in relation to the size of the economy – as a proportion of GDP – it peaked around 260 per cent of GDP in 1818–21, shortly after the Napoleonic wars. In the wake of the First World War it reached 135 per cent in 1919, rising to 182 per cent in 1923. It peaked again after the Second World War, reaching 237 per cent in 1946–7. Although the current level of UK national debt sounds high, around 80 per cent of GDP, it is relatively low by historical standards and so we need not panic. Admittedly, it is the highest level in peacetime, and what this should tell us is that in the good economic years governments became too wasteful. A similar pattern has been seen in many Western economies. In the boom years, a number of these also saw rising levels of personal and corporate debt, compounding the problem. Although fiscal policy has been tight in many Western economies, public debt levels have risen as tax revenues have suffered and automatic stabilisers have kicked in. The best way to make inroads into a debt mountain is stronger economic growth. Debt should be looked at in relation to GDP to keep it in perspective.

For the first five years after the crisis, Western economies suffered from a lack of demand, lending and confidence, holding back recovery. During 2013 this was starting to change. Normally economies grow at their trend rates, which can be sustained without running into inflation or trade problems. If economies grow below their trend rate for any prolonged time this results in spare capacity and unemployment. Even allowing for the likelihood that trend growth rates might have been overstated before the crisis, the US, the UK and Europe have been below trend for a long while and so have considerable upside potential in the next few years.

Traditionally when an economy suffers a setback it can rebound quickly, like an elastic band. When the crisis hit, people discussed what type of recovery it would be in alphabetical terms. Would it be a 'V-shaped' recovery, where the downward leg of the V is the impact of the crisis, which reduces spending power and output, and is then followed by the upward leg of the V where the economy recovers quickly? Or would it be more subdued, like a U, representing a slower pace of recovery? Or even an L, where after the collapse in output there is no immediate recovery and things just stabilise? Or, as the successful businessman Martin Sorrell asked at the World Economic Forum annual meeting in Davos in 2010, would it be an LUV recovery, L in Europe, U in the US and V in China? In the years before the 2008 financial crisis the world economy boomed. People were led to believe the good times would last for ever and few had reason to think otherwise. In the US people spoke of 'the Great Moderation', referring to the decline in volatility of both output and inflation. In Europe, because of the euro, investors regarded economies such as Spain and Ireland as being as safe as Germany but offering better returns. And if one believed that, why wouldn't one invest there? In the UK, meanwhile, Chancellor Gordon Brown said his policies had abolished boom and bust. He was only half right.

Even if Lehman Brothers had not collapsed, another event would probably have triggered a crisis; it was waiting to happen. Perhaps the lesson of the crisis is that if something hasn't happened yet, it is more likely, not less likely, to occur. When things get out of touch with reality they have to correct eventually, as in the case of the cartoon character Wile E. Coyote. He would run off the edge of a cliff and keep running on thin air until he looked down, saw there was nothing there, and fell to earth. Before the crisis, parts of the financial sector were like that, defying gravity. At some stage a fall to earth was inevitable.

By 2007, the year before the crisis, the warning signs were there, but few noticed. Between 1995 and 2004 the world economy grew at an average rate of 3.6 per cent per annum in real terms – a healthy but not exceptional rate of growth. Then, in the three years 2005 to 2007, global growth soared, averaging over 5 per cent per year. Yet the danger signals were already evident: as debt levels rose, credit was widely available and the US economy was already losing momentum. Financial markets had almost given up pricing for risk, with investors, borrowers, even analysts looking only at the upside, not the downside – looking at what would happen if things went well, without taking on board the risks.

A year later, by 2008, we were closer than ever to the edge of the cliff but few were driving more safely. Global growth slowed to 3 per cent in 2008, but in the last three months of that year, as the crisis hit, it was as if the wheels had fallen off, as the world economy ground to a halt. There was a collapse in world trade, as demand plummeted. Financial markets, as is their norm, went from one extreme to the other: one minute they believed the good times would last for ever and the next the end of the world was nigh. In the West, companies found it hard to access finance, and confidence slumped. The net effect was that the innocent suffered along with the guilty – the innocent being countries, largely from the emerging world, that had not engaged in the financial excess and mismanagement that had led to the crisis. They were hit hard, just like the countries that had got many things wrong. The innocent also included taxpayers in many Western economies.

To put this in perspective, a rate of growth for the world economy above 4 per cent is strong and below 3 per cent is seen as weak. In the West the economy would have to contract, and GDP 'growth' be below zero for a recession. In India, in contrast, growth below 5 per cent would feel like a recession as it would not keep up with population growth, and in Africa that figure would be around 2.5 per cent.

The year 2009 saw a global recession; initially the data showed the world economy actually shrank by 0.6 per cent but has been revised since to zero growth. That was the weakest economic performance in global GDP since the Second World War. It was dramatic. Little surprise that some thought of the crisis as an economic war that necessitated an aggressive response, as governments spent money and interest rates were reduced. Thankfully, for many economies the damage caused to growth, although significant, proved temporary. Trade and global growth recovered, driven by the East, but the West languished.

In 2010 the world economy rebounded strongly, like the V shape mentioned above, growing 5.4 per cent in real terms. This was explained by strong growth across regions such as Asia, Africa, the Middle East and Latin America, and by the impact of big policy stimulus in the West, which was the economic equivalent of throwing everything including the kitchen sink at the problem. But throwing the kitchen sink can also leave a mess to be cleared up and that is part of the problem now. What was thrown was more government money across the globe, lower interest rates, particularly in the West, and ample liquidity in the form of central banks using their balance sheets – often referred to as 'printing money'.

While this was happening politicians and policymakers were already conscious of how it might be cleared up – there was talk of eventual 'exit strategies' from low interest rates and the need to co-ordinate policies in later years. It is challenging to co-ordinate policies in recoveries, as economies rebound at different speeds and times. Indeed, talk of the US Federal Reserve turning the tap off by not pumping in more money caused major financial turbulence in the summer of 2013 and in early 2014, even though an increase in interest rates was still some time off. This episode showed how vulnerable economies could be when interest rates do start to rise, and reinforces the case for exit strategies from low interest rates to be thought through carefully to minimise the economic fallout. It also highlighted how interconnected the global economy and financial system is.

Cynics observed that it was low interest rates, too much money and high debt that had got us into this worldwide mess, and now the solution prescribed was lower rates, more money and higher debt. Little wonder the policy was not universally welcome. The Bank of England governor Mervyn King later referred to this as a 'policy paradox', whereby the steps that had to be taken in the short term might not be those required in the longer term. That is the worry about some of the present policies in some Western countries.

As monetary policy has acted as the shock absorber in Western economies, the pressure has remained on central banks to keep interest rates as low as possible for as long as possible, the fear being that economies might be too fragile to cope with the shock of rising rates. As growth recovers and balance sheets are repaired, interest rates in the West will eventually be able to rise, gradually returning to normal, as economic growth recovers. Meanwhile, across emerging economies the imperative is for policy to be driven by domestic needs, not overly influenced by the West, and to keep inflation in check.

The period from 2011 to 2013 has seen a steadier pace of global growth, as policy stimulus in the West started to wear off and as high food and energy prices curbed growth across the emerging world. Growth was 4.1 per cent in 2011, 3.4 per cent in 2012 and around 3.3 per cent in both 2013 and 2014. Now things are starting to turn around and growth prospects should improve.

During 2013 Christine Lagarde, managing director of the International Monetary Fund (IMF), talked about a three-speed world: the developing and emerging economies were in the fast lane and although they were slowing they were still travelling at a faster speed than the rest; the US was recovering and gathering momentum; while Europe was stuck in the slow lane. In the future it is more likely to be a multi-speed world, with economies moving forward at different speeds, heavily influenced by a combination of domestic, regional and global factors.

Clearly the numbers matter, but I think it is sometimes more important to understand the story of what is happening, in order to put things in context. In 2008, after the US election, President Obama's chief of staff, Rahm Emanuel, talked of the need not to waste a good crisis. He was referring to the US, but many other countries – perhaps not enough of them – took him at his word and implemented reform.

Some countries took advantage of the last few years to pursue change and make progress. The Philippines, for instance, became a darling of the financial markets as it got to grips with its debt problem and ran its economy well. Two other countries that have done far better than expected this century are Brazil and Indonesia. Despite their positive underlying story even these economies have not been immune to setbacks and swings in sentiment over the last year, linked to worries about higher interest rates at home, tighter US monetary policy and tougher credit conditions globally.

Indeed, the beginning of 2014 saw the currencies and financial markets of five emerging markets suffer. These were nicknamed the 'fragile five' at the time: India, Indonesia, Brazil, Turkey and South Africa. Despite sound future prospects, this highlighted the vulnerability of economies with current-account deficits to a deterioration in international investor sentiment towards them. This should highlight that economies do not follow straight-line paths, and many emerging economies still have a need for further economic reform.

Vast differences also exist within countries, more evident in larger economies. India is one example, where there is a big contrast between the export-oriented, English-speaking west and south, versus the rural, less globalised north and east. In most countries there are huge differences between city and rural areas. This poses policy challenges, as well as reflecting differences in both economic performance and voting patterns.

Within a number of countries there appears to be polarisation of political ideas and economic attitudes. For instance, over the last decade Thailand has periodically seen battles between the red-shirt supporters of the previous leader Thaksin Shinawatra, mainly from the countryside, and the yellow-shirts, largely from the capital Bangkok.

Even in the US there has been a polarisation, reflected in the 2012 presidential election. When President Carter won in 1976, twenty of the fifty states were decided by less than 5 per cent of the vote, reflecting how similar many states were. In the last election only four states were that close, and twenty-seven out of fifty saw a victory margin of more than 15 per cent.

While there may be one particular moment that grabs people's attention, often developments unfold over months and years. Overnight sensations in any field – music, comedy, theatre – are usually years in the making. That certainly is the case with economic change, and that is what is happening now. The balance of economic power is shifting, but in a far more complex and less threatening way than is currently understood.

32, 62, 72

Three numbers explain part of this important story: 32, 62 and 72. These are the size of the world economy in trillions of dollars: $32 trillion at the beginning of this century, $62 trillion at the start of the financial crisis and $72 trillion by the end of 2012, shortly before

I began writing this book. These figures are in unadjusted nominal terms, so some of the rise is inflation, but the vast bulk is real growth, driven increasingly by different regions. Now, at publication, the figure is near $75 trillion, having reached $74 trillion at the end of 2013. Incredibly, despite the biggest financial crisis since the 1930s, and the first contraction in output since the Second World War, the global economic cake has grown. This number will reach close to $82 billion by the start of 2016.

Consider income per head. In the years immediately after the financial crisis – between 2008 and 2012 – a quarter of economies saw living standards fall in real terms. Hardly surprisingly, this included a number across Europe, such as the UK, Cyprus, Greece, Iceland, Italy and Spain, and also a group of smaller Caribbean economies. Since Europe is a bigger economy than the US, this goes some way to explain present pessimism. But before the crisis I was both pessimistic and critical of the structure of some Western economies, particularly the US and the UK, which I felt were saving too little and not investing enough. These structural problems persist and, alongside painful adjustment in the eurozone, have prompted a fear of 'secular stagnation' of little growth in the West and a lost decade, or two, just as Japan has suffered. I understand where such thinking in the US and Europe comes from, given the lack of demand and weakness in recent years. But it reflects a status-quo bias in much of economic thinking, where there is too often a tendency to expect what is happening now to continue in the future. We saw it before the crisis, when boom times were expected to continue in the West, and we see it now. It ignores much of what is happening across the globe, including the likelihood of continued innovation and creativity.

Perhaps what is remarkable is that three-quarters of economies globally saw their living standards stay the same or improve over the difficult key economic period between 2008 and 2012. Since then there has been further improvement. How has it happened? Part of the answer might be that economies have an innate ability to bounce back. Policies have helped, although for some issues the can has been kicked down the road, with problems delayed, not solved. Yet a big part of the answer is that economies outside the West have grown stronger, become bigger and now matter more on the global stage. This can only auger well for future global growth, particularly as economies in the West recover ground lost during the recession and make up for lost time.

The severity of the financial crisis posed serious questions about the unbalanced nature of global growth before the crisis and of growth within a number of Western economies. It also highlighted the need for many economies in Asia, Africa and elsewhere to move away from relying on the unsustainable situation of exporting goods to Western consumers up to their eyeballs in debt. In the future we should expect to see more engines of growth, both across and within economies.

Drawing the right lessons is key. For instance, it is not that debt is bad. That is like saying drink is bad: it means nothing. Too much debt is clearly bad and potentially ruinous, yet the right amount of debt for the right reasons is understandable: for example, borrowing against future income to buy a house; raising finance to start a family-run business; or, at the country level, borrowing at cheap long-term interest rates to build homes and roads. But what should be clear after the Western crisis is that the financial sector should be there to serve the needs of people and business, not to create fancy products. The good news is that large parts of the financial industry do serve economic needs, but the crisis showed that some significant parts did not. The crisis also highlighted other questions about disparities within countries. But perhaps one important lesson to come out of the crisis was that we should not assume the consensus is always right and, as a result, should be prepared for both surprises and shocks ahead.

In the US, the UK and Europe there were many lessons from 2008 and some have yet to be addressed fully. But over the last year signs of progress are evident, not least in the near-term challenge in many Western economies of generating a much needed rebound in demand.

The interconnections of the world economy have become more evident. Before the crisis, there was a heated debate among investors, policymakers and economists as to whether emerging economies were 'decoupled' or not – whether their growth was no longer dependent on what happened in the West.

The crisis showed that countries across the emerging world were not decoupled from one another, because of trade and financial ties. Emerging markets were hit hard for a short while, but the damage was short-lived. Perhaps, more importantly, it showed they were resilient and able to cope as they were less exposed to financial-sector problems and also, because their economies had been run well, they had more room for policy manoeuvre. Emerging economies held two-thirds of global foreign-exchange reserves, as opposed to one-third a decade earlier. Debt levels were also lower.

In coming years, economies across Latin America, Africa, the Middle East and Asia that previously would have focused on exports might prove to be better diversified with twin engines of growth: exports and domestic demand. Those economies might remain not decoupled but move from being better insulated to being better diversified and thus more resilient in the face of future shocks.

Made in China and bought by China

The three key words that define the century so far are 'made in China', as the country experiences its own industrial revolution. The three words that will probably define the next decade are 'bought by China' as it, like some other economies, goes on a buying spree to move up the value curve – moving away from brawn to brain, from producing cheap things to ones based on quality and expertise, and acquiring intellectual property and brands, to help speed up its pace of development. The three key words in the decade after this are likely to be 'paid in renminbi' as the Chinese currency becomes more powerful.

China's scale captures the imagination but this is not simply a story about China; far from it. Think of all the other countries that we have bought or listened to or watched something from. It is an indication of how things are changing. If the world can grow despite the economic turmoil seen in the US and Europe in recent years, imagine what will happen when the legacy issues of the crisis are solved – as they will be. How much will the world grow then?

In the financial markets I was one of a few economists who were talking about the new world order and the shift in the balance of power from the West to the East over a decade ago. The idea of a shift is now widely accepted but there are a number of ideas within the present debate that have become generally accepted but that are likely to prove wrong.

This shift in economic power does not mean that it is all doom and gloom for the West, or anything like it. The US and other Western countries should prosper if they position themselves wisely. Many Western firms have done well exporting to Asia or investing in Africa. Germany is a manufacturing powerhouse and it will benefit from the infrastructure boom and expenditure on capital goods across the globe. The UK, in contrast, should benefit more in the future from exporting financial, business, professional and legal services. The East is set to produce more; the West is likely to innovate more.

While the outlook across emerging economies is good, it does not mean the path ahead will be straight. There will be some significant and inevitable setbacks along the way. However, these setbacks should not be misinterpreted as failure. They are to be expected as these economies become more global and are subject to business cycles.

But those who are critical of many emerging economies, such as China, are like stopped clocks, always saying the same thing. These cautious and pessimistic voices should not be ignored – I shall address them later – but they should be kept in perspective. Stopped clocks might be right twice a day, but they are useless at telling the time.

The essential message is that the outlook is a positive one for the world economy. That does not mean that we should expect everything to go up all the time. The reality is far more complex, which makes the outlook more interesting. Some of the situations in the story have occurred before. The difference now is in the magnitude of the change. We are observing a radical shift in the global economy.

As a result of the crisis, Western politicians have lost the moral economic authority to tell the rest of the world what to do. This might encourage a more healthy view of how the world should proceed – this time driven by domestic and regional needs.

I shall now turn to the key influences on the world economy, the major drivers of global growth, and their likely future developments. For many people, the economic future will not be solely about achieving growth but about how the fruits of success are distributed between and within countries.

2

Superman drives the world economy

Imagine being able to look at the world economy from 36,000 feet, from an aeroplane window. It would look very different. Or imagine being able to see the shifts in the earth's tectonic plates.

If you were to gather a group of economists together, they would be unlikely to agree on the key drivers of the world economy's tectonic plates. This is unsurprising, as there are so many influences to choose from. However, there should be no argument about the first: China. Its global impact is already apparent but how much bigger can it become? Or will it just burn itself out as, after all, there is a fashion in economics as there is in everything else?

Think about the economies that have suddenly soared into our vision, like shooting stars, grabbing the attention and then fizzling out. Over the last fifty years, different economies have taken centre stage. In the 1960s the Russian economic model was much admired, before its faults were plain to see. Then the Swedish social democratic model was all the rage for a while; economists pointed to its strong post-war performance, despite its large public sector, before its star started to wane as we moved into the 1970s.

It is incredible to think now that in the early part of the 1970s in Western Europe even the East German economy – if not its political system – was seen in a positive light. It was viewed as a sporting success: East Germany did well in the 1972 Olympics, and even beat the eventual champions West Germany in the 1974 football World Cup. It was also seen as an industrial success, in contrast to the UK, which suffered from the 1973 energy crisis and the resulting three-day week, and had to be bailed out by the IMF three years later. 'Goodbye Great Britain' was both a *Wall Street*

Journal headline and the title of a successful book reflecting the prevailing mood.

Fashions continued to change, with Japan becoming the economy to follow in the 1980s, as its industrial model took centre stage. Since that high point it has suffered two lost decades. West Germany, too, which had become fashionable in the 1980s, was cast aside at the beginning of this century, and is only now experiencing a justified rebound in the economic fashion stakes. In its social market economy, the German government seeks to guarantee the free play of entrepreneurial activity while trying to maintain the social balance. In the mid-1990s East Asia was the centre of attention, with the World Bank producing a report entitled *The East Asian Miracle*. Yet, by 1997–8, there was an Asian economic crisis. Then, as we entered the current century, it was America's turn to be the economic fashion icon – not for the first or the last time – as its economy boomed and easily weathered a succession of shocks, until it trembled under the impact of 2008.

China, too, could be a flash in the pan. Some think it is, but I am not one of them.

Two hundred years ago, Napoleon said, 'Let China sleep, for when she awakes, she will shake the world.' At that time China, like India, was going through its economic slumbers, but its potential scale would have been obvious. Until the 1750s or so, largely because of their large populations, China and India were the biggest economies in the world. Industrial revolutions then enabled the economies of the West to overtake them. Now it is the West's turn to be shaken. Although China is already the world's second-biggest economy, its catch-up potential is still huge, as its income per head is less than one-eighth that of the US and is on a par with that of the Dominican Republic.

It is in the nature of business cycles and of economic development to encounter setbacks along the way. The business cycle still exists, everywhere. Sometimes it is possible to sustain continuous growth over successive decades, but more often than not a country's economic growth rate is subject to fluctuation. Setbacks are to be expected, as part of the growth narrative, and sometimes they can be dramatic. China and the other emerging economies might be showing an upward trend, but their path is unlikely to be consistently smooth. They will have setbacks.

China

My first visit to China was in 1994. As the plane landed and was taxiing, there was a sudden screech of brakes. To my amazement, as I looked out of the window, I saw a cyclist on the tarmac, riding along as if the runway were a normal road. It was the first in a series of things that would be in complete contrast to anything you would experience there today. The airport at Beijing amounted to one small terminal building; the road into the city on that Sunday morning was a dual carriageway empty apart from the occasional car or farmer's cart. Then, on the Monday, as I awoke there was no noise of cars or trucks, no morning rush hour. Looking from the hotel-room window, all I could see was thousands of cyclists. The air was clear, the visibility good. It was all so different from now.

Beijing today has countless major ring roads. One of its two international airports is one of the biggest in the world, and it is about to build a third. Pollution is high. I have visited China many times in the last twenty years. On one trip, a decade after my first visit, one thing that had not changed was the hotel where I stayed: the China World, on one of the main highways. I met the UK prime minister Tony Blair at a small reception there during the 2005 EU–China Business Summit, when the UK held the presidency of the EU. I spoke in the Great Hall of the People in Tiananmen Square. It was evident then how ambitious China was to grow its economy, to develop its financial sector and to deepen its ties with Europe, its main trading bloc. Now it is doing all three, and more.

At that summit, Blair, supported by the EU commissioner Peter Mandelson, presented a coherent case for why China should trade more with the UK and Europe. Yet the summit demonstrated something that is still relevant regarding Europe's approach to China. One message from the session I took part in was that the Chinese found America's approach much easier to understand than the EU's. The US came as one entity, one country, driven by a single policy agenda. In contrast, the Europeans were far more 'heterogeneous', to use the word of a Chinese official at that time. They came as one in the form of the EU, but each country also pushed its own national agenda.

It could be argued that in the intervening years Germany has dealt with China far more competently than other European countries, seeking to understand what drives Chinese thinking as well as promoting its own economy. Chancellor Angela Merkel, whom I have heard referred to as 'Mrs Europe' in China, has made frequent visits there, on a number of occasions bringing her cabinet with her. In contrast, a lull in Sino-British relations meant it was not until the end of 2013 that David Cameron was able to make his second visit there since becoming prime minister in 2010.

It is possible to cite countless figures on China. Given the size of the country, the statistics tend to sound impressive. Yet there is always debate about the accuracy of China's data. It produces its GDP growth figures more quickly than any other country in the world and – amazingly – they are always in line with official projections! Revisions to historical data are often big, and official data does not capture the informal economy. Growth figures produced by China's different regions, on the other hand, tend to be much higher than predicted. So China's data, like that of many countries, is always best judged alongside other indicators. The data is not the only key to understanding China's economy; it is important to understand what is driving things on the ground.

A few years ago I testified to a UK parliamentary committee on China and, with limited time to get across the key points, I described

China as a Robin Hood, Goldilocks and Superman economy. This description still holds good.

Robin Hood is a heroic outlaw from English folklore, known for stealing from the rich and giving to the poor. China is a modern-day Robin Hood economy, taking from the rich West and giving to poorer regions such as Asia, Africa and Latin America.

In the West, China has been seen as relying on cheap labour, keeping its currency undervalued and taking jobs away from the West. While playing to its strengths as a rapidly developing economy, it was seen as not playing by the same rules as everyone else. Outside the West, China is seen in a different light. For Latin America, Africa and Asia, it is viewed as a big market to sell into, a source of investment and as a driver of growth, helping exports and jobs. This positive view has emerged since the late 1990s: then, when travelling across East Asia, it was common to hear China regarded as a competitive threat. But, over time, as China's economy has grown, attitudes towards it have changed in a positive way.

China is also a Goldilocks economy. For Goldilocks, the temperature of the porridge had to be just right. Likewise with China's economy. Too hot, and inflation will rise, hitting the poor, who spend the largest proportion of their money on food. Too cold, and unemployment rises. Both outcomes would threaten social unrest, adding to the worries of the communist elite, who are mindful of the need to ensure stability and reduce the risk of popular disturbances. Dissent has increased in recent years, largely because of public reaction to local corruption. Achieving economic growth and curbing corruption are central to retaining future stability in China.

The Cultural Revolution of 1966–76 led to the purge of many significant figures, including Deng Xiaoping, who was later to return and become China's reforming leader. China became inward-looking, remote from the rest of the world, despite establishing ambassadorial links with many Western countries such as the US in 1972, and welcoming President Nixon to the country in 1973. The

Cultural Revolution left it with many scars, not least a poor and underdeveloped economy. In 1955 China accounted for 4.7 per cent of global GDP; by 1978 it was only 1 per cent. While others had moved on, China had gone backwards, and the country seemed to hit one problem after another.

The downfall of the Gang of Four in October 1976, one month after the death of Mao Zedong, brought the dawn of China's national rejuvenation, largely because of one person: Deng Xiaoping. At that time the country's leaders came to terms with the poverty of their people and the yawning gap between China and the West. The enormity of the task and the 'race against time' to develop, as Deng called it, became clear. It was at the end of 1978 that the reform process began and China began to open up. Gradually China introduced the market mechanism and business practices into its economy.

In Europe the 1970s are now viewed as a tough time. Yet, when the Chinese visited in 1978, they were astounded by what they saw. China's first ever official overseas economic delegation, led by Vice Premier Gu Mu, spent two months visiting France, West Germany, Sweden, Denmark and Belgium. The delegation was stunned by how far China lagged behind. It was clear that China needed advanced foreign technology to spur growth. But the delegation also discovered the willingness of others to invest in China. This fed into a frenetic policy debate.

In his book *Breaking Through*, Li Lanqing, a senior official who later went on to join the Politburo, reports on a twenty-day brainstorming meeting in Beijing in July 1978 that reflected on how two defeated nations such as Japan and West Germany could rise to their feet so soon. The momentum was with those who wanted to open China up. Reform began in the agricultural sector, allowing private ownership of small areas of land, and was seen in other areas, including the creation of special economic zones for foreign investment. In his book, Li recalls Deng saying to him on joining the central leadership in 1992, 'We have got to reform and open up; otherwise we are doomed.' The success of the reforms was by no means certain.

The Chinese like their slogans. The Four Modernisations have been firmly indoctrinated in policymaking since the reform process began, reflecting the desire to modernise the four areas of agriculture, industry, science and technology, and national defence. 'Harmonious society', 'prosperous society' and 'scientific development' were the key phrases used to describe China by the fourth-generation leadership of President Hu and Premier Wen early this century.* It is an attitude relevant for so many countries across the globe: the need to be open and compete internationally but at the same time to address the concerns, worries and needs of domestic populations. For Hu, scientific development meant that progress should not enrich one part of the economy or country at the expense of another. It was seen as part of 'scientific socialism' and Premier Wen articulated this in a speech at the Party School in early 2004 when he talked of 'economic and social developments that are comprehensive, well co-ordinated and sustainable'. The aim was not to leave anyone behind in the drive for modernisation. Such thinking could equally apply to current concerns in the US and Europe about rising inequality.

The Chinese leadership always faced a challenging time in ensuring economic stability, not least because of the scale of the economy. In any country there are divergences between regions, but in China these differences occur on a huge scale. The same thing can be seen in other large countries, such as Indonesia, with its growth focused on Java, or in India.

* The first generation of Chinese Communist Party leaders (1947–76), was led by Mao Zedong and included Zhou Enlai and others; the second generation (1978–92) was led by Deng Xiaoping; the third generation (1992–2003) included Jiang Zemin, Li Peng, Zhu Rongji and others, and the fourth generation (2003–12), President Hu Jintao and Premier Wen Jiabao. The fifth generation is now President Xi Jinping and Premier Li Keqiang.

Although China is one country, it is a multitude of contrasting economies. Its economic regions include the old industrial rust belt of north-east China, which has been transformed; the Pearl river delta bordering Hong Kong, which has been a centre of consumer exports in recent decades; the Yangtze river delta bordering Shanghai, which is also heavily focused on exports; the Bohai Rim around Beijing, and the huge inland mass of western and central China.

In late 2003 Hu and Wen outlined five imbalances that China needed to address: those between coastal and inland areas, and between urban and rural areas, as well as social, environmental and international imbalances.

Understanding the importance of these imbalances helps to understand the successful policy approach taken by China. Add in the huge population and this goes towards explaining the present focus on developing the western and central part of the country, where hundreds of new towns and cities are being built and where millions are gravitating from the countryside. It is a largely unknown region for the rest of the world but in coming decades the cities there could become household names. Chongqing, in western China, which I first visited in 2006, is probably the biggest little-known city in the world. Six hundred kilometres up the Yangtze from the Three Gorges Dam, it has a population of over 30 million and is developing fast.

China is not the only country to see the benefits of urbanisation, and it is experiencing these changes on a vast scale. China is now part way through the process, planned to take a number of decades, that will see 230 million people moving off the land and into towns and cities.

There has always been concern that migrants from the land could swamp the cities. This is controlled by the *hukou* land-registration system: peasants who move to cities are not entitled to the same benefits as locals. The *hukou* acted as a safety net after the crisis hit in late 2008, when many migrant workers lost their jobs in export-focused factories in coastal cities and had to return home inland. Many were able to return to their small land holdings. Despite this, unemployment among migrant workers rose sharply, adding to the urgency with which the authorities boosted the economy in the wake of the Western financial crisis.

Remarkably, gradualist policy changes in China have gone hand in hand with significant and radical steps such as joining the World Trade Organization in 2001, which was a major factor in binding China's future with that of the rest of the world. Judging from announcements made after the Communist Party's major conference, the Third Plenum, in November 2013, the new leadership looks set to press ahead with further necessary reform. These include: the market playing a bigger future role in the economy, changes to China's one-child policy, and changes to the *hukou* system to bring it up to date and give migrant workers better rights.

For much of the last decade China has grown at a double-digit rate. It was almost the perfect Goldilocks temperature for a booming economy. However, despite strong growth, all was not well. Growth was unbalanced and unsustainable, too geared to investment and to exports to the US and Europe, and insufficiently based on consumer spending. Whenever there is a slump in exports, it hits China's coastal areas hard. In the future, as domestic demand takes on a momentum of its own, confidence might become less dependent on exports and driven more by domestic economic factors.

After the crisis hit, China's policy response reflected strong leadership and emphasised the government's concern with the social and political implications of an economic slowdown. The government pumped around 4 trillion renminbi into the economy, a huge amount. This helped the economy but it also exacerbated problems, some of which still cause concern.

Relaxing the purse strings saw a surge in spending on local projects, including white elephants that looked good but weren't yet needed, such as countless tower blocks. Too much money pumped too quickly into any economy can lead to problems, particularly when a financial sector is still in the early stages of development, as it is in China. There was concern about rising local-government debt and also the financing of local-government investment vehicles, many of which have subsequently been bailed out by the central government in Beijing. It also raised anxiety about the shadow-banking sector in China, which, like its counterpart in many Western economies, is large and unregulated.

The good news is that the authorities are now alert to the problems and unlikely to repeat them, and the government's finances are healthy enough to cope with a shock. One issue in China is that the economy is run in much the same way as it was when it was smaller, from the centre in Beijing. Then, Beijing was able to exert huge influence. With the economy now being so much bigger, Beijing's influence is less and the post-crisis world reflects this. Some say that the large amounts of private money leaving China, into real estate in places such as London, is a desire to diversify by wealthy Chinese in case things go wrong.

Once state-owned firms were unprofitable and unwanted, but as they have become profitable the authorities have been reluctant to sell them off. In some respects this does not matter. As China's economy has opened up and grown, the private sector has become much bigger. On the eve of the 2012 London Olympics I gave a presentation to the delegation of the Chinese Entrepreneurs' Club, which was visiting London at the invitation of the prime minister. The group comprised about thirty people who claimed to run around 7 per cent of the economy. That is a huge change in a short space of time. As the economy grew after it opened up in 1978, first the price mechanism started to take hold, with market demand and supply replacing official pricing, and then the size of the private sector grew. This is continuing and is a good sign, as a market-driven economy has more chance of succeeding.

One of the biggest challenges is to ensure the continuation of the Goldilocks economy. At the beginning of 2011 China unveiled its Twelfth Five-Year Plan, based on moving towards a slower, more sustainable pace of growth. Double-digit growth was to be replaced by a rate of around 7 to 7.5 per cent. The focus was to be on increased consumption, a better social-welfare system and the green economy. China outlined seven industries in which it particularly wants to succeed – alternative energy, biotech, advanced materials, new information technology, high-end manufacturing, clean energy and environmental protection – relying less on cheap labour and more on the quality of input. A year later, at the beginning of 2012, a report by the World Bank and China's Development Research Centre supported the policy but said China was ill equipped to innovate. The message was clear: change was needed to guarantee that the temperature of Goldilocks's porridge remains just right.

The scale of the challenge of moving from strong to more sustainable growth should not be underestimated. At the heart of it is shifting from an economy driven by exports and investment to one where consumption is higher. Investment has been close to 50 per cent of GDP in China. Economies in Asia with high ratios of investment to GDP in the mid-1990s ran into trouble in the Asian crisis of 1997–8. A change in conditions, with investment falling from high levels, can hit an economy hard.

Chinese policymakers are keen to lower the investment-to-GDP ratio to around 38 to 40 per cent – still a high level but justified by urbanisation and industrialisation. A global average is around 22 per cent of GDP. China still needs to consider the impact of such a consistently high rate of investment. It will aid the necessary economic transformation but it still leaves the economy prone to potential setbacks if investment plans slump periodically, which can happen anywhere if demand and confidence take a hit. Evidence of this can sometimes be seen – for example, unfinished tower blocks – in cities across the globe.

China needs to see the ratio of consumption rise sharply so that future growth can be more sustainable. Private consumption is about 30 per cent of GDP, government consumption 18 per cent, and this combined ratio probably needs to rise to around 75 per cent to be on a par with other international economies. That will take a long time, probably decades. It should reinforce China's desire to make technological advances at home, with its capital stock per worker, according to the World Bank, at only 8.7 per cent of the US level.

To return to my triple-icon image, China is also a Superman economy: it is 'up, up and away'. But Superman had one problem: kryptonite. China's kryptonite is its lack of resources. The country's insatiable demand for resources on a huge scale results in global commodity prices having a 'firm floor and a soft ceiling'. The firm floor is the strong underlying demand from China and other emerging economies, which underpins prices. The soft ceiling is the vulnerability of supply to disruption: caused by geopolitics when it comes to energy, and weather when it comes to food.

Over the last two hundred years the price of commodities has tended to fall. The marginal cost – the cost of producing an extra unit, an important concept in economics – is key to the success of business. As more is produced, the cost of an extra unit falls. Over time, the cost of producing an extra unit of a commodity also falls, and that has allowed prices to fall. Increasing demand from China has altered this trend.

The end of 2012 saw fresh leadership of the party and in March 2013 of the state: President Xi Jinping and Premier Li Keqiang respectively. They face the task of implementing the Twelfth Five-Year Plan and navigating the next stage of economic development. China has to overcome the 'middle-income trap'. When countries develop, it is easier to go from low income to medium income than it is from middle income to high income. Of the 101 middle-income economies in 1960, only 13 have become high income and these include Equatorial Guinea, Hong Kong, Israel, Japan, Mauritius, Puerto Rico, South Korea, Singapore, Taiwan, Ireland, Portugal, Spain and Greece, although the last of these is now in danger of experiencing the process in reverse.

The report by the World Bank and China's Development Research Centre outlined the enormity of the task ahead, and the necessary steps to take to allow China's growth rate to slow to 7 per cent by the end of the decade and to 5 per cent in the late 2020s, consistent with a healthy future performance for what would then be a much bigger economy with an ageing population.

If China can achieve such a global impact, why can't other countries? There is no reason why some other large economies – such as India, the world's biggest democracy, or Indonesia, the world's biggest Muslim economy and also a large democracy – can't have a global impact, particularly as they increase in size and as their middle classes and domestic demand grow. Size need not be the only factor. There is a long list of candidates that could have a global impact, but China's scale puts it in a different league.

It is important to acknowledge that many Western economies will continue to exert considerable economic influence, with the US likely to reinvent itself, aided by its scientific and technological skills. Despite its poor performance in recent years, the EU has the potential to rebound and have a huge global influence, although it needs to embrace innovation in the way the US has.

What should businesses seeking to benefit from China's rise make of this? China's middle class is already a big market to sell into. It will undoubtedly get bigger, as too will consumer markets in other parts of the world, from Brazil to Ghana to India. As incomes rise, families tend to spend more on education and health, while young people, with increasing purchasing power, are attracted to brands.

Economies need more capital goods in the early stage of strong growth, helping exporters from economies such as Germany, while demand for business and financial services comes later. Measuring exports to China is not the only way to see who is making inroads, as in some businesses it makes more sense to set up operations inside China instead. If a US firm moved some of its legal partners from New York to Beijing, that would not show up in exports to China but in a different part of the firm's balance sheet, as profits to be transferred back to the US or, more likely, to be reinvested in China to grow the business there.

One challenge for a foreign business trying to break into the Chinese market is that competition is now intense from domestic Chinese firms, as well as from other international companies. Breaking in takes time, and it is often necessary to work closely with local partners or, as in other markets, to understand how things work on the ground. Equally, the impact China is having is also felt in other countries, benefiting from China's Robin Hood effect. So international firms of all sizes might want to avoid the competition of the Chinese market by investing in other strongly growing emerging economies, such as those in South-East Asia or South America. The point is that international firms, when they think about the benefits of China's growth, do not have to confine themselves to China as their only potential market.

This leads us on to the next key driver: trade.

Trade

Trade transforms the pattern of interaction between countries, the way international firms behave, and what people can buy. Perhaps more than anything else, it reflects how the world economy is changing.

The Silk Road of the eighth to fifteenth centuries was the trade route between the West and the East. In recent years there has been talk of a new Silk Road. New trade corridors are opening up, as goods, commodities and people move across the world. There are more financial flows with people working abroad and sending money back home as remittances or investing in markets overseas. The World Bank estimates global remittances will rise from around $550 billion in 2013 to more than $700 billion in 2016. In addition there is direct investment as more firms invest in overseas markets. Increasingly more of this trade is taking place between regions such as the Asia-Pacific, Africa, the Middle East, Latin America and Eastern Europe, often with China at the centre of the web. A dramatic rethink is happening in how some regions see the world.

Twenty years ago this would have been termed 'South–South trade', with the North representing the advanced economies, and the South the developing and emerging world. Along the Andean coast of South America, economies such as Chile and Peru increasingly look to Asia and China as the key market. Central and South America together now see a quarter of their exports going to Asia, with the same proportion of their exports heading for North America, which was once their dominant market. The growth in Asia is also bringing greater ties with the oil-rich Gulf economies of the Middle East as demand for energy changes.

The countries of South-East Asia as well once saw the US, and not their neighbours, as their target market. That is changing. The Association of Southeast Asian Nations (ASEAN) has an economy the size of India and looks set to thrive as Thailand, Singapore, Indonesia, the Philippines, Malaysia, Vietnam and even Myanmar continue to grow. More of its future trade will be within rather than outside that group of economies.

The development of new trade corridors also means rising intra- as well as inter-regional trade. South America, the Middle East and Africa have traditionally been seen as commodity-producing regions. All have low intra-regional trade: it is as low as 8.8 per cent in the Middle East, as there is little point selling oil to those who already have it, and only 13 per cent in Africa. There, the idea was to get the resources from the mines or crops from the fields straight to the coast in order to export, predominantly to Europe. The aim was not to sell resources, goods or produce to neighbouring countries. A demonstration of that rush to the coast was highlighted by the 2005 report of the African Commission pointing out that in sub-Saharan Africa there was not one uniform rail gauge but three, so that even the basic rail-transport infrastructure was not conducive to intra-regional trade. Things are now changing and as Africa urbanises and domestic demand grows, intra-regional trade across Africa will rise.

Asia's intra-regional share is 53.4 per cent, up sharply from just a few years ago. Europe sees the highest intra-regional proportion, at just under 70 per cent. Europe's high intra-regional trade goes some way to help explain why, when demand is weak in Europe, it affects all European countries at the same time. Weak demand in one European country means weak exports from another. It was also a key contributory factor to sluggish global trade in 2013.

Economies rich in resources, such as those in Africa and Latin America, specialise in commodities. A vital aspect of both the developing pattern of trade and of global geopolitics is that there has been a resources grab across much of the globe. In some respects this is nothing new: it is a common motif of colonial history. But this time it is different, as it is leading to significant investment in many commodity-producing regions, with Russia and China leading the surge and Africa as the central focus of this grab for resources.

Some commodities have become strategically more important than ever: for example, rare earths are essential for high-tech production in Japan, an industry almost brought to a standstill when exports of rare earths from Inner Mongolia were temporarily halted in 2009.

Increased trade has exposed countries more to events in other parts of the world – as the financial crisis demonstrated. The growth in world trade tends to outstrip that of global GDP, and that was certainly the case in the years before the financial crisis. From 1995 to 2004 world trade grew 7 per cent per annum versus 3.6 per cent global growth, and then in the three years from 2005 to 2007 world trade boomed, rising annually by 7.6 per cent, 9.2 per cent and 7.9 per cent. By 2008 the growth in both trade and GDP had slowed to 2.8 per cent. But in 2009, as world GDP contracted 0.4 per cent, world trade collapsed, falling 10.6 per cent.

Export-oriented economies were hit hard. It is remarkable how open to trade and supply chains a number of countries are, and it is thus no surprise that they prosper and suffer with fluctuations in trade. In East Asia, the total amount of exports and imports exceeds the size of the economy in Hong Kong, Singapore, Taiwan, South Korea, Thailand and Malaysia. If demand from the West is strong, their exports grow strongly and their economies do well; if demand is weak, they underperform.

Since the crisis global trade has recovered, but there has been a divergence between sluggish trade in the West and solid trade in emerging economies.

Trade integration looks set to intensify and production networks to expand further. As trade rises, it will show that emerging powers share the EU's and the US's aim for an open global regime for trade and investment. This is because it is a win-win situation.

For international firms the talk is of vertically integrated supply chains. As companies develop, specialise and grow they become focused on fine-tuning processes, reducing costs. Many products may well have been assembled in factories across many different economies. It is the modern-day equivalent of the production of pins that Adam Smith wrote about in *The Wealth of Nations*. Specialisation becomes key.

In some respects it is a version of the Toyota model that became fashionable with firms across the globe when Japan was the fashionable economy. Japan's economic ascendancy came to a head in the 1980s and if there was one embodiment of it, it was the international focus on the Toyota 'just in time' system. The idea was to operate a production process as efficiently as possible. It was called *kaizen*, or 'continuous improvement', in which three things were eliminated: *muri* (burdens), *mura* (inconsistencies) and *muda* (waste). As it allowed Japanese exports to flourish, the idea was copied across the globe. Firms became more efficient in managing inventories and in production. This is an economic version of slim and trim.

Now, as a consequence of vertically integrated supply chains, there are increased flows between countries at different stages of production. While this has helped firms keep costs down and production flows up, it has one drawback – increased vulnerability to disruption in the supply chain. 'Don't put all your eggs in one basket' is the age-old adage. Examples of the vulnerability of supply chains to shocks were experienced in 2011, following the earthquake and tsunami in Japan and later the same year with the floods in Thailand. While the importance of Japan and the disruption caused by the horrific quake and tsunami there might not be surprising, perhaps the disruption triggered by floods in Thailand is more unexpected. Firms have cut costs so much that it could be that just a few factories in the world produce a particular component without which the end product cannot reach its customers. Since those 2011 disruptions, one issue has been how to get more redundancy or slack back into the production process, providing some shock absorbance, and to do it without raising costs too much.

The scale of the rise in trade is remarkable. In 1948, the world total of merchandise exports was $59 billion. In 1973 it was $579 billion. By 2003 it was up to $7,380 billion and by 2012 $17,930 billion. There has been a phenomenal shift in global trade since the Second World War, and there is every likelihood of further change. Perhaps the most dramatic change over the last half-century has been seen in Western Europe, particularly in Germany and the UK. From 1948 to 2012 the UK's share of global exports has continued to fall, from 11.3 to 2.6 per cent. Germany's share, meanwhile, rose from 1.4 per cent in 1948 to 10.3 per cent by 1993, and while its share has slipped in recent years it remains high, at 7.8 per cent in 2012. Likewise, the US accounted for 21.7 per cent of global exports in 1948 but this was down to 8.6 per cent by 2012. Even so, the global reach of US firms has risen, not fallen: the top global exporters are China, the US, Germany and Japan. China, naturally, has seen its export share rise, from 0.9 to 11.4 per cent.

In the future, trade will increasingly be more about services. Western firms that specialise in business and professional services will export their services and skills, opening operations on the ground in new markets. Two economies that lead the way in trade in services are the US and UK. When we think of trade, we tend to think of the selling of goods around the world and global brands, but the increasing global exchange of ideas and thinking is also crucial. That is why I call the next global driver 'inspiration'.

Inspiration

I said earlier that a group of economists would probably not agree on the key economic drivers – but what might appear on their lists? Scale, perhaps, given how much is happening across the globe, but that is more an outcome than a driver. Some might focus on macro-economic stability, as without it growth will not be sustained, in which case indicators such as jobs, trade imbalances and inflation become the focus, but while these are important I see them as policy issues, not drivers. Likewise with potential economic challenges such as excessive debt levels. There could be policy issues linked to the supply side, including improving the efficiency of public-sector institutions and boosting private-sector productivity and competitiveness. Over time some of the consequences of stronger growth, such as increased financial resources to fund investment as firms and countries become wealthier, can themselves then help drive future growth.

Consider the periods in history outlined in the previous chapter. After the Second World War, drivers included the recovery from destruction, the spending power of the US consumer, the baby boom in the West, the rise of Japan in the Far East. Energy, too, played a major role: the focus on nuclear power, and by the 1970s the surge in oil prices that brought growth to a halt. Investment and research spending prompted by many things, including the Cold War, was important. And, of course, ongoing technological change, another key driver.

Exciting new technology has continued to improve the quality of products we take for granted, such as cars or phones, and the quality of people's lives, whether it be keyhole surgery for operations or the advent of new robotics. Technology has always helped to address economic challenges, such as the need for greater energy efficiency.

The various industrial revolutions have reflected supply-side change. Industry, steam and railways had a transformational impact in late eighteenth-century Britain. Then electricity, steel and heavy engineering, plus continued improvements in communication, helped drive the second revolution in the US as well as in Germany and Russia in the second half of the nineteenth century.

Through the twentieth century there have been further advancements: in energy, cars and mass production, the growth of petrochemicals and plastics, telecommunications, information technology, and the workplace revolution as the use of the computer took off. There seems to be no consensus about how to define the industrial revolutions that have occurred over the last century, with different periods of development being referred to as the third and fourth industrial revolutions. What lies ahead is a fifth industrial revolution – and it could be more dramatic than those before, as it has a number of components each of which could lay claim to be a revolution in itself. These include a green revolution, clean technology and biotech, nanotechnology, and the ability to produce customised goods in remote places using digital technology.

At the London School of Economics in March 2011, I was the respondent to a public lecture by Lord Stern in which he outlined why 'green' would be the fifth industrial revolution. The case was compelling, namely the need to reduce greenhouse-gas emissions to prevent significant global warming. He felt greenhouse gases were a market failure and that business should, and would, invest in low-carbon technologies. Greenhouse-gas concentrations have risen from around 285 parts per million (ppm) in the 1800s to over 430 ppm. The figure for US annual emissions per person is twenty tonnes; for China the figure is seven. Emissions will need to average four tonnes per person by 2030 and two by 2050 to keep global warming to below a rise of two degrees Celsius above 1880s pre-industrial levels (currently we are 0.9 degrees above), the level widely seen as being of vital importance to avoid dangerous climate change.

It is often only when there is a shock that progress is made. Japan's improvement in energy efficiency after the 1970s oil crisis is a good example of this. The issue is the need to incentivise business to adopt new green technologies; this has yet to take place but it might in the future.

Industrial revolutions and new innovations cannot be whistled up on demand. It is not possible to predict creative genius. The best that can be done from an economics perspective is to create the right conditions. Investment, a trained workforce with universities near by, openness to global ideas, low tax as well as tax incentives, the right regulation, good infrastructure and access to finance are all factors that can help foster a dynamic private sector. The ideal is to create an environment in which a general-purpose technology that transforms economic and everyday life – such as the telephone or the computer – can be discovered. Some economies, such as Singapore, are endeavouring to produce these conditions.

However, the discovery of a new technology does not guarantee its widespread use. Money is needed to finance its development and it has to be something that people need or want to buy.

There is a body of opinion in economics that holds that innovation is slowing down or even not happening and as a result Western economies will not see strong future growth. This view would be consistent with the secular-stagnation idea of weak growth referred to earlier. I disagree. There are many factors likely to encourage future innovation, including continued creativity, increased trade and the exchange of ideas, continued investment by firms, more universities funding research and greater competition. In any period, the bulk of inventions or innovations could rarely be predicted beforehand. There is no reason to think this will be any different in the future.

Perspiration

If technology is the inspiration, it is people who provide the perspiration. Consider the population paradox. Most if not all of us like the idea of living longer but are wary of the consequences of lots of other people living longer as well.

Is it possible to say in advance if population growth will be a demographic dividend or a demographic disaster? A dividend as more people work and spend; a disaster as there are more mouths to feed, and too many people trying to cram into already overcrowded trains and looking for houses where supply is already limited. Many see it as a problem, following in the footsteps of the nineteenth-century economist Thomas Malthus, who earned economics the title of the 'dismal science' (coined by historian Thomas Carlyle), as he projected that population would grow at a faster pace than the food supply, resulting in misery and hardship. Were he alive now, it is difficult to know whether Malthus would be alarmed by the latest population trends or impressed by the way the world has coped.

There is every likelihood the world will continue to cope. The world's population keeps growing. It reached 1 billion in 1804. It then took 123 years to reach 2 billion in 1927, and another 32 years to hit 3 billion in 1959. Fifteen years later, in 1974, 4 billion was reached, then 13 years to 5 billion in 1987, 12 years to 6 billion in 1999 and 13 years to breach 7 billion in 2012.

It is often said the one forecast that can be made with accuracy is population growth. That is because the key variables are predictable: fertility or birth rates, mortality or death rates, and life expectancy. In many respects this is true. But, even here, things can change. There are pleasant surprises – advances in medicine and health care – that can extend life. And there are also shocks. The Spanish flu in 1918, for instance, killed 18 million, a higher death toll than the First World War. There are also behavioural changes that are not always expected, such as the baby boom in the West following the Second World War. If that has happened once, it can happen again. So even in population projections there can be shocks and surprises.

What are the economic implications of population growth?

People are living longer. The economist John Llewellyn points out in *The Business of Ageing* that, since the 1840s, life expectancy has risen by two years per decade. Fertility rates have declined in many countries for a variety of reasons, including birth control, improved child mortality rates and changes in women's working situations in the advanced economies. It appears that lifestyle changes can increase life expectancy. Studies of the Mormons show they have a longer life expectancy than others in the US population; this is attributed to their healthy lifestyle, including absence of alcohol. Llewellyn discusses the 'technophysio' theory that life expectancy will rise as, increasingly, there will be unprecedented control over the environment, including food production, public health and personal hygiene.

There are examples of active policy overcoming health issues, even ones that seemed insurmountable at the time. In Finland in 1972 the North Karelia Project was introduced in a region that suffered about 1,000 heart attacks a year in a population of only 180,000. The medic Pekka Puski spearheaded a project that radically transformed eating and smoking habits. A healthy food choice had to be an easy choice – labelling foods and removing dairy subsidies were additional factors – and soon the plan went national. Coronary deaths in the region fell over 80 per cent in four decades. Healthy eating was seen as key. All of this highlights the important and positive role policy can play.

As the world's population grows, different things are happening across the globe with significant economic implications. Some regions of the world have very young populations; other parts are getting older.

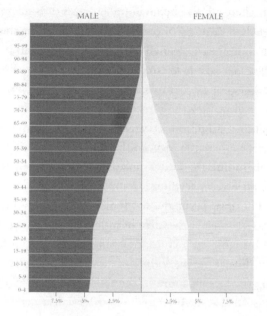

Population pyramids show a country's age profile, with the youngest at the bottom and oldest at the top, and split between men on the left and women on the right. They are called pyramids because ideally that is what they should look like. A pyramid that looks too skewed to one side or has too small a base and a bulky top will be unstable. It is the same with populations. A population pyramid that is skewed to one side means much more of one sex than the other, and a pyramid that has too small a base to support a bulky top has too few young and many more older people. An 'expansive'

age pyramid means a wide base and the need to find jobs for young people. A 'constrictive' age pyramid means a bulky top and the need to cater for the pension and health needs of the old.

It is remarkable how different and dramatic population developments are in some parts of the world. Although fertility rates have economic implications, economics is only one of many factors influencing birth rates. Traditionally, poorer countries have much higher birth rates and hence younger populations – because of high mortality rates, lack of birth control, societal norms and the fact that their economies are often driven by agriculture and it is beneficial to have more people to work on the land.

There is also some impact from the economic cycle. The US saw birth rates decline after the Great Depression and also after the recent Great Recession, to a 25-year low in 2012. Europe also saw birth rates decline between 2008 and 2011, as recession hit. But some countries, including the UK, France and a handful of others in Europe, are now seeing fertility rates rise.

Perhaps not unsurprisingly, economic incentives can influence population. This can take the form of cash allowances to help reduce the cost of bringing up a child, or even incentives to discourage births. Over time, different countries have used incentives to curb population growth. Singapore in the 1960s and India in the 1970s offered transistors, at the time a sought-after consumer durable, to encourage men to have vasectomies. China, in turn, has a one-child policy, although this is now changing. A confluence of factors including economic prospects might influence fertility rates, but it is a complex picture.

The most interesting economic aspect of population growth is that the world is getting older as the fastest-growing part of the world's population is not younger but older people. Those aged over sixty-five are likely to move from 1 in 14 now to 1 in 6 by 2050. According to the UN's population prospects, the world's median age was 23.9 in 1950 and by 2050 is expected to be 38.1, ranging from

28 in Africa to 41.5 in North America and 47.3 in Europe. Within this the number of people over the age of eighty will grow fastest. Two regions stand out: Europe and North-East Asia.

The challenge will be greatest in Europe, and by 2050 over half of the populations of Spain, Portugal, Italy and Greece will be over sixty-five. The problem in Europe is that the welfare system is generous and the fast future economic growth rates needed to fund such a system are not guaranteed. So the longer Europe leaves it to address its expensive pension problem, the greater the challenge will be.

Asia's ageing population should also not be overlooked, with Japan at the forefront and South Korea not far behind. Both are moving to slower phases of growth as older populations produce, trade and consume less. Japan, in turn, has been at the forefront of research into robotics, health care and domestic services, all of which are important as populations age. This demonstrates how investment and innovation can generate opportunities out of a potential problem. In these countries, older people tend to be well off and spend on areas that make life easier for them. With such a growing market in which to sell, more research and investment into new consumer products is to be expected.

China, too, will start to move into the ageing camp around 2015, a process that will play out over the next few decades. It used to be said that China will be old before it is rich. It is now getting older and richer at the same time. While the one-child policy allowed China to manage its population growth, it triggered other un-intended consequences such as the 4–2–1 problem. Four grand-parents and two parents can have only one grandchild, so the danger is that the children will be spoilt and not be team players when they join the workforce. At the same time, a lot of attention has been given to the child's upbringing and many are well educated.

China doesn't just have an ageing problem; it has a gender mis-match too. It is usual for the ratio of males to females to be 101:100, but because of what is happening in the most populous economies, the norm is rising, often being cited as 103–107 births of boys to 100 girls globally. In China, this sex ratio has reached 118:100. It is also high in some poorer Indian states. Culture has favoured having or keeping boys, and now the ability to predict the sex of a baby and the phenomenon of sex-selective abortion means that it is possible to make this preference a reality.

There are also some very young parts of the world's population. This too has significant economic implications and, given economic advances, this will, one hopes, be a population dividend.

The average age in India is about twenty-seven, so half of its 1.2 billion population is below that age. With a world population of just over 7 billion, that means that 1 person in 12 in the world is an Indian aged under twenty-seven. This is the crux of India's opportunity and challenge: while there are many potential positives to having a young population, not least a growing labour force, there is the need to generate jobs and make inroads into the country's high poverty rate. Notwithstanding India's ongoing economic battle over inflation and trade deficits, there are enough reasons to be positive about India's prospects, as I discuss elsewhere. Africa's population is also young, although the factors contributing to this have not always been desirable: famine, war, viruses and disease. But these population dynamics can be overcome. Over the last decade, AIDS has remained a killer, but it is now easier to control.

In June 2013 the United Nations released its latest population forecasts, which divided the world into three groups: 48 per cent of countries were low fertility, with fewer than 2.1 babies per woman; 43 per cent medium fertility, fewer than 5 babies, and 9 per cent – thirty-two countries, of which twenty-nine countries were located in Africa – were high fertility. Over the next forty years Africa's population is projected to more than double, from 1.1 to 2.4 billion, with Nigeria's rising from 158 million now to 440 million by 2050. Nigeria's population will then exceed that of the US, which will both grow and stay relatively young, rising from 312 million in 2010 to

400 million by the middle of this century. With Mexico replacing Russia as one of the ten most populous countries in the next two decades, the US and Mexico trade zone will contain a large young population, an economic plus.

There are so many opportunities that arise from such population developments. Imagine, for instance, a US manufacturer. In the past it would have been tempted to move production to Asia. Now it could potentially have some eye-opening opportunities closer to home, with a large young population in both Mexico and the US, both parts of the North Atlantic free-trade area. This is a potentially large, skilled and competitive workforce. This should encourage the US authorities and US firms to ensure an effective apprenticeship scheme, perhaps along the lines of Germany's, to feed this future. Add the benefits of a cheap, secure supply of energy through shale, and it might encourage a manufacturing renaissance in North America. New technology and robotics could reinforce this, demonstrating that the West need not fear the changing global picture.

The challenge, perhaps illustrated by the case of Africa more than anywhere else, is that population growth does not guarantee economic success. In some respects it is asymmetric. Getting it right helps, but does not guarantee future success. In contrast, getting it wrong is likely to doom an area to failure. Africa was in this latter category as its economy flatlined at a low level of income and growth. In contrast, Japan flatlined over the last two decades at a high level, as a high-income, slow-growth economy. That is not too bad a place to be, particularly as low inflation allowed Japan to enjoy real income gains over this time. The good news for Africa is that now it faces rapid population growth in a more favourable economic climate, helped by better macroeconomic policies at home and access to finance and technology that it previously did not have.

Increasing longevity suggests businesses and people need a paradigm shift in order to change the mindset about age. Too often there is a tendency to think people are past it at a certain age. Winston

Churchill did not become UK prime minister for the first time until he was sixty-five and he was seventy-six when he took office for the second time. A US president has to be at least thirty-five years old, but Ronald Reagan was sixty-nine when he was inaugurated. Moraji Desai was eighty-one when he was elected Indian prime minister in 1977. Age has not proved to be a barrier to success in the past, and there is less reason to think it will be in the future. Experience has important benefits. These demographic changes also pose interesting questions for universities and others involved in the provision of education. How can they provide for a new market of people who, because they are living longer, might wish to retrain or change careers mid-life, with shorter and perhaps online courses to help?

China's ageing means that its working-age population will shrink dramatically, reinforcing the need for China to become more innovative and productive. In contrast, India's working population and labour force will rise rapidly. Therein lies a challenge. Where in India will the jobs come from? Does India need to move into large-scale manufacturing? Or can its service and retail sectors provide the necessary jobs? Or is the answer a combination of these? Similar issues and opportunities face Africa.

In China rising wages have boosted consumption, a key aim of policy and rebalancing. In coastal areas rising wages have encouraged firms to move into higher-value-added production, which is less dependent on low labour costs and needs better-skilled workers. Rising wages have encouraged firms to move jobs inland, where costs are lower and employment is needed. And they have allowed international firms to recognise the opportunities for investing elsewhere, such as in Vietnam and Bangladesh, where there are young populations and low labour costs. India might be the next beneficiary, but it will need to keep its wage growth in check.

Many Western economies have assumed that they will attract and keep high-income jobs, with low-income jobs elsewhere. Certainly some countries with young populations will make the most of this.

That is why it is perfectly possible to see the success China achieved in low-cost manufacturing being repeated elsewhere. And in India, particularly if the infrastructure is improved, farming productivity is increased and issues over land use addressed. Africa could benefit from its sizeable labour force and access to water and commodities. Trade will also play its part. Many economies want to move up the value curve, so there will be greater competition for high-skilled jobs. And while high-value-added jobs will be desired in the West, the reality is that a range of low-skilled jobs will also be needed.

It is interesting to consider whether a further future advance in longevity is possible in population dynamics and, if so, where it might come from.

'X-factors' are plausible events that if they occurred could have a material impact. At the 2012 World Economic Forum's 'summer Davos' in Tianjin, China, I attended a session where we discussed possible X-factors. Thirty years ago this might have seemed like science fiction, but now it is realistic thinking. One X-factor is the possibility of large-scale advances in medicine. Stem-cell research is one likely area for breakthrough. This would imply a step change upwards in life expectancy, as happened at the end of the nineteenth century through advances in the provision of clean water and sanitation. The combination of medical advances and rising incomes suggests life expectancy will continue to rise.

In contrast, there are warning signs, such as the SARS virus, a lack of new investment in pharmaceuticals and antibiotics, rising obesity rates, diabetes and dementia in certain countries. These certainly pose an economic risk.

What you put in influences what you get out. In economics there are four key inputs, known as the factors of production. These are land, labour, capital and skill. These broad terms encompass a great deal. Population heavily influences labour, which is the number in work. In an era before mass production and any green revolution in agriculture, population size was key. Then it changed, with the various industrial revolutions highlighting the importance of other factors, including total factor productivity. This is a measure of an economy's efficiency and technological ability to get the most out of its labour and capital, and produce more.

Sometimes the influence of population has been overstated. During the rise of Asia, before the 1997–8 Asian crisis, and in Russia during the 1960s and 1970s, too much emphasis was placed on population alone as an economic driver. It is important, but other drivers matter too and it has to be judged alongside them.

Responding to a talk I gave to the Cambridge Society for the Application of Research in February 2013, Professor Robert Rowthorn of King's College suggested that at some stage in the not-too-distant future population size would again become the dominant driver of economic performance. He made the interesting point that once other factors – such as technology – are available to all countries then population will again become key in determining output. If so, there might then be renewed focus on the economic incentives that can be used to influence population growth. This leads directly into the next key driver: the growing middle class.

The growing middle class

In Europe and the US the recession saw wages squeezed. As a result there is much talk of this generation being poorer than the previous one. Those who hold this view have similarities with those expecting little innovation in the future. The mindset seems to be that the recent hard times will continue. This is the same bias towards the status quo as was seen in the period before the crisis, when it was assumed that the good times would continue indefinitely. I think this prevailing attitude will change along with recovery, as Western economies emerge from recession, and as firms based in the West begin to perceive the opportunities afforded by a growing world economy.

By contrast, across large swathes of the world, income levels are rising, generating increased demand for all types of goods. As income rises and future prospects improve, spending will be boosted. This three-stage effect is called the S curve: low affordability, take-off and then saturation. Across emerging economies incomes will be rising at all levels. For some this will mean a movement away from subsistence incomes and out of poverty. The number of people in poverty is declining but it is still too high. For others it will mean a move from low to higher incomes. The picture may vary across countries, but the end result will be the same: a staggering increase in the size of the middle class.

It is easy to picture a greater number of people with more money to spend. Before the crisis, the American consumer was seen globally as the person the rest of the world could always rely on to spend. While the US consumer is still vitally important, in future the world will be less dependent on big spenders in just one place. There will be more consumers across many countries. In addition to older, wealthier spenders in the West, the combined increase in people willing to spend their disposable income in China, India, the Middle East and other emerging markets will make those areas every bit as important as the US has been. And, let us not forget, Americans, like Europeans, will still be spending too, as their economy recovers and grows.

Hence global firms are looking to sell both into established markets in the West, where older groups are already high spenders, and into growing markets of younger, new consumers across the emerging world. Take India as an example. It took India thirty-two years between 1971 and 2003 to see its per-capita income rise from $100 to $500. It then took only five years to see it double again to $1,000, and the trend is continuing. According to projections from the Organisation for Economic Co-Operation and Development (OECD), India's middle class will surge from just under one in ten people to nine out of ten by 2039 – a phenomenal rise.

Similar developments, although not on the same scale, will be seen in other countries. A November 2012 World Bank report focused on economic mobility and the rise of the middle class in Latin America, a region that is often overlooked. Across that part of the world the middle class had risen by a half in a short space of time, from 103 million in 2003 to 152 million by 2009, representing a third of the population. A number of factors contributed to this, including macroeconomic stability, employment in the formal sector, education, urbanisation, the number of women in work and the proportion of smaller families. The level of income used to identify the middle class in some regions can appear small, at between $10 and $50 per day, but this relatively small amount can make a difference in economies where the cost of living is low.

Coca-Cola, Pepsi, Google, Facebook, Twitter, McDonald's, Swatch, Rolex: one thing no traveller can fail to notice is how global some brands are and that these universally recognised identities are predominantly Western. This suggests that the West has less to worry about than it thinks. It also reflects economic change. Big Western firms have become global. Now new players are emerging from across the globe: Samsung, Superdry, Tata – the list is already substantial. Consider how Hong Kong has changed. When I was growing up, 'made in Hong Kong' was synonymous with cheap, low-quality goods such as plastic toys. Now goods from Hong Kong are still competitively priced but they are of higher quality.

Economies, like companies, are changing with the times. The *Forbes* top 500 companies include 368 firms from Western economies, including Japan (68), Australia (9) and Canada (11). Almost one in three is from elsewhere, with 73 from China, 13 from South Korea, 8 each from Brazil and India, and 7 from Russia. Global brands are seeking out lucrative new markets, such as younger people in the East and older wealthier people in the West. It is not just brands that reflect globalisation. People are adopting new behaviours too, from visiting fast-food restaurants and coffee shops to the use of social media.

As we use technology and social media more, we encounter the connectivity paradox. The increased ability to communicate, for instance through Twitter, helps the flow of information, bringing insight and empowering people. However, too much connectivity can lead to overload and confusion. I see it in a positive light, as it brings networks of people and groups together and changes consumer behaviour. The UK, for instance, is at the forefront of people using technology to buy things online. This is likely to be a trend that is followed elsewhere. It could have many implications: one is that the high street starts to change, as goods we used to buy in shops are now delivered by vans. Towns and cities need to work out new systems of distribution, to ease traffic flow, and perhaps there is a need for advance planning to recast high-street shops to serve their communities in other ways. Too often people – including economists – don't see the new opportunities in front of them. As Henry Ford once said, if he had asked people what they wanted, they would have said faster horses. He gave them cars instead. Imaginative forward planning and flexibility are essential.

We love cities

Urbanisation is already having a huge impact and will continue to do so. Perhaps in the future we might become used to the idea of 'gross metropolitan product' and not just 'gross domestic product', as cities become a key driver of growth. GMP not GDP.

In 2008, for the first time, the number of people living in cities exceeded those living elsewhere, in the countryside or in villages and smaller towns. This was a tipping point; there is no going back. The world has moved into an urban age, and this is set to continue and probably gather speed. Urbanisation, like population growth, is a big plus for the world economy, but only if it is handled properly. Just as a demographic dividend could become a demographic disaster if unplanned or badly handled, the same is true of urban growth. But there are good reasons to think urbanisation with have a positive effect, probably with different shades of progress across the globe.

Regions of the world have urbanised at different times. For Britain and Europe it was in the eighteenth century, for the US in the nineteenth, for parts of Latin America during the second half of the twentieth century, and it is happening now in large swathes of Africa, China and India. It is the speed and scale of the present urbanisation that differentiates it from the past.

Before the Common Era, the huge cities of the world were located in Egypt and Iraq – the centre of civilisation as it then was – although they were soon overtaken by Rome, which became the first million-person city. Then, over time, the rise of cities in Europe reflected the growth of empires – Spain saw Córdoba, Seville and Granada become Europe's biggest cities before Paris and London emerged centuries later. During the rise of its empire, Portugal even moved its capital to Rio de Janeiro for twelve years. Now the centre of gravity of cities is changing again.

An analysis by McKinsey of the biggest 600 cities in the world found that while these are home to 1 in 5 of the world's population they drive more than half the world's output. That would mean that people who work in cities produce more with higher productivity, largely because of economies of scale. Yet, as with most things, it is essential to get the balance right.

Of the 600 largest cities, 157 are situated in the developed world, with 443 scattered across the emerging world. This is likely to change. In this top 600, about 137 Western cities are likely to be displaced by the same number from the emerging world, with China leading the way and adding around a hundred. Many of these are effectively new cities, with new housing, transport and infrastructure, and many of them are green cities, as they have been newly constructed and can benefit from advances in urban development.

The hot spots expected to have a growing population of younger high spenders in 2025 include Lagos, Dar es Salaam, Dhaka, Ouaga-dougou, Khartoum, Ghaziabad, Sana'a, Nairobi and Luanda (the capital of Angola and the third-largest Portuguese-speaking city in the world). Some names are unfamiliar and hard to say; most are difficult to locate on a map. Over the next few decades, urban growth will be concentrated in Asia and across large parts of Africa, but it will be apparent everywhere. Much of the new growth will come from emerging 'middleweight' cities such as Belo Horizonte, the third-largest city in Brazil; Puebla, the fourth-biggest in Mexico, or Pune and Kochi in India.

Urbanisation helps to reduce poverty, although it might not seem so given the shanty towns and slums in many cities across the globe. However, there is a strong correlation between urbanisation and rising per-capita income; average living standards are higher in urban areas than elsewhere. Scale is one reason; planning is another. The effect of a reduction in poverty is helped by the fact that cities attract younger people from rural areas, and they often provide a hard-working, cheap and ready labour force for the businesses that are also attracted to cities. It is also possible to provide services, particularly education and health, more effectively and cheaply to people living in urban areas, in contrast to catering for scattered countryside populations.

Models of economic geography help explain why some things agglomerate in cities and why others do not. Where people want to live, as well as where they end up living, is a consequence of this. For instance, as younger people choose to live in cities, it is more likely that the jobs and leisure activities they want will also be in cities; this in turn reinforces the desire and need for others to live there. There are other issues linked to this, including the size and scale of cities in relation to each other within a country, and the concept of clusters.

Capital cities and dominant megacities are likely to emerge. In the European Competitiveness Index 2013, produced by the Commission, eight of the top ten regions are centred on a capital city or large conurbation. Even the two that aren't, it could be argued, are linked to London: Berkshire, Buckinghamshire and Oxfordshire, in third place, and Surrey and East and West Sussex, in fifth. London was second, Stockholm fourth, Amsterdam sixth and Darmstadt, which includes Frankfurt, was seventh. Utrecht was the most competitive region. A polycentric picture emerges, of growth centred on capitals and metropolitan regions.

Large cities, particularly capital cities, can also have an indirect and direct impact on the rest of the country. Sometimes the capital city is moved, as happened with Brasilia in 1956 or the decision to make Canberra the capital of Australia in 1908 in order to head off competition between Sydney and Melbourne. The idea of moving Japan's capital from Tokyo was widely discussed after its economic bubble burst in the 1990s.

It has always been the case that particular industries cluster together – for example, the film industries in Hollywood and Bolly-wood, and now Nigeria's Nollywood, the tech industry in Silicon Valley or IT in Bangalore, diamonds in Antwerp, fashion in Milan and Paris, or global financial centres in New York, London, Hong Kong, Singapore and Tokyo. There are positive side effects to be gained from industries requiring similar skills working together, as well as economies of scale. This does not apply only to big cities: there are many examples of smaller cities and large towns where the combination of universities and specialist firms results in increased research and development – Cambridge and its tech and science base being one example in the UK.

Increased global trade is reinforcing this trend, as vertically inte-grated supply chains lead to regional specialisation and innovation. The implications are that national boundaries could break down, as the competition becomes less between countries and more be-tween cities. There might, in turn, be increased regional disparities within countries but at the same time the trend will be towards centres of excellence highlighted by the appeal of cities across the world.

Smart cities also look set to become a reality. And this is perhaps the most exciting prospect, with greater use of technology and sharing of information resulting in efficiencies in housing, transport and other services. Take Abu Dhabi, where there is already extensive research on smart, ecologically friendly cities. In April 2013 I visited Masdar City there and it was eye-opening. It was like finding myself in a dream or in the future. This is an eco-friendly city, in the desert, powered by solar energy. Heat from the plentiful daytime sun is stored in molten sand and used to provide energy at night. Masdar also has a personal rapid transport system, otherwise known as driverless cars. The cars turn up at designated stops, you get in, the door shuts, you say where you want to go and the car drives down the road, directed by magnets. As with anything else, all this needs finance and scale to become viable, but Masdar is an interesting vision of a possible future that can be experienced now. And in many respects it reinforces the arguments in favour of a new green industrial revolution.

While cities have the potential to develop in exciting ways, it is vital to ensure that the rural poor do not simply become the urban poor. That will require a combination of factors to be right: jobs, housing, transport, and governance addressing issues including education, social mobility, health care and sanitation. This means devising policies to respond to the needs of diverse demographic groups within cities. The best way to think about urbanisation is as a stepping stone to increased prosperity.

So the next time you get on a plane to fly out of a city, look down at the world economy. Instead of looking at it from five or six feet, as we do in our daily lives, imagine looking at it every day from 36,000 feet and observing all its moving parts. This is what I have tried to do.

To my mind, the world economy has a number of key drivers, starting with the emergence of China as a Robin Hood, Goldilocks and Superman economy; increased global trade both within and between regions, and the inspiration found in new technology. The other drivers are linked to people: population dynamics, as more of us live longer; the growth of the global middle class, and continued urbanisation. There are certainly policy challenges such as poverty, income disparity and distribution, and the cost of living, but I shall come to these later.

Each of these drivers is important, and the combination of all of them is particularly impressive. Not everyone will agree with me, and some economists might assign higher importance to one rather than another. But all six combined, alongside credible macro-economic policies, point to further economic growth and a growing global economic cake. All of these drivers have a part to play in how people's lives are changing and how business opportunities are evolving. In any economy, any high street, the single factor that drives shops, factories, offices and businesses is the ability to sell to customers who want to buy, at home or overseas. The growing global middle class and the new, expanding trade opportunities will be part of that. Singling out China is deliberate, as it is already having a transformational impact across the globe, and not just in East Asia. Not all firms have a US strategy, so not all firms need to have a China strategy, but there is a need to be aware of the impact China is having.

But on this journey into the economic future, recognising drivers and the positive opportunities that follow from them is not enough. We also have to be aware of the risks, and as on any journey risks need to be overcome, avoided or addressed. That is what we shall explore next.

3

Facing up to the risks

What do India and the UK have in common? There's the English language, of course, a love of cricket, perhaps even a love of regulation! But one important thing the two cultures share is pessimism. Britain's biggest export is pessimism; the same is true for India. Both countries are always self-critical, a quality perhaps reinforced by their open media.

While India and the UK may be pessimistic, the US is usually upbeat and self-confident. The can-do attitude of the US has to be a major asset in allowing its economy to rebound from setbacks. This is often seen in terms of how American companies reinvent themselves – for example, Apple with its iPhones and iPads. Australians, too, like the Americans, are seen as being positive. Just as confidence can play a role in an economy's near-term performance, it is worth asking whether some countries have particular traits that influence their longer-term behaviour. The Germans, for instance, work less than many others in Europe but are more productive; this reinforces their strong competitive position. Is that something inherent in German attitudes, or is it linked to the country's economic model, particularly its investment and education system?

Is it possible to change a national trait or a deeply held mindset about what is achievable and how things should be done? This could be one of the greatest challenges but there is no reason why it cannot be met. It might require political leaders to provide a clear vision of what is possible and to convey this message, encouraging people to spend and firms to invest. Let's not forget there are other influences at play, such as the tax and legal systems.

Optimism sometimes needs to be kept in check. As we saw during the boom, there was a tendency, and not just in the US, to believe that the good times would go on for ever. This is illustrated in many property markets across the globe, where a combination of cheap money, leverage and one-way expectations has driven property prices up in the past, and may be doing so again now in some places. But booms do not last.

How do we arrive at the right balance? One way is to keep on top of the risks. So what are the risks we face now?

At any time, it is possible to construct a set of risks or outline a sequence of events that could result in things going wrong. One could attempt to identify how likely such risks are. At the same time, there are tail risks: those that are less likely to occur but that would have a profound impact if they did. Within this group of tail risks could have been included the recent financial crisis, or the future risks attached to the collapse of the eurozone, or the challenges facing the financial sector in China. 'Black swan' events could also be included. These are unpredictable events with a major impact –although they are usually also defined as events that are rationalised with hindsight. There has been a tendency to view any big disaster, as well as inventions and dis-coveries, as a black swan. I disagree. Even though we do not know when a new discovery will be made or what it will be, we can try to create an enabling environment for it to occur. It is not by chance that many advances are made at universities or at other centres of learning. Likewise, even if we cannot predict exactly when an economic crisis or major shock will happen, we can see circumstances in which such a thing is more likely – perhaps even inevitable.

Is it possible to identify risks in advance? An approach followed by the International Monetary Fund, for example, focuses on early-warning signals, trying to identify things that would provide early guidance as to what could go wrong. The IMF also provides an annual 'Spillover Report' on the five most systemically important economies: China, the euro area, Japan, the UK and the US, and in its latest report it judges that, within them, severe tensions and risk have begun to abate.

Ever since I started my career as a professional economist, I have found large and deteriorating trade deficits to be a reliable early-warning signal of potential problems to come – for instance, in Thailand where it sparked the 1997 Asian crisis, or in the UK ahead of the late-1980s Lawson boom and bust. But there are other indicators. Rapid or at the other extreme stagnant monetary growth can never be ignored, and neither can any indicator that seems too good to be true. Forecasts from economic models can help, but a feel is needed for what is going on in order to put things in perspective.

An alternative approach is the stress tests now common in the financial sector. These project what would happen to a firm's balance sheet or to its investments in scenarios where key variables, such as interest rates or currencies, change. Stress tests need to be tough and rigorous.

Of course, even though a forecaster might be right about an upcoming problem, there is no guarantee that the predicted timing will be correct. But one doesn't have to be an economic forecaster to appreciate this.

Take a housing bubble, where prices keep rising. It might be observed that prices are out of touch with reality and that it is not wise to buy a property just yet. However, the increase prompts others to rush in to buy, fearing they will be priced out of the market. So prices keep rising. It starts to feel like a bubble. Eventually prices correct but a long time after it was thought they should, by which stage they are still much higher than when buying was first considered and the potential purchaser will have probably spent a lot on rent in the meantime. Of course prices could then plummet, but the fear that they might could trigger the government or central bank to step in and change policy to put a floor under prices or to slow their pace of decline, providing help to buyers through cheap loans or massive cuts in interest rates. So the initial thinking about the bubble could have been right but it didn't really help the potential purchaser since so many others bought anyway, forcing prices up, and policy action intervened to limit any correction. Of course, a true bubble would eventually burst and, if there was no policy intervention, prices would then fall sharply. But often policy intervenes. Policy needs to be long-term in its thinking and economically beneficial, but too often is short-term and populist.

The other point to take from the housing example is that risks are not just about things going wrong. There are also risks associated with not being prepared for things that are about to go well. A current example is being ready for stronger global growth. Emerging economies might not be prepared for the inward investment they could attract, and so need to deepen and broaden their capital markets to absorb inflows without causing inflation problems. Likewise, with huge infrastructure needs in many countries there is an opportunity to fund these by attracting savings from longer-term investors across the globe, such as pension funds. All of these become problems when they are not prepared for.

Considering how personal risks might be handled can help with an understanding of the risks facing an economy. There are risks that people would be prepared for, specific to certain circumstances, such as taking up mountain climbing or diving. While there are random risks that cannot be catered for, such as being exposed to freak weather or being in a plane crash, these can be minimised – for instance, by limiting exposure to such risks, whether it be avoiding unnecessary travel or not booking with airlines with poor safety records. Then there are core risks that would harm livelihood, health or home. And while an individual might try to be prepared for these, he or she can control only what is controllable, not what is done by others, although it might be possible to try to influence their actions. An individual can ensure that he or she is as healthy, physically and financially, as possible. It is the same with an economy.

There are always going to be things that happen unexpectedly or go wrong. That is the nature of complex systems such as economies, where so much is happening. From a policy perspective, it could be said that since it is hard to predict everything, the best objective is to be in good shape and resilient to cope with shocks. A healthy lifestyle for an economy would be to have a sound macroeconomic policy framework, with low inflation and unemployment, sustainable growth and sufficient shock absorbers if something does go wrong. I think these include high currency reserves, sound fiscal positions and small, well-capitalised banks.

As with everything, balance is crucial. In the wake of the crisis too much debt was seen as the main challenge. In reality the combination of too much debt and too little economic growth was the problem. I outline here six major plausible risks, divided into two distinct categories of 'too much' and 'too little'. The first risk is linked to health. The second is environmental. Both are heavily influenced by human behaviour and result largely from it. The same is true of the third risk: corruption.

Take health, with antibiotics as an example. We should be concerned about the rise of antibiotic-resistant strains, with the risk of a surge in premature deaths. But, at the same time, we know there is a solution. The nearest major hospital to where I grew up was St Mary's in Paddington. Here in 1928 one of the greatest medical discoveries took place. By accident, Sir Alexander Fleming discovered penicillin. In some ways this was a good economic lesson: if the right environment (in this case an experiment in a lab) is created, something positive yet unexpected might happen. Penicillin was known as 'the wonder drug' and ushered in the era of antibiotics and modern medicine. Unfortunately, its efficacy might not last.

The SARS virus in Asia in 2003 was disruptive enough to raise concerns about how the world economy could cope if there was a global health scare.

Because antibiotics have proved so effective there may be an element of complacency, with the general assumption being they will still be effective for a long time to come. The trouble is, a combination of bad economic factors is leading to the overuse and misuse of antibiotics. In India, for instance, antibiotics can be bought over the counter, without the need for a prescription. People might not buy the appropriate antibiotic and even if they do, they might be able to afford only one, two or a handful of tablets. But even in health systems where there is a requirement for antibiotics to be prescribed by doctors, problems can arise. In many systems doctors are incentivised to recommend medication. For instance, in China, there is high use of antibiotics, often for conditions for which they are not needed. Likewise, in the US there are strong ties between the pharmaceutical companies and those who prescribe. Such health worries figure regularly in discussions at meetings of the World Economic Forum. The net effect is that globally some bacteria are now becoming resistant to antibiotics. In addition, there are genuine fears that scientific developments are not keeping up with what is happening: one concern is the long time lag between the discovery or development of a drug and its introduction.

Incentive is the real issue here. How do you incentivise the right type of behaviour, as well as research into new types of antibiotic medication? Regulation is needed for how doctors prescribe antibiotics, which would then require proper policing to ensure this is followed. In addition, people need educating about what antibiotics can do and the dangers of using them in the wrong way, and the drug firms need incentivising to invest and discover more. Those processes require huge co-ordination, but often the most important factor is raising the level of awareness of the issues to begin with, before action is sought.

Pharmaceutical companies might find it more lucrative to produce drugs for older people in high-income countries where substantial numbers are suffering from chronic diseases or diseases such as diabetes. This potential market might offer higher returns on investment. How could this be addressed from the drug companies' side? Patenting new products is the natural answer, as they allow a firm to protect the secrecy of the discovery in order to boost profits from it. Patents can reward a firm for funding and carrying out research, but the flipside is that information is not shared. In the academic, scientific and health fields there might be more scope for big breakthroughs if there is sharing and pooling of ideas, as if in a giant incubator, and complete transparency might help. It is an open-universe approach.

In economic terms there is likely to be faster progress with a maximum information set that results from sharing data. The problem, though, is where does the funding come from? Producing a drug is a long, drawn-out, expensive process. That is why patents were granted to drugs companies for long periods, allowing them to make money and recoup their investment. Longer patent periods might maximise profits, but not the sharing of information, and they favour large firms over smaller firms.

The private sector is often the best place to do things, but not always. Market failure takes place when the outcome is not in the best interests of the economy and what is termed a 'Pareto-inefficient' outcome occurs. This effect is named after Vilfredo Pareto, an Italian economist of the late nineteenth and early twentieth century, who also popularised the term 'elite'.

A Pareto-efficient outcome is the best there is, where resources have been allocated so that one person cannot be made better off without making someone else worse off. Market failure means a Pareto-inefficient outcome. With pharmaceutical drugs, government and public institutions need to be mindful of the dangers that can arise from market failure, and step in to sort out the problem.

All this is a reflection of wider concerns about health. There are economic lessons to be learned from such possibilities as the ever persistent risk of a pandemic arising from a virus. We need to promote research into this area, and also into effective monitoring by and funding of the World Health Organization.

Too much pollution

The second major risk is too much carbon dioxide (CO_2), the major concern associated with climate change. Whether the world is getting warmer or colder is a keenly contested debate, yet it seems to me that the arguments of those who say there is climate change are powerful. I think the world is getting warmer and, from an economic perspective, we should take action. This can best be thought of in terms of risk versus return, a sort of insurance approach. If there is climate change the risk is considerable, and if it is left too long then by the time action is taken it may be too late, triggering severe and irreversible problems such as sharply higher sea levels, flooding, crop failures and extreme weather across the globe.

It is easy to understand why there is disagreement over climate change. The world's temperature has been subject to significant fluctuations over time, often linked to solar flares or other solar activity. There was a medieval warm period around the year 1000, and then a little ice age around 1650. During the last century there were two warm periods, between 1920 and 1940 and since 1975.

A combination of factors, including deforestation and economic growth, has led to increased demand for and use of fossil fuels. This has meant a significant rise in CO_2 emissions since the late 1950s. So, unlike the past, the current phase of climate change appears to be heavily influenced, even driven, by human activity.

The earth is a natural greenhouse. The atmosphere traps solar radiation, warming the planet and preventing it, and us, from freezing. Carbon dioxide has reinforced this greenhouse effect.

In 1938 Guy Callender suggested global warming was caused by humankind, but not everyone agrees. Despite the current bout of climate change, the longer-term trend over thousands of years is that the world might eventually be heading back to another ice age. The Clash even sang about the ice age coming in their late-1970s song 'London Calling', reflecting the mood of the time.

The best economic analysis on the subject was the 2006 Stern Report and it concluded that immediate action is needed.

This leads on directly to the next stage of the argument: mitigation versus adaptation. Do we try to prevent climate change – mitigation – or wait and, if necessary, adapt to it when it happens?

In his report, Professor Stern suggested we should spend 1 per cent of global GDP each year to prevent temperatures rising too far. Since then, as fears of a bigger temperature rise have emerged, he has suggested spending 2 per cent of global GDP each year on mitigation. This might sound expensive but, to put it in perspective, the IMF calculates that the world already spends 2.5 per cent of global GDP on energy subsidies.* The point is that the amount Stern has suggested is not that high, especially given what is at risk. Furthermore, this expenditure could have positive spin-off effects, triggering innovation and jobs in areas such as energy efficiency.

In the future, as the world economy recovers and grows, we shall become wealthier. This forecast encourages an alternative view: rather than spend now, why not wait and spend later when we shall have become wealthier and shall know if the outlay is needed? After all, this argument goes, we might be wrong about global warming.

The 'Y2K bug' could be cited as a reason for waiting. Ahead of the year 2000 there was widespread fear that computers across the world would fail when the clocks moved from 1999 to 2000. It might be hard to imagine now, but for a while the fear was that planes would fall out of the sky, or devices, including nuclear ones, would fail. A small fortune was spent on IT experts – and nothing happened. Many said this was because preparations were made, but even those who did nothing did not encounter any problems. While the Y2K episode might support those who counsel waiting, the risks suggest that, when the potential impact is huge, it is better to act. I agree with Stern.

* See speech by IMF head Christine Lagarde, 'Stability and Growth for Poverty Reduction', on 15 May 2013.

A 'free rider' is someone who doesn't contribute to solving a problem but rather relies on someone else to do it and benefits when it is done. We need to solve the free-rider problem in climate-change policy: all countries must work together. In much the same way that some global firms move low-cost production to economies such as Bangladesh and Vietnam, some countries outsource their emissions problem to others, often in the emerging world. So many Western countries can claim to be environmentally friendly when all that is happening is that many of their firms are emitting their pollution elsewhere, bypassing costly environmental standards.

But even in these countries the same thing can happen. Take China. A number of inland regions account for a significant amount of emissions while much of the output is consumed elsewhere in the country, particularly in the more affluent coastal cities. The dirt is not being cleaned up; it is simply being moved to poorer regions of the world where jobs are needed and in consequence less environmental cost is imposed on firms.

We need a better way of measuring the problem. One suggestion is a consumption-based accounting of emissions. This might reveal that the West is not that environmentally friendly after all. A global approach is needed, with accepted and enforceable standards.

A positive development is an environmentally friendly approach to business and the green economy. This might be based on quality-of-life arguments, reducing pollution to improve public health. We see it in the construction of environmentally friendly cities around the world, and even in China it is evident in the Twelfth Five-Year Plan's emphasis on the green economy.

The Stern Report held that the issue of climate change demonstrated a clear case of market failure and the need for government intervention. The recommendation was that strong early action was better than waiting. An additional reason to act was the complex negative-feedback loops that exist as pollution reinforces warming.

One part of the world where such feedback loops might already be evident, and where there is dramatic change that could have a major economic impact, is the Arctic. It remains to be seen whether the cooling there over the last year continues or whether the melting of the ice seen in previous years reappears. That melting was having a positive economic side effect, opening sea lanes previously closed to shipping for most, if not all, of the year. In August 2012 the Chinese ice-breaking research vessel *Xuelong* ('Snow Dragon') sailed from China to Iceland via the Bering Strait and the Barents Sea. Around the Arctic, new sea routes are opening that could have a transformational impact on trade, particularly for economies such as China, Russia and Iceland.

Two new routes might become commercially viable in coming years. One is the Northwest Passage, with its romantic historic image of bravery and adventure as explorers tried to navigate a route. If the ice melts, this route around the northern coast of Canada would soon connect the Atlantic and Pacific oceans for large parts of the year, perhaps for all of it. Then there is the north-eastern route, around the north of Russia. Melting snow and rising water levels have meant this passage is becoming navigable by bigger ships. There is also a channel that might emerge closer to the North Pole, in international waters, if the ice continues to melt.

The future economic benefit of faster sea routes contrasts with rising sea waters leading to flooding in coastal areas around the world. One consequence of rising population and stronger growth in many emerging regions is that there will be more people and more economic activity in these high-risk areas. This moves the economic focus from mitigation to adaptation. Singapore is already taking action by planning for a one-metre rise in sea levels this century. Others could learn from this example and take preventative action in coastal areas.

Too much corruption

The third risk is corruption. It is already happening and the danger is that it will get worse. This corrosive influence is like a cancer, eating away at the very fabric of an economy and society. It under-mines behaviour and distorts incentives, and the result is a worse economic outcome.

Corruption is hard to quantify, but it is an issue many countries must face up to. There is a tendency to think corruption is a devel-opment issue, endemic in poorer countries, and that over time, as their economies grow, it becomes less of a concern. It is often seen as operating at the intersection between the public and private sector, especially where public officials have discretion over expenditure or awarding projects where the private sector might be involved.

Transparency International carries out an annual survey that ranks countries by the scale of corruption. In 2013, 177 countries were monitored. The bottom three – in equal 175th place – were Somalia, North Korea and Afghanistan. There was a mixed picture for some of the big growing economies, with Brazil in 72nd place, China 80th, India 94th and Indonesia 114th. Those figures feel right. European and Western economies did well.

In India, the need to confront corruption head on caught the pop-ular imagination during 2011. Anna Hazare, a man in his seventies, decided enough was enough and embarked on an indefinite hunger strike to exert pressure on the government to bring in a stringent anti-corruption law. His action was immediately supported by widespread public protests. In 1969, the first attempt to introduce an anti-corruption bill in India failed; it was not approved by the upper house of the Indian Parliament. This established a trend that was, incredibly, to last for over forty years. Eventually a Lokpal – roughly translated as 'protector of the people' – Bill was passed by both the upper and lower houses in December 2013. The aim of the Bill was to establish an independent super-judicial authority with powers to investigate and prosecute ministers and bureaucrats. Having taken decades to pass this Bill, the start of 2014, an election year, saw the different Indian parties calling for more anti-corruption bills, This is going in the right direction, but there is still a long way to go.

In the past, as long as ruling elites around the world provided stability and growth they could by and large rule as they wished. Now, with increased openness and transparency, habits need to change. And change is possible. Over the last decade, two economic success stories have been Brazil and Indonesia. Previous fears in both countries that political leaders would be extreme have proved misplaced and anxiety about corruption has eased, particularly in Indonesia. The challenge is to sustain this trend as political leaders change. In Indonesia the 2014 presidential election will be important, and it needs to show recent gains are sustainable. Brazil, meanwhile, must deliver on the 2014 World Cup and 2016 Olympics, and show that it can tackle its twin issues of poor infrastructure and inequality. Economic success continues to bring new challenges.

In economics, any amount of corruption is bad and should not be tolerated; on a larger scale it can threaten economies and society itself. On the face of it the West is not corrupt, and this is reflected in international comparisons. But the reality is the economic system as it has evolved is dominated by vested interests. Big firms are extraordinarily powerful. Huge amounts are spent on public relations, often to ensure the status quo remains unchallenged.

It is essential that there are safeguards in place to protect against oligopolistic and monopolistic behaviour. If not, the rules of the game don't provide a level playing field for all. The dangers include consumers paying too much, and competition suffering as new firms find it hard to enter. In the wake of the 2008 crisis there has been increased financial regulation, often designed to protect the public, but such regulation can be expensive to implement. A serious unintended consequence is that this protection will make it more expensive and harder for new firms to enter parts of the financial industry. And that is not healthy. Capitalism works when existing firms fail and new firms form – a version of nature's survival of the fittest. The last thing that should happen is for failures to be shored up and for new entrants to be faced with insurmountable obstacles.

Curbing corruption often requires a cultural shift. But it also highlights the importance of having the right institutional infra-structure in place. This requires openness and transparency about public procurement processes, improved governance and greater accountability of company boards, an open and free media, and a legal system that operates above the heads of politicians and rulers.

We have now considered the 'too much' risks. What are the 'too little' risks?

Too little energy

Over the last decade demand for primary energy has risen 30 per cent, predominantly from emerging economies. In four of the last five years, demand from OECD economies has fallen, a reflection of the poor post-crisis recovery and lack of demand. Increasingly, many initiatives we pursue, including new technologies, are energy intensive.

An easy-to-understand four-sector diagram demonstrates the energy outlook. Demand for energy is captured along the horizontal axis, so a movement to the right reflects rising energy demand, and to the left falling energy demand. Price is captured on the vertical axis, with rising prices going up and falling prices going down. Global growth and energy prices are interlinked and, along with energy supply, determine which sector the world is in.

The bottom-right sector of the diagram shows rising demand and falling prices. This is outcome A for Ample supply. It means a favourable outlook with demand met easily by new supply. It also reflects a declining marginal cost of energy production, which contributes towards the falling price. The top-right quadrant is outcome B, where B stands for Bright future. The lights certainly wouldn't go out in this future, but unlike in scenario A, prices would rise, not fall.

One way to understand this is by considering the oil and commodity situation in recent years, where for a time there was a firm floor

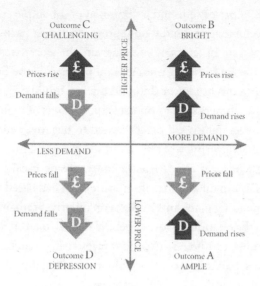

and a soft ceiling. The firm floor reflected strong underlying energy demand from across the emerging world, sustaining prices. The soft ceiling was because prices could be pushed up by energy shortages or geopolitical problems – for instance, with Iran or Saudi Arabia.

The top-left quadrant of falling energy demand and rising prices is not the place we want to be. But as with all four outcomes here, it is possible to construct a scenario in which it might occur. C stands for Challenging. It is the peak cheap oil outcome. It also reflects the feedback loops that exist between energy and world growth. If supply is tight and energy prices rise, this dampens demand and hits confidence. It is remarkable how many growth phases in the past have had cheap energy, land or labour contributing to their success. These factors remain important, alongside supply-side issues such as technology and innovation.

Outcome D is a Depression scenario, where demand and energy prices fall. It is worse than outcome C. So in terms of this four-sector diagram of the energy landscape, A is better than B, which in turn is better than C, and D is worst for the world economy. In late 2014 a sharp fall in prices reflected a combination of ample supply and an expectation that demand would grow at a slower pace than previously expected. In terms of the diagram, the worry was that this reflected D when in fact it was A. If oil prices collapse because of ample supply and not lower demand then it should be good news, provided the winners such as oil users spend some of their extra income. However, falling oil prices added to negative sentiment in many places, triggering worries about deflation in Europe, adding to financial concerns about Russia and exposing fiscal difficulties in Middle Eastern oil-producing countries that had based their government spending plans and budgets on oil prices remaining high.

Many in the oil industry don't believe in peak oil. But it is a valid worry, as oil is a finite resource that faces rising demand. In economic terms, I am more comfortable with calling it peak cheap oil as opposed to peak oil. If oil prices stay high, this provides an incentive for energy companies and oil producers to develop new fields that would not be profitable at lower prices. So more oil comes on stream – but it is not cheap.

Decarbonisation is seen as a necessary trend for the future. An important concept mentioned by Sanders Research is energy return on investment: Sanders thinks that the amount of energy required to extract energy is rising. If so, it reinforces the peak cheap oil debate, and adds to the incentive to find technological solutions.

There are three possible responses to a rise in demand for oil: price, supply or technology response. Or, more likely, a combination of all three. Technology can cover many areas, aimed at improving energy output and efficiency. It can make it economically viable to produce new forms of energy.

Global growth leads to increased energy consumption. Higher prices increase the incentive to look for new sources of supply, such as offshore Brazil, the west of Africa, in the Arctic, or oil and gas from shale, as well as increasing the incentives to devise new technologies and improve overall energy efficiency.

Consider the benefits of affordable energy, and in turn the challenges caused by high energy prices in recent years. It is often overlooked how high energy and commodity prices were ahead of the financial crisis. In 2007–8 these high prices contributed to the US slowdown by curbing spending power. High energy prices before the crisis provided a clear signal of the lack of previous investment in commodity-producing regions.* Then, by the time investors and the industry were waking up to this situation, the financial crisis was in full flow, acting as a hurdle to investment, and finance and funding were no longer available. As the world started to recover, pent-up investment in commodity-producing regions began to take place.

There is always a danger going from a famine to a feast in investment spending. This is true in any sector, especially in energy and commodities, as it might take a long time before investment results in higher output. As a result, commodities are sometimes subject to violent cyclical swings. Low prices discourage investment but encourage demand. Higher demand raises prices, in turn encouraging investment; that takes time to come on stream and, by the time it does, demand has often eased, either because an alternative supply has been found or, more usually, because high energy prices have led to a slowdown in growth.

Given all these challenges, it is interesting to observe that it is the international energy company Shell that has gained a reputation for scenario planning. The company's first major scenario-planning exercise was in 1972, and since then it has carried out a regular scenario plan every few years, where it publicly presents its overall thinking. Their latest scenario considers the water–food–energy nexus, as they see demand for these rising by almost half by 2030. This feeds nicely into the second 'too little' risk: clean, unpolluted water.

---

* Also speculators contributed to a rise in the price of oil from $70 a barrel in summer 2007 to $145 a barrel during July 2008.

Too little clean, unpolluted water

The price mechanism is a central feature of economics, vital for sending signals. Yet there are some essentials that are free in many places or not priced properly in others, and water is one of them. When commodities are not priced properly it leads to a misallocation.

Take basic services. Provision of basic services has to be paid for, and in some countries the costs are met by general taxation or government borrowing. This includes a multitude of areas: for instance, the provision of sewers to carry away waste, pipes to bring drinking water, or health provision. But once you create a disconnect between the person who pays for a service and the person who receives it you have a potential problem, and if something is free or too cheap it is often not valued or not used properly.

The provision of water should be seen in this light. We must price water by charging people and companies for using it. It needs to be priced properly to discourage the wrong type of behaviour, to encourage the right type, and to avoid penalising the poor in the process.

With water, the problems are multiple: shortage, location, pollution. These problems are not being addressed properly, so many wrong behaviours continue.

The scale of the problem is considerable. Across the globe, one person in eight lacks safe drinking water and four in ten lack adequate sanitation. There is a 'water gap' between those who have it and those who don't. Twelve per cent of the world's population consumes 85 per cent of its water. As the world economy grows and incomes and aspirations rise, the demand for water will increase. It is an issue that needs to be addressed sooner rather than later. Pricing water properly is one important step.

There are various ways in which water can be collected for use. The cheapest is the catchment of rainwater: rivers are the single biggest source and reservoirs are plentiful. Next cheapest is recycled or reclaimed water, where sewage or waste water is treated and purified for reuse. More expensive is the provision of desalination plants to convert sea water into usable water. These are to be found in the Gulf countries in the Middle East, but while desalination helps with the water shortage it is energy intensive. Then there is the importation of water from neighbouring countries. Singapore, for instance, has had a long-standing contract since 1962 to import water from Malaysia, but aims to have achieved self-sufficiency long before the contract expires in 2061.

Greater awareness of this issue has also focused attention on other ways to address water-shortage problems: the easiest and quickest benefit is achieved by upscaling the pipe infrastructure to prevent leakage. Just as preventative medicine is better than intensive care, preventing water loss might be the best way of conserving it.

Other than capturing rainfall, perhaps the most important concept in the economics of water is 'virtual water'. Virtual water refers to the amount of water used to produce both foods and non-foods. Most of us don't have a clue about how much water is used to produce something – in part because we have not been taught to think in those terms, and also because virtual water is hard to measure and the use of water is not priced properly.

One problem with water is that it is difficult to understand the variety of units in which it is measured. Rainfall is calculated in inches or centimetres; personal consumption in litres, and agricultural use in cubic metres. Comparing like with like is hard. Globally, there are a number of regions that face extreme water shortages, including the Gulf, the Middle East and North Africa. The countries hardest hit include Bahrain, Qatar, Kuwait, Libya, Djibouti, UAE, Yemen, Saudi Arabia, Oman and Egypt. Then there are particular regions of other countries where there are extreme problems, including parts of China such as the North-East, Beijing, Jiangsu, Shandong and Tianjin; parts of India such as Haryana, Uttar Pradesh, Gujarat and Rajasthan, and parts of the US Midwest and Southwest.

In many high-population areas there is overexploitation of groundwater resources, such as the Ganges and Indus river basins in India and the Yellow River basin in China.

What is the answer? Globally 69 per cent of water is used by agriculture, 23 per cent by industry and 8 per cent by individual people. Agriculture is one area in which it should be possible to make major changes, but moderating all water use will help. Among potential solutions are more effective irrigation, including systems such as the drip lines used in Australia to provide precisely the right amount of irrigation or the minimum water needed by particular crops. Support for small-scale farmers, who are not using large-scale irrigation methods, or who grow diverse crops to suit local conditions, should be encouraged. Agroforestry, aimed at building root systems and avoiding soil erosion, is of interest. As is replacing intensive grain production with other crops in more water-stressed regions.

Having attended various sessions on water across the globe, it is clear to me that an increasing number of people are aware of the problem and more is being done to address it. Countries such as Singapore and Australia are allocating more time and resources to the issue. Insurance companies and big agricultural and commodity firms are funding more research into water management. There is also sophisticated statistical modelling to determine optimal cropping patterns, a shift to biodiversity and to an optimised agricultural policy in various countries. As awareness rises, progress is made, but there is still a long way to go.

Although some economists say there is little innovation, they should look at what is happening on the ground in many areas, water being one of them. It is not just about farming or drinking. Data in 2009 showed the number of children globally who die each day from a lack of access to clean water and sanitation is equivalent to the number of passengers that would be killed were six jumbo jet planes to crash. While there might have been some improvement in that figure since 2009, it is still likely to be high. But whereas air crashes make the TV news, water problems rarely do.

The pricing of water is key, both to reflect the cost of getting it to where it is needed and to reflect its scarcity. For a start, subsidies should be dropped in many areas, as they distort perception and encourage the wrong behaviour. The 2011 annual budget in India had an opportunity to address three big subsidies – food, fuel and fertiliser – but fell short on each. In India electricity subsidies led farmers in some states to pump too much water. Globally, subsidies should be reduced and water costs should be charged at point of use. The issue in the West is not personal drinking water; flushing toilets, washing clothes and taking showers are the high-volume activities. The key is effective water management, in both demand and supply.

Water security has also become a new buzz phrase. But it would be better if there was co-operation rather than confrontation in tackling this issue. The building of dams, for instance, was once vital for hydroelectricity, but it might now not only have an impact on local ecosystems but also cause tensions with neighbouring countries, particularly if they lie downriver. The UN declared 2013 its international year of water co-operation, no doubt with one eye on countries working together to address issues.

As big a problem as the shortage of water is, it is always possible to find a solution. Flying into Bermuda helps one appreciate this. The vista below is a most picturesque manmade scene, with beautiful white-topped roofs scattered across the island. At first it seems that the architecture is for cosmetic reasons – like a perfectly manicured Disneyland – but the square residential buildings with stepped white roofs serve a purpose. These roofs are made of the limestone that is plentiful in Bermuda and which also happens to be a purifier. Bermuda has sufficient rain for its needs but its land mass is small, so capturing water as efficiently as possible is essential. When it rains, water falls on and flows down the stepped roofs, being purified naturally by the limestone and then flowing into a storage facility in the house, for personal use. It works.

Too little awareness of the risks

The final danger is too little awareness of possible macroeconomic risks and not pricing properly for them. The economic outlook is neither completely predictable nor completely random. Recently I heard a discussion about climate and the weather and what struck me was how relevant some of the points were for the current economic discussion. The scientists were making the point that it is difficult to predict the weather over days and weeks but far easier to analyse longer-term climatic trends for years to come. It is the same with economics.

It seems obvious that if something is closer it is more predictable and if something is further away it is less predictable. Yet that is not always the case. Economies are complex systems with many variables and sometimes the further ahead one projects, the clearer the outcome – perhaps like everyday life. With specific events that are months away, such as a big family occasion, we might have a better idea of what we'll be doing than on a given date in a few weeks' time.

It is also possible to look at the future in the way that seamen once looked out from the crow's nest, surveying the horizon. When we survey the economic horizon we can imagine things that are more or less likely to appear on it. But we don't know when, or where.

A few years ago US Defense Secretary Donald Rumsfeld received much coverage for talking about the future in terms of knowns and unknowns. He referred to 'known knowns', 'known unknowns' and 'unknown unknowns'. It was received with merriment in the media, which was a shame, because some of the risk debate in the years preceding his speech had been conducted using these terms. There are some things we know could happen and some things we don't know.

The example I used to use – before Rumsfeld spoke – was Mount

Vesuvius. When Pompeii and Herculaneum were big towns, people thought Vesuvius was just a mountain, not a volcano. This was an unknown unknown. The first unknown was they didn't know it was a risk and the second unknown was that there was no way of predicting when it would explode anyway. After the eruption Vesuvius became a known unknown: they then knew it was a risk (known) but they didn't know when it would erupt again (unknown). The financial crisis for me was a known unknown: it was no surprise there would be a crisis but it was unclear when it would occur. And at some stage there will be another.

Ahead of the financial crisis, interest rates in many Western economies were too low, so borrowers and lenders did not price properly for risk. The interest rate is the price of money. If it is too low, money is too cheap. At the same time, financial markets became worried about too much money in the world economy – in other words, too much liquidity. Low rates led to a search for yield, as investors sought higher returns. The result was lax financial conditions and increased vulnerability to shocks.

Diversification used to be thought of as a way to insulate against possible risks. Yet recent years have provided reasons to think otherwise. Singapore, for instance, prides itself as an economy that plans ahead and protects against risks. Diversifying its economy was seen as both providing the country with many different engines of growth, such as manufacturing, retail, business services, finance and insurance, or transport and storage, and giving it greater protection on the downside, as each sector of the economy might have had different growth drivers. Yet what we saw was that when a big enough shock hits, with demand falling, it impacts the whole economy.

The lesson here is to improve our own resilience by accepting that shocks will happen and they are out of our direct control. For instance, a country with a coastline is not able to stop a tsunami but it can improve its defences and early-warning system in order to move people to safety by the time the tsunami hits.

The International Monetary Fund tries to have sufficient early-warning signals in place to spot potential macroeconomic or financial risks. But as it is hard to plan for all scenarios and be aware of all dangers, resilience to shocks may be a better way to proceed. Risks and potential problems can be addressed in many ways: a combination of the right governance structure, incentives and information sharing. The more information there is about potential problems, the better prepared we can be. The perception of risk is subjective. There is no hard and fast rule and, to make it worse, it is usually only when a risk hits that we find out whether the economy is resilient enough to cope.

There are significant changes in the risk landscape that offer opportunities for those in the risk business, not least Lloyd's of London, but also others involved in the monitoring, assessment and placement of risk. To quote the speech of John Nelson, the chairman of Lloyd's, at the Lloyd's 2013 City Dinner:

> No major economy has ever been able to prosper, on a long-term basis, without proper risk transfer. That means we have extraordinary opportunities for growth in the emerging economies, which are starting to use formal risk-transfer mechanisms. I will give you one figure: less than one per cent of the damage caused by the earthquake that occurred in China in April was in fact insured.

He's right that people should start to take more responsibility. But it is not just in the emerging economies. As the welfare system in the West changes, and as people grow older, there is the opportunity for insurance to evolve and cover not just cars and homes, but other areas of people's lives.

It is always possible to think of something that could go wrong, but that doesn't mean it will. The economic lessons are to improve domestic resilience to cope with shocks, to encourage the right long-term behaviour, and to work together with other countries.

4

An Apollo 13 moment for the financial sector

There is a saying that nothing is certain except for death and taxes. Most of us would probably agree. Perhaps it should be revised to cover death, taxes and financial crises. We all die; governments find ways to tax us more and more, unless you live in one of the Gulf economies or a tax haven, and financial crises occur with increasing frequency.

There is no strict definition of what constitutes a financial crisis. Normally it involves a large fall in stock markets, a collapse in the value of a currency, or major problems with a bank. There can be other elements, but these are the most usual.

Why are financial crises inevitable? Is it something about the way banks and financial markets operate; the greed of the people who work within them; poor management and governance, or ineffective policing and regulation? Or is it that, as the financial system is now so complex, it is far more difficult to manage risk? Or is it a combination of all of these?

Economics teaches us that incentives really matter. Economics also shows that the financial system plays a central role in allowing an economy to grow, as people and businesses borrow for their future needs and savers invest. As with the circulation of blood within a body, when a financial system is working properly it ensures that money goes to where it is needed. But, after the 2008 crisis, faith was rocked. Many felt the financial system had moved out of touch with the rest of the economy, that it was no longer servicing its customers and was instead looking after itself. Credit is at the heart of the financial system. In Latin, *credo* means 'I believe'. Belief and trust are essential for a banking and financial system to work properly.

There can be many triggers for crises, and often it is hard to pin-point the catalyst precisely. However, often there are warning signs. Growing economic imbalances can be one indication, especially if a country is running a large current-account deficit, meaning that it is dependent on foreign financial inflows to fund it. This is made worse if the deficit is needed to finance domestic spending rather than investment, and if it is funded by short-term 'hot money' inflows, as has often been the case in crisis-hit countries. Such hot money is fast-paced speculation on variations in interest or exchange rates, and it can leave an economy just as quickly as it arrives.

Sometimes the early-warning sign of an impending problem can be financial, with bond and equity markets behaving in a way that is out of sync with either economic reality or prior market perform-ance – such as when a stock market keeps reaching ever new highs, or if bond markets continue to rally, with yields falling to ever new lows.

Perhaps we could do with a form of Richter scale to measure financial shocks. The Richter magnitude scale measures the energy released by an earthquake. It is a logarithmic scale, meaning an 8 is ten times as powerful as a 7, which in turn is ten times as powerful as a 6. A financial Richter scale would allow us to assess the scale of financial crises. A crisis would be registered when it was powerful enough to be noticed and caused economic damage. We might con-clude that financial crises are now more frequent and extreme and ask why that is the case. Are there enough early-warning signs and are economies able to cope?

With earthquakes it is possible to gauge the damage in terms of the loss of life and the cost of reconstruction, but it is less easy to do with financial crises. When an earthquake strikes, it is clear what is needed in order to return to normal. Its economic impact can be represented as a V shape, with the downward part of the V being the damage and immediate impact after the quake, when buildings collapse, transport grinds to a halt, mobility is limited and dis-cretionary spending is hit. The upward leg of the V represents the return to normality. The depth of the first stroke of the V relates to the extent of the shock. The trouble with financial crises is that it is not always clear what the response should be, and so the length and angle of the second stroke of the V is difficult to predict.

Here is a list of a selection of financial crises. It is not intended to be comprehensive but to illustrate that they have occurred all over the world over a considerable period of time. A table covering all financial crises would go on for pages. I have categorised the crises by impact, as one would an earthquake. Many earthquakes are scarcely noticeable, falling into the categories of 'micro' (less than 3 on the scale), 'minor' (3 to 3.9) or 'light' (4 to 4.9). There are about five hundred 'moderate' quakes a year (5 to 5.9), causing slight damage; about a hundred 'strong' ones (6 to 6.9), causing potentially lots of damage depending on where they hit; about twenty major quakes a year (7 to 7.9), and one great quake every five years, measuring more than 8 on the scale and causing severe damage.

Micro (< 3)
1979–87 Frequent realignments in Europe's exchange-rate system.

Minor (3–3.9)
1870   Argentine economic crisis
1884   Panic of 1884, one of many that characterised that time, in New York and Europe
1992   Banking crisis in Scandinavia and Finland
1994   Mexican economic crisis
2001   Argentine currency crisis

Light (4–4.9)
1989–91 US savings and loan crisis
1993   Currency crisis in Europe, the legacy of Black Wednesday the previous year
1998   Russian financial crisis

Moderate (5–5.9)

1890   Panic of 1890 involving Argentina and Barings

1987   Black Monday: stock-market crashes across the globe

1992   Black Wednesday currency crisis; sterling collapses
        and leaves Europe's currency system

Strong (6–6.9)

1893   Panic of 1893

1907   US Panic of 1907; contributed to creation of the US
        Federal Reserve Bank in 1913

1982   Latin American debt crisis, triggered in Mexico

1997–8 Asian economic and currency crisis

Major (7–7.9)

1990–97 Japan bubble bursts, with aftershocks until 2010

Great (> 8)

1929   Wall Street Crash followed by Great Depression

2008   Western financial crisis, centred on banks

If there was a Richter scale for financial crises, the one that hit at the heart of the global economic network in 2007–8 would have registered a 9.5. It was severe and the damage extensive. In the West it is seen as a once-in-eighty-year event, on a par with the Great Crash of 1929 when the US stock market collapsed.

On the financial-market Richter scale there have been many crises, minor tremors and shocks, in fact too many to comment on. Since starting work in the financial sector in October 1985 I have observed, up close, five major financial shocks, and a number of others from afar. I would have had to be living on the earthquake-prone Pacific Rim of Fire and contriving to be in exactly the wrong place at the wrong time to have experienced so many major earthquakes in such a short period. But in the world of finance there was no need to move anywhere. I was simply working at the heart of the biggest financial centre in the world: London.

Below I outline the major financial crises that have occurred since I started working in the City of London and what they reveal about the way markets work, economies cope, those in the financial sector react, and how politicians and policymakers respond. The lessons we take from these events are relevant to an understanding of the future.

Black Monday

The film *Wall Street*, released in 1987, captured the optimism and excitement of that era in the West. Gordon Gekko was the film's central character, believing 'greed is good' and that the end justifies any means. After the depressing 1970s, littered with economic crises and energy shocks, and the recession of the early 1980s, there was a sea change. The mood turned positive. Success was measured by financial reward, not personal fulfilment.

So many changes were happening in the mid-1980s.

In the US and UK, under Ronald Reagan and Margaret Thatcher, there was a shift in favour of free-market thinking and policies. Their economic policies resulted in lower inflation; lower taxes, especially for high earners; an easing of controls on credit, and a resurgence of confidence. The biggest beneficiary was the financial sector. Thatcher, in particular, took on vested interests, including the City of London, and in October 1986 the 'Big Bang' of financial deregulation took place. London and New York established themselves as the world's pre-eminent financial centres, ahead of Tokyo. It was the start of an era of light regulation that continued up until the 2008 crisis. Financial markets were off the leash, but this was not to be without consequence.

It was also the time when the world economy started to become smaller because of improved communications, including telecommunications. Things were very different then.

Soon after winning the UK general election in 1979, Thatcher abolished exchange controls, which were complex and intrusive. Before 1979, an individual could not take more than £50 out of the UK. The movement of money was freed up. Another big change was in communication and technology. Nowadays, on the right tariff, it is possible to use a mobile phone to ring the other side of the world. Back in 1984 this could be done only from a landline, but it wasn't possible simply to pick up the phone and dial an overseas number. To ring many countries from the UK a call had to be booked via the phone operator; to places such as Australia it had to be booked a day in advance.

Much of the world has moved on since then. In 1990, visiting South-East Asia for the first time, I was struck by how the main hotels in Thailand and Indonesia had just one international television news channel. This was not broadcast in real time but with a delay of many hours so that any undesirable items could be censored and not shown. As for getting the latest football results from England, whereas now one would just go online instantly, in those days one had to search them out days later in the *International Herald Tribune*, the one available international newspaper. It seems like a different world, and it has changed so quickly.

Since the 1980s there has been increased capital mobility as money has flowed around the globe. There has also been financial deepening as more products in which to invest and save have become available. This has contributed to the intricate interconnections we now see across the financial world.

In the mid-1980s the good times rolled. Then, suddenly, there was a jolt in the form of the first major Western financial crisis in modern times: Black Monday, 19 October 1987, when global stock markets crashed. Having started work two years earlier in the City, I had also just bought my first flat in London not long before. It proved the peak of the property market for a few years. It was also when I first heard the saying that banks will happily give you an umbrella but they will ask for it back at the first sign of rain. Banks had lent generously and then became cautious; public confidence was hit, and, soon after, the Chancellor realised he needed to tighten policy to curb the boom. Interest rates were to double from 7.5 to 15 per cent.

I was fortunate as I was one of the few City economists predicting aggressive interest-rate hikes and had fixed my borrowing costs at the bottom. It is said that property prices can't fall, but they did then, not showing signs of life until 1993–4. I also realised the problem lay not only with the first-time buyer – the person needed to start the market moving – but also with the first-time mover. If there is a need to move to a bigger place because, say, of a growing family, it might be difficult to do so if prices have fallen. The flat I owned at that time is currently worth about eight times its value then, illustrating rampant house-price inflation in London. Perhaps Mark Twain was right when he advised, 'Buy land. They've stopped making it.'

One story from Black Monday is that that evening, Alan Greenspan, chairman of the Federal Reserve, the US central bank, stepped off a plane after an internal flight. The first question he asked waiting officials was where did the US stock market, the Dow Jones index, finish? 'Down five zero eight' was the reply. Greenspan looked relieved. After all, 5.08 was not such a bad performance, particularly given the turbulence of the market the previous week. Seeing that the chairman had clearly misunderstood, the officials hurriedly put the record straight. 'No, five hundred and eight, not five point zero eight,' they said. Relief was replaced by shock and horror.

The previous record stock-market fall was just the week before, when it fell 95 points on the Wednesday, following poor US trade figures; 58 points on the Thursday and, another record, 108 points on Friday, 16 October. So the collapse on the Monday, 508 points, was dramatic. A quarter of the net worth of all US firms – and with it the wealth of many savers and investors – was wiped out in one day. Stock markets worldwide collapsed.

If ever a financial-market event caught the public attention, this was it. There were headlines across the globe. Comparisons with the US stock-market crash of 1929 that preceded the Great Depression were everywhere. Black Monday provided many economic lessons we would see repeated over the next twenty-five years. It also gave an insight into the triggers that could destabilise financial markets, and showed how these same markets could move out of line with reality and overreact to news.

Three related issues triggered the fall on Black Monday. All are relevant today. One was public disagreement between the Americans and the Germans over policy, after a prolonged period of agreement. Germany raised interest rates on 6 October, sending the message that – for the Germans – domestic needs rather than global concerns were the key influence on policy. The lesson was that financial markets don't like policy disagreement, instead preferring to believe that there is someone in charge. The second trigger was a poor US trade deficit that fed concerns that the US might be living beyond its means. We've seen this many times since. Third, there was a deterioration in US inflation expectations, which pushed bond yields up and made the stock market look expensive. In short, the macroeconomic environment sets the mood of the moment, heavily influencing outcomes. And, ahead of Black Monday, that was changing.

Markets can overreact, with excessive volatility. Black Monday was also the first real sign that the financial market's tail was wagging economic policy's dog. The crash in stock markets led politicians and central bankers to respond: America cut rates; even the German Bundesbank lowered its discount rate to a then all-time low of 2.5 per cent, and the UK cut its interest by 0.5 per cent on three occasions in the following weeks. It was these interest-rate cuts and not the crash in stock markets that had the bigger economic effect. The world economy recovered and did not slump as feared. The power of monetary policy was underlined, as central banks not only lowered interest rates but also pumped in money to help out banks and financial institutions. They have been doing it ever since.

The markets were reassured: the belief was that if something goes wrong in the financial markets, politicians and policymakers will step in. It became known later as the 'Greenspan Put'. Using terminology from options markets, it expresses how the financial markets expected Greenspan and the Federal Reserve to respond to problems by cutting interest rates or adding liquidity. Greenspan's policy reflected the pressure on policymakers and politicians to provide instant solutions to problems, rather than take a tough non-interventionist stance.

One lesson from Black Monday has also been apparent in many financial crises since. There is no reason for markets to fluctuate so much. The fact that they do makes many people question whether markets are out of touch with economic reality.

There are other ways to look at this. One is the sheer scale of transactions. Take the foreign-exchange markets. The 2013 *Triennial Central Bank Survey* of foreign exchange showed that daily turnover had reached $5.3 trillion in April 2013, having continued to climb from $4 trillion in April 2010 and $3.3 trillion in 2007. In many respects, these numbers are so big it is hard to conceive of them, but they show that the size of these markets is huge relative to any sensible benchmark. Some of this foreign-exchange trading is to finance trade, but a vast amount of it is between one trader and another in the financial sector itself. It is not just the scale of the markets that has become a concern but their complexity as well. This makes it harder for banks and financial firms to manage their risks.

This reinforces the need for the financial sector to be properly regulated, particularly to ensure that contagion is limited when something goes wrong, and even raises the question whether parts of it need to be scaled back in size. It is also possible to understand why there are calls for a financial transaction tax. The economist James Tobin was the first to suggest that a small tax on foreign exchange would deter speculators but not long-term investors. In theory it has attractions, but making it work in practice is the challenge. Many investors do genuinely change their mind and such a tax might be an impediment to them. If the tax is small, it is unlikely to deter much speculative trade and, if large, it might see financial activity move to a location where the tax is not imposed. So we might end up still at risk from any global fallout but without the benefits of having the business in our domain. London accounted for 40.9 per cent of foreign exchange in 2013, the US 18.9 per cent, Singapore 5.7 per cent, Japan 5.6 per cent and Hong Kong 4.1 per cent.

In the years leading up to 2008 crisis, the international economist Dr Zhu Min, then at the Bank of China and now at the IMF, pointed out the risks of a global derivatives market that was multiple times the size of global GDP. The massive growth of the derivatives market highlighted the increasing complexity in the financial system and triggered much debate and some anxiety. What would happen if things went wrong? On a visit to London in 2002 Alan Greenspan was quizzed about this in a question-and-answer session after a lecture to the Society of Business Economists. He replied that there was no need to worry, the scale of the derivatives market was a sign of markets reallocating risk.

The trouble is that when the latest crisis came, instead of reallocating risk, derivatives amplified it. Data from the Bank for International Settlements showed at the end of 2013 the total amount of outstanding derivatives was $763 trillion* and turnover was many times this. They are called derivatives because their value derives from something else. They serve a vital economic need. Farmers for instance can use them to lock in the price of their crops, removing

---

* In June 2013, according to the Bank for International Settlements, the total amount of outstanding Over-The-Counter Derivatives was $682,908 billion, exchange-traded futures $24,967 billion and exchange-traded options $45,119 billion. In June 2008, outstanding OTC Derivatives were $683.7 trillion.

uncertainty. But derivatives on commodities are now a small fraction of this activity, the vast bulk being interest-rate derivatives. While these also serve an economic need, allowing firms to agree contracts, or hedge, based on future interest rates, it is the scale of these that appears too big to be justified by economic growth. It suggests too many derivative transactions are speculative, as financial traders take complex bets on the future. The incentive for them is that such trades can be profitable and rewarding if correct.

Speaking in November 2008 to G20 finance ministers in Brazil, China's central bank governor Zhou Xiaochuan drew parallels between the financial sector, engineering and control theory. There were, he argued, too many positive feedback loops that amplified risk: 'What we need to do is not to totally rebuild the system, but to add a few negative feedback loops which are able to sufficiently change the characteristics of our system.' The point being that in the 2008 crisis the financial system didn't absorb the shock but gave it added strength, like a tsunami approaching a coastline. The worrying thing was we saw signs of this way back in 1987 with Black Monday. But those warning signs were never heeded.

When financial markets grow far more than other economic measures, it should raise questions about the economic purpose and benefit of these markets. By the time of the 2008 crisis a considerable amount of activity was between institutions within the financial sector. Lord Turner, then head of the UK Financial Services Authority, called these activities socially useless once the scale of them became known. That was also highlighted in a 2013 analysis by McKinsey that showed that, 'financing for households and non-financial corporations accounted for just over one-fourth of the rise in global financial depth from 1995 to 2007 – an astonishingly small share, given that this is the fundamental purpose of finance'.

Black Wednesday

The second financial crisis I was able to observe at first hand was a more localised event, but from a political and policy perspective was every bit as dramatic as the collapse in stock markets on Black Monday. This was Black Wednesday, the day the pound sterling went crashing out of Europe's currency system, the Exchange Rate Mechanism. Perhaps these days should have been called Red Monday and Red Wednesday, as that is the colour used to indicate shares are falling.

This taught me how badly wrong the consensus can sometimes be, and also that if one has a strong view based on sound arguments, stick with it. The consensus was not only wrong about what would happen to the pound ahead of Black Wednesday but also about what would happen to the economy after.

In the mid-1980s, *The Times* newspaper had an excellent business section and each Monday contained a column written by a leading economist in the City. It was a must-read. In 1986 I was asked to write for it, even though I was only twenty-five. I joined the other nine or so economists who wrote the 'Gilt-edged column', which meant writing once about every ten weeks. I did this for a number of years. It so happened that during that period I often ended up taking a different view from the consensus, arguing that the UK needed to introduce credit controls to curb rising personal debt, that the economic boom under Chancellor Nigel Lawson would become a bust and, among other things, in February 1992 that a devaluation of the pound was inevitable, whoever won the April 1992 UK general election.[*]

In economics, the majority is not always right. Margaret Thatcher was elected prime minister on 3 May 1979. For the next decade the

* See, for instance, by Gerard Lyons: 'Devaluation on the agenda whoever wins', *The Times*, 10 February 1992; 'The outlook hinges on domestic credit control', *The Times*, 27 June 1988; 'External deficit overshadows Budget surplus', *The Times*, 21 March 1988.

battle against inflation led to many shifts in UK monetary policy. To begin with, the exchange rate took centre stage with an international monetarist model that pushed sterling so high that it squeezed inflation. The trouble was that UK industry was also squeezed in the recession of 1979–82. The currency then took a back seat, but after a series of failed experiments with domestic monetary aggregates it came back to the heart of policy again, heavily influenced by politics. The UK decided, for domestic political reasons, to join Europe's Exchange Rate Mechanism in October 1990 at the central rate of 2.95 Deutsche Marks to the pound.

It was a disaster. The UK joined at the wrong time, at the wrong rate, for the wrong reasons. It was the wrong time because it was obliged to follow German interest rates at a time when their economy was strong and needed high rates and the UK's was weak, needing low interest rates. It was the wrong rate as the pound was tied at too strong an exchange rate to the Deutsche Mark. And it was the wrong reason because it was to get the prime minister out of a short-term political problem, rather than from a genuine desire to become a central part of the European economy. Although the ERM was a peg, which could change, the underlying problem was the same as that faced now by many countries in the euro: a 'one size fits all' exchange rate and an interest-rate policy that does not work for all countries. If the currency can't act as the shock absorber, output and jobs have to.

By 1992 it should have been clear that it was a failure. But the economic consensus was that the UK could not leave and that if it did, interest rates would have to go up, the pound would have to go down and recession would follow. I disagreed and said so. I believed that devaluation was inevitable, and, as I wrote in London's *Evening Standard* a couple of days after it had occurred, I also believed that interest rates would be at 6 per cent by the following spring and that the economy would recover strongly. It did. On Black Wednesday itself the pound came under relentless downward pressure, falling to DM 2.20 once the Bank of England stopped wasting the country's currency reserves trying to defend it. On Black Wednesday interest rates rose from 10 to 12 per cent and it was announced that they were then to rise the following day to 15 per cent, although they never did. That Wednesday cost the UK taxpayer £3.3 billion and the government its economic credibility.

The important thing is to learn lessons from these events, to gauge what will happen next time, what the market reaction is likely to be and what the policy response should be. In many respects, every financial crisis ought to be treated in its own context, as there may be specific circumstances that explain why events turned out the way they did. Having blind faith in an inappropriate currency policy is a recipe for disaster.

Many financial crises since have had imbalances as an important contributory factor. An imbalance is when something unsustainable happens in an economy, such as running up a large trade deficit with imports outstripping exports, or permitting people to run up excessive debts. Often the lesson from a financial crisis is to ensure in future that economic imbalances are kept in check and do not get out of hand. Within European currency systems, such as the ERM or the euro, the central issue is usually competitiveness as the country at the centre, Germany, is far more competitive than others in the system.

There is also the need to get the balance right between domestic and external policy requirements: setting policy for domestic ends and yet recognising there are times when it is vitally important to co-ordinate policy with other countries.

The events of Black Wednesday and the response to them were very telling. Late on the previous Sunday evening, Germany announced its plans to cut interest rates marginally, to help take pressure off the lira. This was the catalyst for the turmoil of the following days. For domestic reasons the Germans did not want to cut rates, but the resultant easing achieved the worst of all worlds –

it confirmed to the markets that something was wrong, yet at the same time it was clear that the response was not substantial enough. If politicians are to act, they must act decisively – they need to get ahead of the markets and not play catch-up. All too often they fail to realise this.

Black Wednesday also demonstrated that the UK's approach is fundamentally different from that of the rest of the Continent. The UK tends to look at the euro debate from an economic perspective, and hence events such as Black Wednesday leave a lasting legacy, whereas across much of Europe the euro issue is seen in political terms and economic setbacks are handled within a political climate of simply moving on towards ever greater integration.

For British people Black Wednesday was a saviour. It meant moving from a policy that was not working to one that would, boosting demand. On the Continent, however, the problems suffered within the ERM system were to persist, with further turmoil over the following year.

Japan's bubble bursts

Of all the crises of the last few decades, it is the bursting of Japan's economic bubble that sends shivers down the spines of many people today, as they fear it is a forerunner of what is unfolding in the US and Europe. When Japan's crisis hit, I was chief economist and executive director for DKB International, at that time the biggest bank in Japan and in the world. While there are many things to heed from Japan's crisis, it might be premature to conclude that events will unfold in the same way elsewhere. The Japanese did not believe their economy could go sour so quickly, and when it did, they suffered from a lack of confidence that the situation could be turned around.

At the end of the 1980s the Japanese were buying assets across the globe. In much the same way as China is now. The grounds of the

Imperial Palace in Tokyo were then valued at more than the land of the entire state of California – clearly that could not be right. Land prices peaked in Japan in 1989 and didn't stop falling until 2003. The Japanese stock market also peaked in December 1989 and is still well below that level, although thanks to the current reflationary policies of 'Abe economics' the economy and market are recovering.

Back then, Japan had two problems: a demand-side problem in that they needed to ensure spending to head off the threat of deflation, which would cause prices to fall, and a supply-side problem requiring changes in the structure of the economy and in the cosy relationship between inept politicians, big business and the civil service.

To tackle two problems, two solutions are needed. But the Japanese only ever responded by trying to pump demand into their economy. They made little attempt to address the supply-side issues and structural problems. As a result, Japan's economy flatlined – albeit at a high level. It was a high-income but low-growth economy. Despite sluggish wage growth, real incomes rose as inflation was so low. Perhaps that reaction added to a sense of complacency there, although many policymakers would argue that they were doing everything they could. Japanese people had saved during the good years and the high savings of an ageing population also allowed the economy to cope. Visitors to Japan sometimes found it hard to believe there was a crisis.

The Japanese failed to act quickly or decisively enough, always believing the economy was on the verge of recovery. That expectation deterred them from taking sufficient action – unlike the central banks in the West who quickly opted for unconventional policy in response to the 2008 crisis. In part this might have been because Japan's debt problem then was different from the West's now, as it ran current-account surpluses by exporting more than it imported and was able to fund its debt easily at home. In the years since the 2008 crisis the US and the European periphery did not have that luxury and so had to face up to their problems sooner than Japan ever did. The immediate challenges facing the West in recent years, with little growth and low interest rates, have been worse than those confronting Japan. But the West has shown itself more likely to reform, aimed at boosting productivity.

Japan was not the first economy to have a banking crisis. Just as Japan tried to learn from the experience of previous crises, such as those in the Nordic countries in the early 1980s, in recent years the US and Europe have been trying to learn from Japan.

The Asian crisis

The crisis in East Asia in 1997–8 was a particularly interesting one. I have always regarded a large external deficit as one of the best early-warning signals in economics. It can reflect imbalances at home, with savings too low, and it can sometimes suggest a currency is vulnerable, ready to weaken. In Asia in the late 1990s, a number of countries were growing too strongly for their own good; euphoria was escalating.

There were many signs of problems. Take investment. There is no ideal level of investment. The Asian economies that ran into trouble in 1997–8 had high investment ratios above 40 per cent of GDP. Not only that, but many firms were borrowing heavily to invest and, to make matters worse, many were borrowing from overseas, in foreign currencies where interest rates were lower. They did this because they thought there was no currency risk – as their countries had informally tied their currencies to the dollar. To compound the risk, a lot of this overseas borrowing was short-term. So if interest rates rose or currencies fell there would be trouble for the borrowers. Both were to happen, and at the same time.

All good things come to an end. The booms were not sustainable, and neither were the currency levels. As the currencies fell, many of those who had borrowed from overseas went bust. The East Asian miracle came to resemble a mirage. But the good news is that the region learned its lesson, and rebounded. The Asian crisis also taught China some useful lessons. Although China was left unscathed at the time – largely because it had its own ups and downs earlier in the 1990s – the high rates of investment enjoyed by the crisis-hit countries were a warning to China to lower its investment ratio and to keep its financial system in check.

Some of this overseas borrowing at low rates might have recurred in recent years in a number of emerging economies and, although the scale is low and emerging economies are in stronger shape, it suggests a fluctuating path for emerging economies when US rates rise.

How countries respond to crises is always revealing. While it is better to avoid a crisis in the first place, once it hits the best thing is simply to respond and move on. South Korea refused to admit it had a problem during 1997, and was only five days from going bust before it came clean to the IMF about the scale of the country's debts. As the crisis unfolded across East Asia, confidence plummeted, international creditors panicked, currencies fell, interest rates rose, foreign debts soared, stock markets collapsed and economies fell into recession. A number of crisis-hit countries were helped out with loans from the IMF, including South Korea, which borrowed $60 billion in December 1997.

Then something quite remarkable happened in South Korea. In January, the government, with the support of three chaebols (conglomerates) – Samsung, Daewoo and Hyundai – initiated a national campaign called 'Collect Gold for the Love of Korea'. People began donating their gold, including their wedding rings, to the government. The aim was to sell this gold to help repay some of the country's loan. The response was incredible as people queued to donate – it is hard to imagine it happening in many other countries. Such public self-sacrifice was perhaps symbolic and reflected the gravity of the situation South Korea found itself in. It also made it easier to understand how the country had made such economic progress over the previous thirty years. Since the crisis, South Korean firms have gone from strength to strength globally. While not all countries can reflect Korea's nationalism, they all need to have an understanding of why reform is necessary, an appreciation of the pain being worthwhile, and a vision of what success might bring.

It is remarkable how often some of the biggest problems in a financial crisis are the unintended consequences of earlier economic policies. The Asian crisis is a case in point and, in an indirect way, has relevance for understanding potential problems today in America, Europe and the UK as a result of quantitative easing and cheap money.

The pace at which the Asian crisis unfolded caught politicians and policymakers unawares. In September 1997 the annual meetings of the IMF took place in Hong Kong. Even though the crisis had already begun, there was a sense of disbelief about what was happening. The choice of Hong Kong was highly symbolic, as on 1 July that year the former British colony had returned to Chinese rule. There was much misplaced nervousness about this. But the Hong Kong handover on 1 July was followed, almost by chance, by the Thai baht depreciation on 2 July. This was the event that signalled the start of the crisis. The dominoes started to fall and, as they did, politicians refused to acknowledge the potential crisis and appeared more intent on finding someone to blame than on getting ahead of events. Malaysia's leader Mahathir Mohamad publicly blamed George Soros. I met Mahathir in his office a few years later, and he was a clear advocate of an interventionist policy, distrustful of markets.

As the currency crisis spread across the region, the markets felt they were pushing against an open door, as it was easy for speculators to attack one currency after another. The Hong Kong peg proved the exception, as the scale of its currency reserves allowed the authorities to defend their currency's link to the dollar. In contrast, as Indonesia's currency fell, few seemed worried to begin with, as it had high reserves, a trade surplus, low inflation and the banks appeared in good shape. But their firms had borrowed heavily overseas, the full scale of which became clear only later. Within a year, the Thai baht had fallen by over a third, along with the Philippine peso and Korean won. The Indonesian rupiah collapsed, and within a year was worth less than one-fifth of its prevous level, as huge currency mismatches were exposed on corporate and bank balance sheets. By May 1998 Indonesia's economic collapse had forced dictator Suharto out of office.

The widespread regional economic, social and political fallout from the Asian crisis was not without benefits. Many countries across Asia strengthened their economies, improved their fiscal and debt positions and reformed their banking sectors, which proved invaluable a decade later when the global financial crisis hit, and they were able to bounce back quickly. The Asian crisis also provided valuable future lessons for the rest of the world. As Dr Zeti, governor of Malaysia's central bank, commented in 2012, 'The financial restructuring and repair, the fiscal consolidation and structural adjustment urgently needs to be complemented with wide-ranging pro-growth policies.' The lesson, in short, was the need for a comprehensive solution.

The crisis

Anyone familiar with the board game Monopoly will have probably, perhaps inadvertently, learned the most important financial lesson of all. The learning of this lesson would have helped in 2008, as it would in every financial crisis.*

Pro-cyclicality means adding fuel to the fire or continuing to dig when in a hole. It makes an existing situation more extreme. Ahead of the 2008 crisis there were many things that were pro-cyclical. Many Western economies had excessively low interest rates. The

---

* Lehman Brothers filed for bankruptcy on 15 September 2008. See paper by James Bullard listed in the bibliography outlining how the first stage of the crisis began on 9–10 August 2007 when markets began to lose confidence in banks.

incentive structure within the financial industry contributed to a culture of greed. Then, when the crisis hit, the role of ratings agencies and the use of mark-to-market accounting created a vicious cycle, triggering asset write-downs and panic selling, as prices fell and expectations deteriorated during the downturn.

Ahead of the 2008 crisis there was much discussion of the savings glut, whereby savings flowed from Asia to economies in the West, whose growth was driven by debt. Normally – as is happening now – savings would be expected to be attracted to emerging economies where future investment returns are higher. At that time the US, UK and Spain received the bulk of inflows. Interestingly, though, a fascinating piece of work by the Bank for International Settlements after the crisis pointed out that the picture was more complex – largely because of the role of the financial sector – and that it wasn't just the East financing the West. Amazingly, the UK, despite running a large current-account deficit, was one of the big providers of funds to the US. The US, a debtor, was being partially financed by another debtor, the UK.*

Helping the economy is one of the most important elements in a financial system. Managing risk is the other. For banks and financial firms the holy grail is to minimise risk while maximising return. Ahead of the crisis many banks and financial firms thought they had achieved this. Most were wrong. The capital reserves that banks held to call on in a crisis were too low, based on artificially low default levels. The low yields available on low-risk investments also encouraged many to take on more risk in a search for yield and higher return.

The biggest financial crisis of our lives – so far – was caused by the four Gs: Glass–Steagall, Greenspan, Governance and Greed.

The first cause was the repeal of the Glass–Steagall Act in the US. Although we are talking about a financial crisis, the root cause of the problems lay with the banks. The Americans don't muck about when something goes wrong. They don't feel they have lost

* See the paper by Borio and Disyatat listed in the bibliography.

face in the way that the British or the Asians do. They act, sort out what went wrong and move on. So it was after the Wall Street crash. The Banking Act of 1933 was aimed at making it impossible for another financial crisis on the scale of the 1920s to occur. And a key component of making the Banking Act work was the Glass–Steagall Act, named after the two senators who sponsored the Bill.

The aim was to separate out the risky from the less risky parts of banking: it divided commercial banking, which deals with the day-to-day needs of private individuals and firms, from the investment banking activity, which can lead financial firms to take speculative positions in financial markets. The Glass–Steagall Act made the financial sector more stable. Yet during the era of deregulation this act was repealed, with the Senate voting 90–8 to repeal it in November 1999. It was a disastrous move.

It is interesting to note that the major post-crisis report in the UK – the Vickers report from the Independent Commission on Banking – called for a modern-day version of Glass–Steagall in the form of a ring fence. It is a great idea, naturally resisted by the banks, as the needs of clients may straddle both sides of any ring fence, creating a grey area. The report also called for greater competition – again a good idea. Given the global nature of the financial crisis there has been a desire for a global response with simple rules and clear directives. While that makes sense, different approaches have emerged, with a lack of agreement on reinstating Glass–Steagall but a genuine desire to curb speculative activity, from the Volcker Rule in the US, to the Liikanen Report and also Commissioner Barnier's proposals in Europe.

Glass–Steagall deals with a key issue: the structure of the banking industry. It has been argued that repealing Glass–Steagall cannot be directly blamed for the US financial firms that failed as they were not covered by the original act. Also Glass–Steagall would not have prevented banks investing in residential mortgages and one of the big problems in the crisis was low-quality sub-prime mortgages –

nicknamed NINJA loans, as they were sometimes made to people who had no income, no job and no assets. All this is correct but I think it important to differentiate between regulation, culture and structure. Excessive regulation is wrong; the right regulation is needed. But repealing Glass–Steagall contributed to both structural and cultural changes central to the crisis.

When investment and commercial banks merge, the investment-bank culture dominates. The size of institutions also grew. The tone for this was set by the merger of Citibank and Travellers to create the world's biggest financial services company. Although this took place in 1998, it was on the expectation that Glass–Steagall would be repealed within the two-year review period of proposed mergers.

Reintroducing Glass–Steagall would mean that the traditional commercial activities of banks would be less risky and so offer lower returns. Banks, it has been argued, would be more like public utilities and so should pay their high earners much less. The investment-banking arms would have to stand on their own two feet, not posing a risk to depositors or to taxpayers.

The Greenspan factor refers to US monetary policy being inappropriate ahead of the financial crisis. Hindsight is a great thing in economics. And to criticise Greenspan is difficult, as he presided over strong economic performance. Yet he made some fundamental mistakes. In particular, he kept interest rates too low for too long. He was not the only one. Although inflation was low, asset-price inflation was a problem and should have led to higher rates. As a result, before the crisis, the biggest single problem in the financial sector was that markets were not pricing sufficiently for risk. The dominance of the US at the heart of the system led to a lack of pricing for risk around the world.

The Bank of England's financial stability division hosted a well-attended seminar in December 2006 entitled 'Pricing for Risk' and, among other things, stressed the dangers of 'crowded trades'. A crowded trade is where many people are doing the same thing in a market where it would be hard to escape if everyone tried to get out at the same time: an analogy would be a theatre audience needing to get to the emergency exit after a fire has broken out. Traders effectively thought they could do the impossible and pick the exact moment when they could escape before risks became reality. They thought they could make it to the exit first.

Such behaviour not only reflected Greenspan's errors but also, in a bizarre way, confidence in his ability. The market was not pricing for risk because rates were too low and it expected Greenspan to react if things went wrong. Mervyn King, governor of the Bank of England, termed the economic period leading up to the crisis 'the NICE decade', of non-inflationary continuous expansion. And markets behaved accordingly.

The third G was the lack of Governance. Boards did not hold their executives to account. The banks and financial firms that ran into trouble had taken on too much risk, or had unsound business models. The extent of poor governance – as well as ineffective regulation – was seen a few years later when the scandal over the rigging of the London interbank offer rate (Libor) came to light. Libor is the reference rate for interest-rate contracts across the globe and that scandal further eroded trust in banks.

The fourth G was Greed. Or, to put it another way, the incentive system in the financial world encouraged behaviour that contributed to the crisis. It was not that people wanted to cause a crisis, or that they ever imagined they would, but the reward structure in the financial system encouraged and incentivised short-term thinking and excessive risk-taking. Some of this is now being dealt with. Capping bonuses is not the answer, as that just leads to higher basic salaries, but not linking them to sales or revenues that have suffered from mis-selling and also deferring bonus payments over years might be a start.

The trouble was, greed was endemic in the behaviour of many people, not just bankers. This was linked to low inflation and the search for yield, as investors sought higher returns. The consumer price index, CPI, measures inflation. One of the many consequences of the opening up of China was that it exported low inflation to such an extent that CPI figures could have been renamed China price indexes. China not only exported cheap goods that people across the world bought; it also boosted the global labour force to such an extent that the wages of unskilled workers in the West were suppressed as firms tried to remain competitive.

In turn, because inflation was low, central banks in the West kept interest rates lower than was justified by domestic credit conditions and thus lower than they should have been. That in turn contributed to greed: investors wanted higher returns; so too did savers, and the financial industry became incentivised to sell higher-yielding products that were often more complex and risky. Now there is more of an inflationary impact as China's labour force starts to shrink and wages as well as commodity prices rise.

At the Bank of England, outside the key committee room where interest-rate decisions are made, is a lovely nineteenth-century painting, *Dividend Day at the Bank of England*. It shows people queuing up to receive their dividend income in 1859. Dividend day was the quarter day when dividends were paid on bank stock and government securities. 'Consols', consolidated government annuities, paid a 3-per-cent rate per annum and were the only investment permitted to trustees of widows and orphans. The painting shows the animated faces of people receiving their dividends. Perhaps ahead of the crisis, expectations needed to change to reflect the mood of that painting, with people – as they were back in 1859 – being delighted with a more realistic and lower return.

The lesson from Monopoly is that liquidity is king. Apart from the luck of the dice, the person who builds the most houses and hotels is not always the one who wins. The winner is usually the person who is able to pay his or her bills when going around the board. Liquidity is familiar to anyone who has played Monopoly, and it was a key issue in the crisis. If people believe a bank has enough money, there will not be a run on that bank with people rushing to take their deposits out, as happened with Northern Rock in the UK. If a counter-party financial institution has enough liquidity, others will deal with it. If a country has enough liquidity in the form of foreign-exchange reserves, speculators will not attack its currency. Liquidity is the essential line of defence, and it is backed up by confidence.

The future

What of the future? Finance has a vital role to play, but how effectively it fulfils it depends on many factors. Not least will be whether we can learn the lessons of previous crises. We also need to see finance cope with the increasing needs placed on it by the growing global economy. Perhaps the key question is whether or not the present proves to be an Apollo 13 moment for the financial sector. What do I mean by this?

Apollo 13 was due to be the third manned lunar landing but it never reached the moon, encountering a crisis en route that threatened the lives of its three astronauts. As the crisis unfolded Gene Kranz, who was head of mission control, was confronted with the accusation that this was NASA's worst ever moment. On the contrary, he replied, if the astronauts returned safely to earth it would be NASA's best moment, and so it proved.

Is this the financial system's Apollo 13 moment? Will our economic system be stronger after a crisis that saw it almost crash? That depends on whether one believes the right lessons have been learned. As bad as the crisis might seem, provided the problems can be sorted out, then it might prove to be an important turning point for the financial industry.

As with the NASA disaster, the actions in the wake of this crisis prevented something even worse. Economic depression and financial meltdown were avoided – but at a price, and the full consequences of that are still unclear. There has been a loss of trust in finance. Many emerging economies that need to develop their financial systems have become wary of doing so. Policies adopted across the world since the crisis could have added to future risk, as some banks now believe they are too big to be allowed to fail. And increased regulation aimed at making the system safer might increase the costs of doing business to such an extent that new firms could find it hard to enter parts of the financial industry. When the barriers to entering any business, including banking, are placed too high, future competition can suffer. Such unintended consequences need to be addressed, with finance focused on supporting future global economic growth.

Apollo 13 was followed by four successive lunar Apollo landings. Can the financial industry similarly rebound? I think it can, and it is important that it does. Let me outline some ways finance can influence the unfolding economic outlook.

Learn lessons

First, learning the lessons of history should make us optimistic about the future role of global finance. If death, taxes and financial crises are inevitable, then we need to ensure we can live with each of them. It makes no sense to say we can stop all types of financial crisis, any more than to say that we can stop boom and bust in an economy. Anyone who makes such statements fails to understand the complexity either of the financial system or of an economy. There has been a well-trodden path of crisis being followed by reform. The challenge is to ensure that the reforms this time go far enough to make the banking sector safer. As important as the financial sector is, it cannot be allowed to blow up again as it did in 2008. Reassessing the structure of the financial industry is one aspect of this. But even though safety needs to improve, there will still be future crises. So, we need to anticipate problems sooner, ideally to stop them and, if they do occur, then to ensure the economy is resilient enough to cope.

One area that merits particular attention is the relationship between finance, real estate and the economy. As the Bank of England noted in its 2011 discussion paper on macro prudential policy, 'Excessive credit expansion, often in the real estate sector, has characterised the build-up to most financial crises in the past, from the Great Depression, to emerging market crises in Latin America and East Asia, to recent crises in developed countries.' Often it is commercial real estate, not just residential. It is vital to prevent the combination of cheap money, leverage and one-way expectations where banks and people think property prices can only rise. This points to the need for monetary policy and macro prudential policy to work closely together, the latter including the ability to place specific curbs on how much can be borrowed or lent to residential and commercial real estate.

One lesson, surely, is the vital role monetary policy has played, both in terms of limiting the downside after a crisis hits, but also in terms of sowing the seeds of problems in the first place. On the positive side, following the 2008 crisis central bankers eased policy and so avoided some of the policy mistakes made in the Great Depression of the 1930s. But the role of monetary policy in contributing to crises is a future lesson to avoid.

Ever since the 1987 stock-market crash, monetary policy has been used aggressively to head off prospective economic downturns, or to respond to actual financial-sector shocks. In Western economies, monetary policy has become the modern-day shock absorber. There are a number of reasons for this: it can be altered quickly but also because of the growing scale of the financial sector and of personal credit, its effects can impact quickly. The net effect is the markets expect monetary policy to come to their rescue if something goes wrong. But perhaps the key point is one that is often overlooked. That is, in most phases of monetary easing in the last quarter century, the biggest problem was not the reduction in interest rates but that the subsequent tightening in policy was not enough, and was often less aggressive than the preceding easing. As a result, in the good times, interest rates did not rise enough; money was too cheap, leverage too high. Just as I think governments should run budget surpluses when the economy is growing strongly, central banks should ensure money is expensive in such times, with high interest rates.

Although there are similar themes, each crisis can be different. So it is important to address not only the factors that led to the 2008 crisis but also other areas that could be a future cause for concern, even if they did not cause problems in 2008. A few stand out. Although banking is just one – albeit vital – part of the global financial industry, it was central to the 2008 crisis and so much of the post-crisis regulation has focused on banking.

There is now agreement that banks need to be well capitalised, liquid, have effective risk models and low rates of leverage. The trouble is, if leverage is too low, growth may suffer. There is less agreement on the issue of size. But size does matter: the larger the size of the financial sector in relation to an economy, the greater the risk it imposes. Size was not the factor that determined who got into trouble in 2008 but needs to be addressed as banks must not be so big that they cannot be allowed to fail. One response would be to split banks up and in the process increase competition, but there are economies of scale with large institutions that we might not want to lose. So splitting up institutions has not been adopted across the globe.

Instead the focus has been on resolution schemes and living wills. The idea is that if things are outlined in advance, as in a will, it will be easier to sort out a crisis that leads to a bank dying. It sounds good in theory; whether it works in practice is the issue. In life, even when wills are straightforward and uncontested, they are not always settled quickly. So in the complex world of finance, there is no guarantee living wills will work smoothly.

Another idea is to cast some light on the shadow-banking industry. This little-known area was shown to be vitally important at the time the 2008 crisis hit. It is the part of the financial sector that is outside regulation. As a result it is hard to measure. Since 2008, increased regulations have added to the attraction of shadow banking. The regulatory pendulum has swung from one extreme of light regulation to the other extreme of heavy regulation, when it would be better to stop in the middle, with the right degree of regulation. Shadow banking is likely to have grown further, and the Financial Stability Board calculates its size as $71.2 trillion at the end of 2012, being at its largest in the US at $26 trillion, in the euro area $22 trillion and the UK $9 trillion. The UK was one of three countries, along with the Netherlands and Switzerland, where their 'non-bank financial systems' were more than twice as large as their respective GDP.

Because it is opaque, it is difficult to say how much of it is good, and how much of it is bad. Non-banks can have a legitimate role to play in increasing the finance available to borrowers experiencing funding shortages. Some multinational companies provide finance to key firms in their supply chain. This part of shadow banking is good. In contrast, some banks who are part of the regulated financial sector might carry out off-balance-sheet activities in the shadow-banking industry. It is the lack of transparency that is the worry as it makes it hard to detect any build-up of risk.

Openness and transparency matter, but a stable, thriving and successful financial system also needs a clear set of rules. This does not mean that global markets need to be overburdened with controls, but rules imply accountability. The success of capitalism has always been based on winners being rewarded for their success and losers suffering. Banks and financial firms that screw up should be allowed to fail, and to do so without bringing down the system and being bailed out by taxpayers.

Paying for one's sins is necessary, so it has to be clear that government bail-outs cannot be relied on. In recent years the financial markets operated a 'heads we win, tails you lose' approach. When things went well, huge profits generated large bonuses, but when things went wrong, and problems were seen in the wider economy, the government stepped in. In economics, this is called moral hazard and it must be avoided, because, if it isn't, problems are created for the future. Moral hazard encourages risk-taking, because if something goes wrong someone else picks up the tab. It means not taking full responsibility for one's actions. In the insurance industry, moral hazard plays a central role. If someone drives a car carelessly and crashes, he or she pays higher premiums. It is about people taking responsibility for their own actions, rather than loading the cost onto others. So learning lessons is the first future financial driver.

State capitalism

The second future financial driver is the role of the state increasing in the financial sector. This is not simply about the need for effective regulation. It is more about ownership. Across Europe and in the US there has been the need for the government to step in and bail out the financial sector. The scale of this state intervention might be temporary. But across large swathes of the world the scale of state intervention might prove longer lasting. 'State capitalism' was a phrase I used in a piece I wrote in the *Financial Times* in 2007 on the rising role of the state in financial markets – an example being governments using their currency reserves or their sovereign-wealth funds to buy overseas assets. I testified later to both the US Congress and the Senate on this topic, as there were genuine concerns about foreign ownership.

But if the rules of the global system are clear, with level playing fields around the world so discrimination is kept to a minimum, then whether ownership of a financial firm is domestic or foreign shouldn't matter. It might, of course, matter in a strategic industry such as defence or surveillance. In contrast, in finance, state owner-ship as opposed to foreign ownership could matter, as it changes the rules of the game. A foreign private firm buying shouldn't matter; a foreign government could.

Government-controlled funds might be opaque rather than transparent, strategic rather than commercial. Thus they bring a new dynamic to global finance, particularly if open markets allow a government in one country to use its money to make purchases in another country. Resource nationalism and the acquisition of commodities is one aspect of this.

Sovereign-wealth funds were established originally by energy-rich economies, planning for the time when their oil and gas would start to run out. This made sense. The economic benefit was that the country investing in a diversified portfolio of international assets could draw a future return from it. The first sovereign-wealth fund was set up by Kuwait in 1953. In the last few decades, the number of countries setting up such funds has risen sharply and the amounts at their disposal have grown. They have also been set up by countries without energy resources.

In 2008 an article by US Deputy Secretary of the Treasury Robert Kimmitt in *Foreign Affairs* talked of 'the four sovereigns', comprising sovereign-wealth funds, foreign-exchange reserves, government pension schemes and state-owned enterprises. The last were particu-larly relevant to China, but the other three are important across many parts of the world.

Helping growth

The third future, and vital, role that finance has is in economic de-velopment. Progress is already being made. The main role of finance is to serve wider economic needs, not to make the people who work within it rich. This matters. There are so many exciting ways that the financial sector will be able to drive future global growth. In any economy a properly functioning global financial sector can help achieve and sustain future economic growth. Innovation will play an important role here, as in other industries. Financial innovation needs to encompass a broad range of areas, inclusivity being one of them. As economies grow, incomes rise and companies expand, all reinforcing the need for capital markets to develop. There will be both push and pull economic drivers attracting money to new economies and opportunities. The push drivers include the search for yield and growth opportunities, the need for increased returns, risk diversification, particularly taking into account interest-rate and exchange-rate movements. The pull factors attracting money include infrastructure and development needs, growth opportunities and better economic fundamentals.

The global infrastructure boom is a positive development and has already begun but it needs to be financed. There is no doubt this is problematic. At the February 2014 G20 meeting in Sydney it was said that $57 trillion was needed for global infrastructure until 2030. Although the sums involved are huge, there are tremendous opportunities. Governments can issue bonds, as they do now. The ironic thing is that it is the countries with big government-budget deficits that issue bonds to finance themselves, whereas many investors would sooner put their money into countries that have budget surpluses rather than deficits. Singapore, for one, issues bonds, even though it has a surplus, as it allows the country to borrow long-term money cheaply and develop its financial markets.

One area that could take off is thematic bonds, issued to investors to fund specific infrastructure projects, such as toll roads or ports, often having a guaranteed future return.

Perhaps the best opportunity is to make the most effective use of the large pockets of savings dotted around the world. Many people keep their savings at home, under the mattress, in gold, or just sitting passively in banks, earning low interest. There is a phenomenal opportunity to develop the savings and investment institutions that already exist in the West, and also across emerging regions of the world that will need them in the future. When savings can be placed with professional managers not only is it safer, but it should allow people to earn higher returns on their savings and, collectively, these could then be directed in a more efficient way towards investment opportunities – both in infrastructure and in the private sector.

Pension-fund assets globally total around $31 trillion, but in emerging Asia, one of the fast-growing regions where savings are high, they total under $600 billion. A small figure that could grow phenomenally. Likewise with mutual funds, the size of the mutual-fund industry in Asia, excluding Japan and Australia, is less than one-twentieth that of the US. Asia, certainly, should continue to develop its own capital markets.

As financial markets deepen, and broaden, this will not only allow savings to be directed to investment opportunities but it will allow some of the basics of global finance to become commonplace across more countries – such as people borrowing against future income and firms having access to finance. Savers in the West, too, will have access to a wider array of global investment opportunities.

Then there is the great unbanked. As many as 3 billion people lack access to the traditional banking sector. I wrote a paper on this for the 2005 Commonwealth Finance Ministers Conference. They were very engaged in the idea of making banking and finance available to people on all incomes and to firms of all sizes. This does not mean lending to people with no income, no jobs or no assets to buy properties, as mentioned above, instead it is about micro-finance, servicing micro-industries, providing basic banking across the globe, such as saving and withdrawal facilities to aid consumption and spending flows. In many parts of the world it has the ability to help empower women, who often control the family budget.

The banks meanwhile need to get the three Rs of Resources, Risks and Returns aligned in this area so as to provide cost-effective services. They need to dedicate more resources – consistent with

Hertfordshire
Libraries

Harpenden Library
Kiosk 2

Customer ID: ******5264

Items that you have borrowed

Title: Letting go : how to plan for a good death
Due: 05 September 2022

Title: The consolations of economics : how we will all benefit from the new world order
Due: 05 September 2022

Total items: 2
Amount outstanding: £0.00
Items on loan: 2
Overdue: 0
Reservations: 0
Ready for collection: 0
15/08/2022 14:43

Thank you for using Hertfordshire Libraries
Enquiries / Renewals go to:
www.hertfordshire.gov.uk/libraries
or call: 0300 123 4049

the idea of banks being utilities and providing a service. Risks are always higher when the information set is small, and the lender does not know who is being lent to. But often the banks believe the returns are too low and the resources required to service the unbanked too high to yield adequate profits.

The contagion and fallout from financial crises necessitates a global response. One concern, expressed by Tim Adams of the Institute of International Finance, and which reflects the valid concerns of the banking industry, is the need to avoid the unintended consequence of excessive regulation, namely a fragmentation of the global financial system in which cross-border financial flows suffer. We can take comfort from a couple of recent developments.

One is that the Financial Stability Board has grown in stature as a result of the crisis and has behaved in a sensible and mature way in seeking to establish a common global approach. Another is the way issues with sovereign-wealth funds have been resolved. The creation of the Santiago Principles in 2008 to address concern over governance, accountability and code of practices among sovereign-wealth funds showed that it is possible to reach international agreement in areas where previously there were none. There is a need for countries to collaborate, co-ordinate and co-operate.

Currencies

The final key area to focus on in the future is currencies. Economists sometimes disagree strongly on the topic of currencies. There is no ideal currency policy. Stability is preferred to volatility but flexibility is always needed, with a weaker currency boosting competitiveness and helping exporters, and a stronger one helping curb inflation.

It is important to avoid currency policy being viewed as an easy option. Firms can compete on cost or quality, or both. Firms shouldn't be able to rely on a cheaper currency as an easy way out.

Economies such as Italy and the UK, for instance, too often relied on currency depreciation to help their industry. The alternative is to become competitive with increased investment or working more productively, as in Switzerland and Germany. Labour-intensive economies will want to keep their currency cheap, while high-value-added economies should seek rather to improve competitiveness in other ways, which can often be difficult and time consuming, such as economic reform, as opposed to currency weakness.

Markets discount information quickly. That can create problems, as well as benefits. For emerging economies, the benefit is that it attracts inward investment when sentiment towards an economy turns positive. The problem is that money can be attracted too quickly as investors discount too much news too soon. Examples are the optimism about Africa now or about Brazil in recent years. The optimism is justified but the outcomes might take longer to be realised. In recent years the combination of low interest rates in the West and increased optimism about emerging markets has seen money flow fast into some countries, resulting in rapid currency appreciation. The Brazilian finance minister even warned of 'currency wars' as money flowed into Brazil, forcing its currency, the real, to appreciate too much, harming competitiveness. It didn't help Brazil's economy. Sometimes, in order to deter such inflows, interest rates can be kept low, but this can feed other problems, as Japan's bubble economy of the late 1980s shows.

The alternative, sometimes tried in Brazil, is capital controls aimed at deterring speculators. These controls work by stopping certain types of money coming into a country – and so prevent a damaging currency appreciation. They are not ideal but are understandable in certain situations. The ideal situation is if a country can have deep capital markets that are able to absorb inflows, but this is not realistic as it takes time. The dilemma with controls is that investors don't reward countries for using them. Controls can mean money already in the economy becomes trapped, and in the future investors either become wary of investing there again or demand higher returns for thinking about it.

Too often it can be smaller economies that need the controls to protect themselves and yet they are the ones who are penalised most for using them. Bigger economies – such as Brazil or India – would be less likely to be penalised by investors, as at some stage they will need to invest in these markets. Arguably the IMF and regional-development banks should work with smaller economies to adjust, and investors should accept controls are part of the necessary tool-kit for economies in transition.

Perhaps the key issues are what will happen to the world's major currencies, especially the dollar and the euro. The biggest surprise about the financial crisis was the performance of the dollar. Before the crisis, there was rising pessimism about the dollar. Yet the crisis told a different story. Instead of deserting the dollar, in a time of trouble people trusted it.

It was in 2007 that the central bank governor of China called for a change to the existing currency order, which he felt was dominated by the dollar. In the past there was a strong attraction to the idea of pegging a currency to the dollar: the country concerned effectively tied its interest rate to that of the US, and linked itself to the cred-ibility of the US Federal Reserve. It made sense for countries whose economic cycle was tied into that of the US. Many economies such as Hong Kong and the Gulf economies pegged themselves success-fully to the dollar. Nowadays, however, new trade corridors and the emergence of bigger and stronger economies across the globe favour a shift in this thinking. The dollar is no longer the only game in town.

Admittedly, the dollar is likely to remain the major currency, reflecting the importance of the US economy and of its macro-economic policy. This is also an effect of the dominance of the US in other areas, including hard power, which enhances its attraction as a safe location in which to save and invest during times of trouble.

What currency should we expect to rival the dollar? That is more difficult to predict, but as trade flows change it would make more sense for countries to measure and manage their currency not just against the dollar but against a basket of currencies with which they trade. So India might manage its currency against its major trading partners and so not just focus on the value of the rupee against the dollar, as it does now, but instead measure it against a basket of currencies including the euro, the dollar, the yen, and currencies in South-East Asia, as well as the Chinese yuan. The weight and hence the importance of each of these in the basket would depend on the trade flows with India.

In Chapter 1, I suggested we could go from 'made in China' to 'bought by China' to 'paid in renminbi'. Now, as China's trade has grown – and as people have expected its currency to appreciate – more of China's bilateral trade has been paid for in renminbi. This will continue, even though the Chinese currency is definitely not a one-way bet. It was also interesting to note that at the end of 2012 the Nigerian central bank governor signalled a new trend when he indicated his central bank was prepared to hold Chinese currency even though it is a heavily controlled and not fully convertible currency, and that this move was in response to seeing Nigeria's private sector settle more of its trade with China in renminbi.

Others will follow and holdings by central banks of the Chinese currency should rise. The growth of the offshore Chinese currency market in recent years, largely in Hong Kong, but also in other financial centres such as London, will continue. Once the dollar is perceived as being less robust, more countries will naturally reassess their currency policy. In the future, a basket of currencies might form the natural way in which investments occur, and by which many countries will set their currency policy, as opposed to tying it to any one currency.

Another factor that will favour greater use of a number of currencies will be increased flows of savings and investment across the globe. In his book *Emerging Markets in an Upside Down World*, Jerome Booth argues that international investors currently have a herd mentality that creates a bias towards investing in the euro and dollar but in the future the need to have a balanced portfolio of investments will favour more money going into emerging economies. I agree. China would be one of many beneficiaries of this, but I would also expect money to flow in the other direction. Currently China tightly controls its capital account and so limits how much money its people can take out as well as how much money foreigners can bring in. This has some benefits as it protects China from the full impact of financial shocks elsewhere and it also insulates the rest of the world from inevitable, temporary, setbacks in China. As part of its necessary economic reform China will need to ease controls on its capital account, and this will also make it easier for Chinese money to leave and buy assets elsewhere. The scale of Chinese savings means this future impact could be huge.

I have remained wary of the euro from the beginning. My view has always been that there should be a two-speed euro – a hard euro, in the fast lane for the economies in Northern Europe that are relatively similar, and a softer euro, in the slower lane, for the rest. Going at the speed to suit your domestic economy makes sense. The root cause of the euro's problems is that its main driving force was political, not economic. In a fixed-currency system, economies should have similar economic characteristics and so form an 'optimal currency area'. But that did not happen. The Maastricht entry criteria were not rigorous enough and were not enforced. So too varied a group of countries was joined together. In the good times, money flowed from the centre to the periphery, feeding property booms in Ireland and Spain, among others, and then, in the bad times, the money has flowed back to the centre, which could feed future inflation there.

In Europe, as across the globe, it is important not to build up imbalances. Economies with current-account surpluses need to spend more; those with deficits need to spend less. Outside Europe, imbalances also mean currencies adjust, but in Europe economies cannot rely on currency devaluations to boost competitiveness, instead having to adjust, often squeezing demand. From an economic perspective I cannot believe that all the current members of the euro can remain within the system. It would not surprise me if eventually it were to collapse. But it is a political project, and on that basis, if Europe moves closer to political union, the survival of the euro not only becomes possible but it will also remain an important key future global currency. Indeed, if Europe were to reform, addressing current issues such as high welfare spending and resistance to innovation and change, and then take a leadership role globally, the euro could indeed become the major currency many wanted it to be. But it does require significant reform.

It is too early to say if this is an Apollo 13 moment in the financial crisis. But there are reasons to suggest that it is a turning point, if the right lessons are learned. It is work in progress. In economics, as in life, it is only when things go wrong that we see what needs to be done and who we need to rely on to sort things out. One of the lessons has wider global interest, beyond the banking and financial world, and that is a key question facing political institutions: who runs the world economy?

5

Invisible influences

I remember visiting Manila in the early 1990s. The media was full of anti-American sentiment. One of the US military bases in the Philippines – Subic Bay – was about to be closed. Rising nationalism in the Philippines among the politicians appeared to have been a key factor. Whatever the real cause, reading the media and speaking to senior policy people, as I did on that visit, I could sense the anti-American feeling. Yet I soon saw at first hand that the reality on the ground was very different when my driver took me past the American Embassy. There was a queue that stretched a long way. I discovered that it was the queue for visas to visit or work in the US, and the queues were that long every day. Moreover, I was told, given half a chance, the whole of the Philippines would move to the States. Despite the domestic politics of that time, the people wanted more, not less, America. Why?

There are many reasons behind America's global reach. Soft power is one of them.

The term 'soft power' was coined by Joseph Nye, and he defines it as 'the ability to get what you want through attraction rather than coercion or payments. It arises from the attractiveness of a country's culture, political ideals, and policies. When our policies are seen as legitimate in the eyes of others, our soft power is enhanced.' In testifying to a House of Lords select committee in 2013 Nye also described it as 'whose story wins in an information age'.

The term is used primarily to refer to global politics and influence, but I think it has global economic significance too. In a nutshell, it is the spread of a country's influence through non-military means. Soft power might be difficult to picture – and thus to measure – but if it is conceived of as the opposite of hard power, it becomes easier to visualise. Hard power is the ability to influence through military means or the use of physical force. Soft power is any influence that is not hard power. It is a great concept and can be applied to a wide array of areas and ideas. In Nye's analysis, and in its interpretation, soft power is viewed as distinct from economic influences. Here, however, I would like to examine the overlap: soft power stems from the image and perception of a country, yet it has very strong economic implications too. Moreover, many of the factors now referred to as soft power are very economic in nature and may be broader than Nye's original definition. As a result, I have interchanged the terms 'soft power' and 'soft economic power', in order to highlight soft power's strong economic implications and benefits.

Soft power is one of the four powerful influences and drivers in the modern-day world economy that I have focused on, alongside economic and financial power, politics and policymaking power, and military power. All four are changing, but not in the same way. Soft power is supportive of some Western economies, such as the US, but it is a competitive space as well, not least in education, and future change here is always possible. In bygone days, it was as a consequence of war and hard power that countries subsequently succumbed to soft power. Not now, as it has its own dynamic. It is connected with hard power, but nowadays it is possible to win the war but lose the peace.

Soft power is the ability to influence through ideas, thinking, culture, education, media, sport or creativity. The key thing is that many of these are where advanced economies in the West do well. They are also areas where others will aspire to catch up. In a changing global economy, where ideas and knowledge can provide key value, it is an important influence. It has the ability to attract followers.

A visitor to any country in the world can hear Rihanna, Daft Punk and One Direction on the radio and then watch American movies, buy global brands and watch one of the global sports: Spanish or English football, American basketball or even cricket. The literature might be more regional, with many great writers in different countries. The cars people will aspire to drive are likely to be Japanese or German, even American. Drive down the main road in Beijing and it is full of Buicks, Audis and Volkswagens. And white goods such as fridges or cookers that people want in their homes: German. The top fashion shops are probably French or Italian. Of course, there is a need to appeal to different budgets so alongside the top designers there will also be Superdry, Topshop or Nike. Western firms dominate.

Countries are also able to implant their economic power elsewhere. When Japanese firms invested in the UK in the 1980s and 1990s, their focus included research, design and development (RD&D).

There are many different measures of economic success. But all too often these are heavily influenced by quantifiable things such as sales of goods or exports of machines. While some aspects of soft power can be measured – such as when people buy tickets for cultural events or travel to a tourist site – it is not clear that all aspects of soft power are accurately caught in economic data.

Perhaps, given the difficulty of capturing what constitutes soft economic power, one of the biggest challenges is to measure it. People recognise soft economic power when they see it.

Surveys

Let's consider a few surveys that give us some insight into soft power. In the fourth annual *Monocle* Soft Power Survey of November 2014, carried out with the UK-based Institute for Government, the US was top, displacing Germany, which had been top for the first time in 2013. The top ten were:

1	USA	6	Switzerland
2	Germany	7	Australia
3	United Kingdom	8	Sweden
4	Japan	9	Denmark
5	France	10	Canada

The trouble with surveys such as this is that there is often some built-in bias, which in this case probably accounts for the Western focus. Some regions were missing, such as the Gulf economies and India. However, the results, and reasons, can tell us something about soft-power issues.

Fifty measures are used in the survey for each country, from diplomatic missions to sport and culture. Germany, ranked second, benefited from economic leadership and its business strength in Europe plus academic and footballing excellence. The UK had been ranked first in 2012 because of its hosting of the Olympics and Paralympics, as well as its strong showing in music. As if to highlight how the definition of soft power is now used more widely, one of the factors helping France into fifth place was 'luxury retail'. In addition, France, is ranked highly for art galleries, cuisine and museums. Although Germany tops this survey in Europe, it feels to me that the UK – and certainly London – is more of a global leader in soft power, helped by the English language. The US, ranked first, benefited from pop culture and Silicon Valley's ability to allow it to lead in many digital areas.

The top Asian country was Japan in fourth place. Although South Korea did not make the top ten, its economic strength has been reflected in its global brands, particularly over the last decade – and if one needed a clear sign of globalisation it was the rapper Psy and his 'Gangnam Style' becoming a global music and video hit in the summer of 2012.

However, as *Monocle* said after the 2012 survey, 'Just because Britain has soft power does not mean it necessarily knows how to use it.' The same could be said of many other countries. It raises the question of how soft power can be changed from a passive thing, a positive reflection of a country, to an active driving force.

Where people work and what they buy are important, but quality of life for many is key. The *Economist* Intelligence Unit has a quality of life survey based on eleven indicators, the 'Where To Be Born Index'. It gauges the best opportunities for a safe, healthy and prosperous life, giving a top ten of:

1	Switzerland	6	Singapore
2	Australia	7	New Zealand
3	Norway	8	Netherlands
4	Sweden	9	Canada
5	Denmark	10	Hong Kong

Interestingly, Germany and the US were equal sixteenth, Japan twenty-fifth, Britain twenty-seventh, China forty-ninth and India sixty-sixth.

Perhaps a better guide is where people migrate to. That would at least give another insight into how attractive some countries are. The trouble is, many things can influence this, including pull factors (some countries are keener than others to attract immigrants) as well as push factors (war, repression or economic hardship among many) that could cause people to leave.

Also, it most likely reflects economic opportunities rather than soft power itself. A migrant might need to move for work, but not want to take his or her family, preferring to send money back home to support them. In those circumstances the prime reason for moving is economic: options might include the ease of obtaining a work visa and a relatively small distance from home. There is a strong regional pull.

As a regular visitor to the Gulf, I always found it interesting to note how many of the car drivers and staff in the hotels were from

Kerala, a region of south-west India, where educational standards are high.

The World Bank *Migration and Remittances Factbook 2011* provides a comprehensive analysis covering 210 countries. The countries that attract the largest number of migrants are the US, Russia, Germany, Saudi Arabia and Canada. That is a good indication of the pull of each country. Admittedly, there are some other places that have higher ratios of immigrants relative to their domestic populations – for instance: Qatar, 87 per cent; Monaco, 72 per cent; UAE, 70 per cent, and Kuwait, 69 per cent – but as these countries are relatively small this cannot be seen as a sign of their soft-power attraction. The largest migration corridors also reflect proximity as well as economic factors – such as Mexico to the US, which is the largest with 11.6 million migrants in 2010, followed by two-way flows between Russia and the Ukraine, and then a one-way flow, Bangladesh to India.

The World Bank report also indicates that small countries are suffering a brain drain, as they have a higher ratio of skilled emigration. For instance, Grenada, Dominica, Saint Lucia, Cape Verde, Fiji, São Tomé and Principe, and Liberia have the highest emigration rates of doctors. This raises the issue of the size of economies possibly being an influence in soft power.

In Chapter 2 I suggested that urbanisation was a key economic driver. Cities capture many things, including soft power. Big cities sometimes have a magnetic pull, it seems, both within countries and across borders, not just because of jobs but because they are fun places to be – the 'London vibe' being a classic example. Indeed, Australia's seventh-place ranking in the *Monocle* survey, above, was partly attributed to its 'world-class cities'. There are many rankings of cities. The financial-analysis company Mercer ranks 460 cities based on ten criteria, showing a dominance by Europe. Its quality-of-living survey has Vienna first, Zurich second and Auckland third, and three German cities in the top seven (Munich fourth, Düsseldorf sixth and Frankfurt seventh). These three German cities also make it into the top six of the Mercer rankings for infrastructure, where Singapore is first and London is sixth. It is easy to see why Vienna does so well – a city that was built to run an empire. But given what is happening to cities across the emerging world, it would not be a surprise if there were changes over time.

To provide an idea of what features some people regard as important, consider the approach of the accountancy and professional-services company Ernst & Young. In its analysis it identified thirteen variables to reflect soft power, focusing on integrity, image and integration with the global economy. The components of its integration index make sense: immigration, tourism, fluency in English and ranking of universities. The components it examines to reflect integrity are a mixed bag; freedom index and voter turnout being arbitrary, although CO_2 emissions and the rule of law make sense. Its image criteria are also rather arbitrary but include 'most admired firms', which is a good measure. Interestingly, among its definition of rapidly growing markets, China ranks first, India second.

One report that is always interesting and which is relevant to an understanding of soft economic power is the World Economic Forum's global competitiveness report. It ranks countries based on a dozen variables, which have a strong economic focus. Let me list them, to give you an idea of what some others see as important: under the heading of 'basic requirements' for so-called factor-driven economies that depend on cheap labour or commodities are institutions, infrastructure, macro-environment, and health care and primary education. Next, for the efficiency-driven economies, are the 'efficiency enhancers', which include higher education and training, goods-market efficiency, labour-market efficiency, financial-market development, technological readiness and market size. For the innovation-driven economies there are innovation and business sophistication. The aim is to try to make allowance for countries being at different stages of development.

Perhaps as a further sign of how European thinking has such a dominant bearing on the categories being assessed, Europe provides six of the top ten. These are Switzerland (first), Finland (fourth), Germany (fifth), the Netherlands (eighth) the UK (ninth), and Sweden (tenth). The other four in that top ten are the US in third place and three from Asia: Singapore (second), Japan (sixth) and Hong Kong (seventh). Although the order has shifted, these countries were the top ten the previous year as well. The strong showing of Switzerland, in first place for the sixth successive year, might not come as a surprise, but it should dispel some old-fashioned thinking in economics that competitiveness is just about the price. It is not; it is also about quality. The fact that Switzerland can be ranked first should reinforce that. Few, if any, think Switzerland is cheap. Its competitiveness reflects quality.

The global competitiveness report includes some fascinating results. For instance, in the category of health and primary education, the top five economies are, in order, Finland, Belgium, Singapore, New Zealand and the Netherlands. I was surprised to see Belgium so high. It also figured in the top five for higher education and training, after Finland, Singapore, the Netherlands and Switzerland. Belgium, as the WEF reports, boasts an exceptional higher-education and training system, with fine education in maths and sciences, excellent management schools and on-the-job training. The US, whose universities are the best in the world and have very good collaboration with the business sector, was seventh and the UK nineteenth.

It is remarkable how well northern European countries always seem to do in these international comparisons. Denmark and the Nordic countries have the best-functioning and most transparent institutional framework. Sweden, like Finland, focuses on innovation-led growth. Nordic countries are very competitive despite high tax rates. Too often this leads to the wrong conclusion: that taxes don't matter. They do. High taxes are a potential hurdle for business and for hard work. But equally it should dispel the idea that low taxes alone guarantee success. This again indicates the need to differentiate between causality and correlation: two things happening at the same time does not mean that one caused the other. Indeed, in this case it is other factors that matter. Finland, for instance, has high-class health and primary education and is also very innovative. Having a well-functioning and transparent institutional framework is vital.

Another country that surprises in league tables is Puerto Rico. In terms of the availability of scientists and engineers, the top six are Finland, Qatar, Japan, Greece, USA and Puerto Rico. Greece might also surprise at fourth. Puerto Rico has provided a significant proportion of the Hispanics who have worked at NASA. The quality of scientific research institutes is high in Switzerland, the UK and Israel. The challenge for many small economies is to retain their skilled workers.

At best one can say these surveys reflect some interesting comparisons, but perhaps one important message is that on many criteria economies in Western Europe and North America as well as Australia and New Zealand do well. Although there is clearly a shift in economic power – for all the reasons we've seen – Western economies have less to fear than is sometimes thought. Soft power reflects aspects of economics that might prove more resistant to change, and so might provide opportunities in the West as the middle class grows and spending power increases across the globe.

There are also certain aspects of soft economic power that underline the importance of longer-term strategic thinking. This covers many areas. If soft economic power makes a country an attractive place to emigrate to then this can bring great rewards if handled properly. It also means that immigrants to an economy, viewed as a collective group, are required to provide a positive economic boost, through work, and not a drain, through receiving benefits. Incentives matter, and to discourage benefit tourism there is an economic case to limit benefits available to new immigrants.

The ideal situation is when a country is able to attract immigrants who are cheap, skilled workers or where they fill a recognised economic need – such as the shortage of nannies in Hong Kong, contractors in the Gulf, or health-care workers in the UK. Immigration itself is an economic boost, but can cause displacement of local workers in specific fields, and if there is a lack of strategic thinking, it can result in increased pressure on housing and on local public services such as education and health. It can also expose a problem of lack of skills in the recipient country, squeezing wages.

There is a danger that the term 'soft economic power' will become used simply to refer to all the major drivers that are difficult to categorise in any other way. Given that, let's identify the key aspects of soft economic power and their importance.

Global brands

Reaching the top of any field is hard. Staying there is even harder. The world's best brands have usually done both. Global brands are part of the soft-power story. To appreciate that fully, it is necessary to think of brands in a wider context. David Beckham is a brand. So too are the Rolling Stones, the iPhone or any other global product. Often we think of brands solely as goods or products; they are more than that. They have the ability to attract and to influence, especially in terms of technology products. Essentially, they are things people might aspire to see, be like, use, wear or be associated with.

A 2013 report on global brands by the World Intellectual Property Organization estimated that the amount spent on 'global brands investments' was $466 billion, a large amount, and in addition advertising expenditure was equivalent to about one-third of global spending on research and development. The top global brands included Apple, Google, Samsung, Coca-Cola, IBM, McDonald's and Microsoft – a strong US bias.

London is a global brand. The 2012 Olympics helped cement its position. It is not just a popular place for tourists but the centre of London has almost become a no-buy zone for locals, as international investors want to buy property there. Why? Some say it is because there is only one London. But, in reality, it is soft power. The UK upholds contracts: its legal system, in enforcing this, means wealthy people from across the globe see it as a safe place to keep their money. Central London property has displaced bank vaults in Switzerland as the place to store wealth. Then there is the attraction of the London cultural and creative scene: its theatre, ballet, even stand-up comedy.

The classic example of London's soft power is the British royal family. Its economic impact is hard to quantify fully, but both directly and indirectly it is significant. Its soft economic power is seen by all – and there are countless examples of it in operation. For instance, over the last few years, twice I was asked to chair business events at St James's and Buckingham Palace, on boosting UK business with Kuwait and with Vietnam. The sizeable audiences were definitely A-list for both events, a sign of the pull of the venue and of HRH The Duke of York, who hosted them and was successfully promoting UK trade and investment at home and overseas. The important thing is to ensure such soft power is not seen as a legacy of the past, but as an economic driver in the future. The way the royal family evolves is a positive reflection of that. Take the Duchess of Cambridge, Kate Middleton: once her picture is on the front cover of a magazine, sales of that issue soar.

The intense and widespread international interest in the birth of the future heir in 2013 reflected this soft power, with celebrations to celebrate HRH Prince George's birth taking place across much of the globe.

As the world economy grows and more countries prosper, there is a growing desire for countries to prove themselves in some way. This is not new, and it is always interesting to observe. In 2010

Shanghai hosted a magnificent Expo, the largest ever, with the most visitors at 73 million, boosted by hordes of Chinese schoolchildren, and the largest ever number of countries exhibiting. Official world expositions or 'world's fairs' are selected by vote of the general assembly of the Bureau International des Expositions. It was not until I visited an Expo, in Shanghai, that I fully appreciated its scale and significance and understood its impact.

The origin of such exhibitions dates back to France in 1798, at the end of the French Revolution. The French then continued with fairs, including the French Industrial Exposition in Paris that ran from 1844 to 1849. Although the idea was French, it was the UK that brought it to a higher level and a bigger scale, hosting the first great exhibition in London in 1851. It was known as the Great Exhibition of the Works of Industry of All Nations, and from May to October that year Hyde Park provided the venue for the first major world fair. Fairs then became common through the nineteenth and twentieth centuries.

The London exhibition was aimed at demonstrating the UK's role as an industrial leader. It had a lasting legacy, spurring innovation, and the profits funded the London-based Science, Natural History, and Victoria and Albert Museums. One would expect the Shanghai 2010 Expo to have a lasting impact too, reflected in its slogan 'Better City, Better Life'. Shanghai, which had no metro in 1995, boasted a 260-mile metro, longer even than London's, by the time of the Expo.

To win the selection for the Expo is a competitive process. Each of the cities that competed to host the 2020 fair chose a topic that indicated what they saw as the key issues ahead. Dubai won with a focus on sustainability and development, a further recognition for an economy that has already repositioned itself, building up its tourism and business sectors. The other cities that competed for the 2020 Expo included Izmir in Turkey, which chose health for all; Ayutthaya in Thailand, resources; Yekaterinburg in Russia, global knowledge sharing; and São Paulo in Brazil, diversity and harmony for growth.

Turkey, which only a couple of decades ago had a poor health system, especially outside its cities, now has ultramodern hospitals that attract visitors from the West, having transformed its health system with a combination of public and private money and a successful social-insurance system. There are many spin-offs from hosting an Expo, as there are from hosting major sporting events. Emerging economies are now wise to this, and there is greater competition to host such events. This is not the MICE market – hosting meetings, incentives, conferences and exhibitions – which although lucrative is hardly power, but rather the aim is to have an impact globally or regionally by hosting a big event that attracts mass media attention, and influences the global agenda, or debate, in some way.

Global sporting events such as the Olympics or the football World Cup can be prestigious occasions that help portray an image of a country. Hence they attract huge interest in hosting them, even though the immediate and sometimes even the longer-term financial returns to the host country are minimal, particularly given the cost of building new stadia.

Infrastructure

Infrastructure is a major ingredient of soft economic power. But not in the way one might think. When I refer to infrastructure here, I refer to three types: hard, soft and institutional infrastructure. Too often when people, including economists, refer to infrastructure, it is what I would call hard infrastructure: transport, such as the road and rail network, the housing stock – both in terms of its quality and quantity – and the schools, sports and health-care facilities to support all this. When roads and houses are built, this is captured in economic statistics – but there is even more to hard infrastructure than this. It is also about longer-term strategic planning.

This does not mean that the state necessarily builds the houses or schools: ideally not. Rather, it is about ensuring the right numbers are thought about in advance, so that the private sector is empowered to build what is needed. But in somewhere such as Singapore, or in some of the new cities across China, there is micro-managing down to the look and feel as well as the location of new hard infrastructure. Thinking ahead and planning are important.

It is the soft and institutional aspects that are often overlooked in the debate about infrastructure. Both are important – and part of soft economic power. Both are areas in which the West does well. This is a vital issue for emerging economies. Soft infrastructure is skills and education. It is not just about educating people but also about ensuring there is the right mix of skills for an economy to succeed. In the West, we desire high-skilled jobs. Of course we do. So, too, do most, if not all, countries. These jobs bring more money, more spending in the local economy and probably more future investment. A 2013 report by the consultants Deloitte suggested certain cities attracted high numbers of 'high-skilled knowledge-based jobs', with 1.5 million in London and 1.2 million in New York, but these were way ahead of the 784,000 in Los Angeles, 630,000 in Hong Kong and 425,000 in Boston. Yet it is necessary to have many low-cost jobs as well, to help provide employment. It is not a case of either/or; both are needed. It is essential not to be dismissive of such jobs. They are indispensable for an economy to operate. In my summers as a student I did a number of low-cost jobs, including street cleaning, hospital portering, and cutting grass in a cemetery. Low-skilled jobs are important for an economy, but having the right soft infrastructure to attract the high-skilled jobs is vital. Skills and education play a vital role in that.

Education is clearly a crucial part of soft economic power. But an interesting question is how the importance of education is measured. Is it the ability of educational institutions to sell their services, in which case their value is measured by revenues received or foreign students attracted to study? Or would it be better to measure it in terms of the ability to educate or the ability to influence? As the Mayor of London, Boris Johnson, pointed out in a speech to the Global University Summit hosted by the University of Warwick in London in May 2013, Margaret Thatcher was refused an honorary doctorate by Oxford University in 1985 because she had passed a law making it possible for higher-education institutions to charge international students for a contribution towards their studies. How ironic, given that that measure now raises a huge amount, allowing UK universities to fund their research.

A few weeks before Mrs Thatcher's death in 2013, there was much focus on the fiftieth anniversary of another former prime minister – Harold Wilson – taking over the leadership of the Labour Party. Wilson said that his greatest legacy was the Open University. It was indeed a great legacy, and in some respects highlights the potential future for teaching and learning if social media can be utilised properly. With people living longer, and with new technology developing rapidly, the ability to utilise the concept of the Open University for wider means is considerable, as people will have the potential to learn and retrain mid-life and study remotely, at the best colleges.

Universities and higher education establish deep-rooted ties between students and their place of study, and raise awareness of other cultures. They have a central role in soft power. Universities in many countries jealously guard their independence, retaining autonomy and their own international strategies. Yet in some places they are an important part of the national economy and its future influence. Many countries want to be major knowledge economies, promote soft power and position themselves for reputation, visibility and influence.

Universities are the most meritocratic institutions there are, although politicians sometimes find that hard to accept and often want to interfere to make them places to carry out social engineering. If poorer people don't go to certain universities, it is often a reflection of problems elsewhere, in primary and secondary education.

There are many surveys of universities, and they tend to show a similar story. The top places are dominated by the US and while universities from a few emerging countries are moving up the list, they are still a long way down it. This is a positive feature for the economies concerned, many in the West, as universities are often associated with clusters of strong economic activity. For instance, in the *Times Higher Education* survey for 2014–15, the top twenty comprises fifteen universities from the US (California Institute of Technology in first), three from the UK (Oxford in third), one from Switzerland (ETH Zurich in thirteenth) and one from Canada (University of Toronto in twentieth).

The top fifty includes more universities from the US, UK and Canada, but let me note the highest-placed entries of other countries: Tokyo is twenty-third, Karolinska Institute from Sweden is forty-fourth, the University of Hong Kong is forty-third, Melbourne is thirty-third, the National University of Singapore is twenty-fifth, Peking University is forty-eighth. Germany's top-ranked institution, Ludwig Maximilian University of Munich, was twenty-ninth, up from fifty-fifth the previous year. South Korea's Seoul National University was fiftieth. Eleven different countries figure in the top fifty, and twelve economic regions, if one counts Hong Kong separately.

Then there is institutional infrastructure. This can sometimes be overlooked as a key part of the infrastructure fabric of an economy. Its importance in developed economies has often been under-appreciated.

Niall Ferguson recently argued that the pillars of Western economies are being undermined, as Western democracy is not addressing certain issues, with free-market capitalism being overcome by complex regulations, the rule of lawyers replacing the rule of law, and uncivil society displacing civil society. Despite the problems in the West, many emerging economies have much to learn in this area, India being a notable exception, with many independent institutions. Having the right institutional infrastructure in place helps encourage and attract investment, encourages businesses to invest and people to live there.

Take the European Union, which has expanded its membership to the east this century. Of its twenty-eight members, ten joined in 2004 and three more since, many of them former Soviet bloc economies. Their attitude to the Union appears very different from that of older members, as membership allows them to adopt the institutional framework, openness and freedom denied to them under Russian rule. In fact the communist countries that embraced capitalism after the Iron Curtain fell saw their economies rebound more quickly. Perhaps it is no surprise the riots seen in Ukraine at the start of 2014 reflected a public desire to embrace capitalism and the West.

The Magna Carta, signed in England in 1215, has remained a key cornerstone of the unwritten UK constitution and of individual freedom. It also reflects how hard won some of the things we take for granted are and suggests that while soft power will evolve, Western economies still have a head start. The question is whether they will retain it.

Crucial to soft economic power are the rule of law, the upholding of contracts and the protection of intellectual property rights (IPR). Each of these on its own is a vital issue, but as a group they are important attractors for business and economic activity. While it is possible to measure the economic benefit of legal services, it is not always possible to capture fully the other aspects, such as the protection of IPR. Yet IPR will constitute a vital part of a decision on where to invest, and also on how to invest. So Japanese firms, for instance, retained or returned high-value-added production to Japan from China to protect IPR. And when a firm operates within a country where it is concerned about the possible loss of IPR, there might be a need to keep parts of any production or supply process separate in order to minimise any potential theft. This concern overlaps with other factors, such as the need to eradicate corruption, or at least to minimise its economic and societal impact.

Morals and ethics

I link the issue of institutions into morals and ethics. There needs to be a moral, ethical code that underpins the institutional structure. I referred to this earlier but it is worth reiterating.

It is often said that there is a right way of doing things and a wrong way. The 2008 crisis threw up some interesting assessments. In early 2009, I returned from Davos, where it was bright and sunny, to a snowstorm in London, where the Chinese Premier Wen Jiabao was delivering a speech at the Natural History Museum. In discussing soft power, he said:

> I always think a noble economy should be closely combined with noble ethics or morality. Every economist, every financial expert, should have the blood of morality and ethics flowing in their veins. In his works on wealth and theory on moral sentiments, Adam Smith mentioned the two hands – invisible and visible. One refers to the market and the other refers to morality and ethics. If we had combined these two, we could have avoided the crisis that we are facing today. This is a heavy and sad lesson.

It was not the first time I had been impressed by the Chinese premier. On another visit to London, he met a number of City dignitaries at the Mansion House. One of the topics was the environment and they gave him helpful, perhaps pointed, advice. In the subsequent round-table discussion, he asked those who had just warned him about the environment what cars they drove. The point was made: practise what you preach. This should apply to the corporate world too. Nowadays many big firms spend fortunes on corporate social responsibility, while other parts of the same firms work hard to avoid paying their fair share of tax. This moral dilemma – otherwise known as greed – means it is best to judge firms by what they do, not just what they say.

Rather than seeing soft power just as one country versus another, one can also view it in terms of empowering a more open or more transparent world, with greater awareness and accountability. Soft economic power can help empower people, in combination with new technologies and their influence, particularly over a younger generation – #softpower – including how they can be used to hold company executives and politicians to account.

The post-war capitalist system favoured the multinational, and soft power in some respects continues and reinforces that through the prominence it gives to global brands. These are the new power brokers – although in the modern era, while we talk of global brands in reference to firms, the concept can be applied to people as well. While soft power exerted through brands might reinforce the importance of big firms, one significant aspect of soft power moves the balance away from firms. And that is because of the way new technology has shifted things. Most industries have barriers to entry – these are exorbitant in areas such as capital goods but even in the media they used to be huge. Now, in terms of the information space, this has changed. The journalist Nik Gowing in 'Skyful of Lies' and Black Swans pointed out how 'the institutions of power – whether political, governmental, military or corporate – face a new, acute vulnerability of both their influence and effectiveness' because of what he calls 'information doers'. He emphasised the need for an active approach and for firms to enter the information space swiftly.

Soft economic power doesn't just lie within countries; it can lie with groups. This makes it potentially more exciting. Just as capitalism put power in the hands of firms, now soft power is putting it into the hands of people or certain groups.

When I worked in the City, 'speed to market' was always important, particularly when economic data was released. You took a view according to an instant analysis based on all your collective knowledge and the information set available at the time, and on outcomes versus expectations. Sometimes when data was released the immediate market reaction would be clear, but often it was more complicated, and it was the view of the economists that set the trend. On my first day at work my boss said there were two things I needed to know about the City: 'In the land of the blind, the one-eyed man is king. And always have a view.' When you have a strong view, you need to make it heard. A clear vision allows you a bearing when events happen and you need to respond.

The aspect of soft power that is changing is the capacity for scrutiny and accountability. Although not talking about soft power, Gowing's booklet captures this, describing how 'in a crisis there is a relentless and unforgiving trend towards an ever greater information transparency'. Basically, big firms and politicians are now put on the spot in a way in which they would not previously have been but even now they don't yet get it. It is, as he calls it, the 'new civilian surge'. A 24/7 real-time information environment. Judgement comes in here: it's not possible to respond to all the inevitable noise, but it is necessary to react to the key things that will affect the brand or have a cumulative economic impact if not addressed immediately. So soft economic power provides a more accountable society. In this information age we see the rise of non-state actors and of individual bloggers.

But what does this mean for democracy? In the West, this is a hard question to comprehend, as democracy is taken as a given. Globally, the Arab Spring uprisings of 2011 showed that people aspire to democracy. Democratic systems are seen as part of soft power, particularly when set alongside the institutional infrastructure and increased accountability mentioned above. But, like all things, it needs to be constantly reassessed.

There are a number of key economic attributes that link into soft economic power. Creativity is one of them. As we have discussed, in the changing world economy the countries that do well will have one of the three Cs: Cash, Commodities or Creativity. With creativity such an important aspect of the changing world economy, we need to know if it is being captured properly. Creativity is central to a knowledge-based economy of the twenty-first century and to an ideas generation.

It is not possible to predict when someone will invent something or whether a life-changing discovery will be made, but it is possible to create an enabling environment in which these things are more likely. We can create clusters to which like-minded people or firms are attracted, as to pools of academic excellence such as universities and research centres. It is also vital to ensure that the market is allowed to operate properly, as this is the best way to allow ideas and inventions to be commercialised and used fully. Central planning cannot do that; the market can.

Finally, soft power includes the power of attraction, which has different aspects. There are the features that attract tourists: the historic monuments or sights to see. In Europe, the magnets of soft power include art, literature, museums, design, fashion and food. And then there are fundamental principles that can often be overlooked and taken for granted in the countries that have them.

In January 1941, President Roosevelt gave his 'Four Freedoms' speech in which he talked of freedom of worship and of speech and the freedom from want and from fear. At that time the US had a non-interventionist stance – as China does now – and while the speech was opposed by some non-interventionists, it is a good reminder of some of the attributes of the US that are vital for soft power.

Soft power's potential importance is not understood by all. The BBC World Service has been a key stalwart in standing up for independent news across the globe. Yet in recent years the World Service has been cut back. Its global influence in turn has been squeezed. Almost mirroring this, the rise of television has become more apparent. Visiting Nairobi in 2011, I was struck by a few things: one was the newly tarmacked dual carriageway from the airport into town, which had not been there on my previous visit and which I learned had been laid by Chinese contractors, and the other was the large television studio recently built there for Chinese CCTV. You could interpret this as a sign of China recognising the importance of soft power, with a news channel, in English, able to broadcast across Africa.

I have heard many different views, or interpretations, of democracy across the globe. In China I attended a lively debate where the point was made that democracy provided accountability but did not guarantee responsibility. And in some respects that fits with a point made by Niall Ferguson about large budget deficits heaping IOUs onto future generations. Politicians' thinking may be too short-term, reflecting their basic desire to be re-elected. The theory of rational expectations suggested that people would see through this, and recognise that the political theory of the business cycle brought short-term temporary help but longer-term problems, and that in turn would force politicians to address the longer-term issues.

Democracy alone does not guarantee economic success. Nepotism is to be avoided. In *Japan: The Coming Collapse*, Brian Reading pointed out that in 1992 'every LDP [Liberal Democratic Party] Dietman under forty, except one, is related to another present or past politician'. It is an issue now in India. Citing Patrick French's *India: A Portrait*, Ruchir Sharma pointed out something similar: 'Every member of Parliament in the Congress Party under the age of thirty-five was a hereditary MP.'

The democracy debate is often raised, usually in private. On one visit to South-East Asia, at a private dinner with politicians, I was asked whether the West would ever contemplate partial votes, with those who are older receiving a fraction of a vote, versus a full vote for working-age voters. The policymaker suggested he was simply thinking aloud about possible ways to stop a built-in bias, particularly if a population ages and lives longer. The idea was to break the short-term mould.

What then are the implications of soft power for the consolations of economics?

The first is that at a time of great uncertainty for the world economy, Western economies should feel reassured that they retain a dominant role in soft power and this remains a positive driver of growth for themselves. This should help them as the global economy grows.

The second is the importance of continuing to invest in brands and for countries to play to their strengths. Indeed, younger people should think of themselves as a brand as they start out in their career.

Third, the importance of hard, soft and institutional infrastructure, all of which are likely to be drivers of future activity.

Fourth, even though morals and ethics cannot be legislated for and might not be viewed as directly contributing to growth, they are important considerations.

Fifth, soft economic power is a new area of focus for more countries across the globe.

Soft power is central to the debate about the best model to follow: the Washington consensus, focused on markets; the Beijing consensus, focused on the power of the state, or even the Mumbai consensus, not often talked about but highlighted by Larry Summers as a people-centric and democratic approach. That leads directly on to hard power, where the US is dominant, and where the alliances it forms as a result allow it to gain widespread support for its free-market policies across the globe. It is the market, provided its excesses are kept in check, that benefits from the combination of soft and hard power.

6

Hard power

What are the two most important words associated with President Obama in his first term of office? The president gives countless excellent speeches on many subjects. It might seem strange to single out just two words, but nevertheless I would choose 'and' and 'pivot'.

It's a fantastic feature of the English language that 'and' can be so vital a word. The US used to have a regular 'strategic economic dialogue' with China. Soon after becoming president, Mr Obama changed this to a 'strategic and economic dialogue' and it immediately made a big difference. Treasury Secretary Geithner and Secretary of State Clinton launched the new dialogue, which was divided into two strands. The economic strand covered commerce, trade and issues such as the currency. 'Strategic' covered pressing bilateral issues such as security and energy, some of them controversial, such as US concern about cyber-espionage by China in 2013. The word 'and' was a clear statement of intent and ensured distinct strategic and economic outcomes from the talks. For the world's two biggest economies to meet regularly and discuss such issues is great, particularly given their growing economic links.

The second key word was 'pivot'. While 'and' was about moving relations with China forward, 'pivot' signified a change in direction towards Asia and a focus on the new centre of gravity in the Asia-Pacific.

In the context of hard power, both words are key. But what is hard power? I have seen hard power referred to as a combination of economic, technological and military power. It is also part of smart power, a combination of the power of coercion and the power of persuasion. Smart power means that soft power works much better when it is backed by hard power, or that hard power works well when it has soft power as a mitigating factor.

At its most basic, hard power can mean the ability of a country to achieve its aims through conflict or the threat of conflict. Hard power is also a hedge against the unknown and for some the justification for a nuclear-weapons capability. So, as with many views in economics, there is no complete agreement on the term, but here I use it to express military might and some future geopolitical influences. Hard power is a perfect complement to the other key drivers that explain how the world is evolving and what lies ahead. Hard power will be an important part of the global outlook in coming decades.

Historically, when there were power shifts across the globe, the changes in economic and hard power would usually go hand in hand. The further back one goes, the more likely it was that war would be part and parcel of the process. Indeed, historically, war often seemed inevitable and it would be worth considering if that is still the case now. It could be argued that the case for conflict might have been lessened by the inability of major nations always to win wars against inferior opposition, despite their firepower, plus, increasingly, the need to have public support before engaging in a conflict. Yet the combination of the War on Terror and constant media coverage of the wars and conflicts of the last decade might make it feel like a dangerous world.

Throughout history the major economic powers were usually the same as the main military ones. As a country's economic power grew, so too did its army or navy, and its appetite to dominate. Napoleonic France and Imperial Germany are good examples of this. The British Empire became the first great economic power of modern times, and in the last major shift, a century ago, the US superseded Britain as both the economic and military superpower.

The Cold War eventually saw the US, thanks largely to President Reagan, with strong support from his allies, particularly Prime Minister Thatcher, outspend and defeat the communist system.

Indeed, for a time, the USSR showed it was possible to be a military power without corresponding economic might, a position that proved unsustainable. Conversely, after the Second World War, both Japan and eventually Germany had shown that it was possible to be a great economic power with no military might.

The global situation is complex. The shifts in power that I have discussed might lead some people to talk about this century belonging to China or Africa or Asia, but it might be more appropriate to think of it as a global century, with a multipolar world, where many regions and countries do well. As we saw in the last chapter, soft power favours the West. Hard power, too, favours the West, although that is changing: the global story grows more complex even as the US still retains the upper hand as the world's major, and for the current time only, superpower.

What then are the key hard-power questions that stand out? The president's two key words cover the vital issues – the future relationship between China and the US, and the outlook in Asia. What does the pivot actually mean and how does it play out with China's regional strategy and with other Asian countries? Will there be a new Cold War and a new Bamboo Curtain? Or could it be even worse, with a new hot war? After all, the US is a staunch ally of countries that might be viewed as possible enemies of China, with potential for territorial disputes – for example, Japan, the Philippines or Vietnam. How events in Europe unfold is the other key issue, particularly as the 2014 Ukraine crisis has fuelled fears of a new Cold War between the West and Russia.

The Cold War

When I was growing up, one issue dominated the news and global debate. It was not economic or financial. It was the Cold War and it meant the risk of a nuclear war was a constant fear. In fact, as a schoolboy it sometimes seemed more likely to happen than not.

That is now a long time ago, but visiting Japan at the end of 2012, I was struck by the feeling there that we were entering a new Cold War between the US and China. Is that really the case? There are certainly rising tensions between the two, but could it really reach the scale of intensity of the US–Soviet stand-off?

It is worth remembering how much the rivalry between the USSR and America at the height of the Cold War dominated everything, spreading into so many other areas of what was going on in the world and its coverage in the media.

One area was the economic divide. The consumer-focused West, where the price system dominated and allowed resources and investment to be directed into many of the right areas, stood against the price-controlled, target-driven system in the East that failed to deliver on strong economic growth. Comecon was the economic gathering of the Eastern Bloc, and its idea of control and direction proved second best to what was happening in the West. Over time this made it difficult, and ultimately impossible, for the Soviets to match the Americans on hard-power spending.

While there was always lots of data to show the West's better economic performance, not least rising living standards, when I visited Berlin in the mid-1980s, before the Wall fell, I always felt the best visual indication of the economic difference was in the centre of West Berlin. There a giant bright Mercedes Benz symbol rotated on top of the Europa Centre and could be seen across much of the city, even from parts of the East, where people were driving about in Trabants. There was no economic comparison between the two systems.

The Cold War saw growing competition between the US and the USSR in all walks of life. There was the Space Race of the 1960s and even the battle for the World Chess Championship in 1972, which made news across the globe as the American Bobby Fisher took on the Russian Boris Spassky in Reykjavik. By 1980 the US was boycotting the Olympics in Moscow in reaction to the Soviet invasion of Afghanistan in 1979.

The US–USSR military conflict was reflected in an escalating build-up of weapons and technology, and was also a factor in many other disputes, such as the Vietnam War or the earlier Korean War, which was the last time China and the US faced each other in battle. Then there were various nuclear close shaves, notably the 1962 Cuban missile crisis.

The positive economic spin-off of increased military spending is often overlooked. It allowed both the US and the USSR to be at the forefront of scientific development and technological innovation, although the communist system never allowed commercial development and wider use, while the US free-market system did. Today, one should not underestimate the positive economic effects of US military spending, which helps finance scientific development and university research. To stay ahead in hard-power terms requires not only money but cutting-edge science and technology too.

For the last half-century the US has tried to ensure it maintains a competitive edge in all forms of research that might affect national defence. It has the Defense Advanced Research Projects Agency to support this aim, which has helped develop technologies with wider commercial use. The UK, likewise, has the Defence Science and Technology Lab aimed at maximising science and technology for the defence of the UK. There is cutting-edge work on all areas of defensive and offensive technology.

Despite the Ukraine, I don't think there will be a new Cold War involving Russia. The ideological divide between Russia and the West today is nothing like it was. Just as before, Russia will not be able to match US military spending, even though the Russian economy has seen a surge in living standards over the last decade. In fact, with savings usually leaving the country Russia is often capital constrained, and even an escalation in tensions tends to leave it in financial difficulty, as we saw during 2014. If there were to be a new Cold War, it would be between the US and China. Recent years do not suggest their relationship is heading that way, but who knows how it will unfold in the future? Naturally, in coming decades, attention will be on how the US and China compete, but also, as the Chinese economy grows in a way in which the Soviet economy never did, I think we shall also see how the US and China can complement each another.

Current hard-power trends

There is no single way of measuring hard power. Instead, we have different comparisons that are variations on a theme. In terms of spending, one might opt for numbers of troops, or missiles, aircraft carriers, nuclear arsenals or other military equipment, or one might want to make allowance for technology, or instead look at track records in war. Global Firepower, for instance, has a ranking based on conventional weapons, with a top four of the US, Russia, China and India. Indeed, India has 22.9 million people who reach military age annually, providing a huge potential military force.

Data can often be a problem when making international comparisons, because not all countries measure things in the same way. This can be more complicated still in hard-power areas as there could be an additional desire for secrecy. Also, the data might not be comparing like with like. Countries might spend money on wildly different things. In China, some of its increased military and defence spending is on wages; and a significant portion might be focused more on internal security than on fighting wars. The UK budget, meanwhile, is heavily focused on expeditionary warfare and mainland defence. Comparing an inappropriate element, such as obsolete equipment, can also lead to an inappropriate conclusion, such as Iraq being viewed as having the third-most powerful army in the world in 1991, when clearly it didn't and just looking at the state of its economy would have led one to question that proposition. Some might say the best guide is power projection capability, a country's ability to use its military either to threaten or to fight, although this too seems hard to measure accurately and might not be appropriate for all countries.

In addition, the nature of new threats can change, so it is not just scale that is important, but adaptability and the intelligence to change in response to any new environment. Recent decades have shown many examples of challenges to hard power.

When we looked at soft economic power in the previous chapter, we saw the advancement of technology allowing people to hold politicians and others to account. Similarly, with hard power, technology has led to a greater need to guard against both terrorism and cyber-attacks. This raises fresh questions about the effectiveness of military spending. The US has found it hard to defeat weaker enemies with much less military capability, spotlighting that it is not just about money. This not only justifies co-operation among like-minded countries but also should ensure continued military spending on areas such as technology and security.

A few current trends in hard-power spending stand out.

The dominance of the US is one. Hard power is changing but it is premature to suggest that there is a significant shift at the top. To understand why, consider who spends what on military and defence. This shows a remarkable concentration among very few countries. The US accounts for 39 per cent of the global total. China spends 9.5 per cent, Russia 5.2 per cent, the UK 3.5 per cent and, somewhat surprisingly in my view, Japan 3.4 per cent. The next ten account for another 21.2 per cent. So the fifteen biggest spenders account for almost 82 per cent of the total, and of this top fifteen the US spends almost as much as the next fourteen countries combined.

There is a group that has a strong modern military because of on-going issues and disputes: this includes India, Israel, Turkey, South Korea and Pakistan. Japan might be set to follow and under Prime Minister Abe seems keen to re-establish itself as a regional force.

Then there are the new kids on the block. These are countries that are building their military capability because they want to and because they can, helped by stronger economic performance. They include Brazil and many economies across East Asia, including China.

China's spending is rising and on current trends it could match the US by around 2025. Even allowing for this, it is hard to imagine the US losing its pre-eminent position any time soon. It is not just the scale of its spending but, as the economist Natalia Lechmanova has pointed out, the quality of it too that gives the US a clear competitive edge. China's military spending grew annually 15.9 per cent between 2001 and 2011, just exceeding its 14.9 per cent nominal growth, so as a proportion of its economy China's spending has remained close to 2 per cent of its GDP.

Although there is widespread concern about China, it would need both a huge catch-up and for China to keep matching US spending once there. At the start of the Cold War, the USSR was spending about half its GDP on defence, far more than the US, and yet despite that it was soon being outspent because the US economy was so much bigger. It could be argued that the US was caught napping by the USSR after the Second World War and it was not until the 1960s that its huge technological advantage allowed it to pull away. There is no danger of that now. And in some respects the US pivot towards Asia is an attempt to make sure it doesn't get caught out in the future.

The US hard-power budget is under pressure, although it is still sizeable. In the wake of frivolous general government spending in recent decades, the US is now squeezing its military budget at a time when others, particularly in Asia, are expanding theirs. But the US lead, in quantity as well as quality of spending, is so large that it will retain its dominant role even with a modest defence budget, and then it always has the ability to increase it if there is ever the need to.

Asia is seeing a phase of military modernisation, in which China is leading the way, with others such as India following. India and China, with their large armies, are now developing their maritime capabilities. Within Asia there are many differences: South Korea, Singapore and Japan have had modern Western-style militaries for some time, while new regional players, including Thailand,

Indonesia and the Philippines, are hoping to emerge. For many, the worry in Asia is between China and Japan.

Europe too warrants renewed attention following Russian aggression in the Ukraine. It highlighted the changing picture across Europe, where there is both a peace dividend and a legacy effect. The end of the Cold War led to the peace dividend, with less need for military spending and the pressure to allocate available money to other domestic areas. For a number of smaller European economies there might still be more of such a dividend to be seen and this positive economic effect might still be underestimated. For instance, Finland's military budget might appear small in global terms but it is still a significant 4 per cent of its government's spending. It spends almost the same proportion of its GDP on defence as at the height of the Cold War, and the question is whether this is necessary. Whereas three decades ago Finland feared Russia, now it allows state-backed Russian firms to buy Finnish companies.

Whether European countries are able to realise such a dividend will heavily depend on how they view Russia in the wake of the Ukraine. That crisis appeared to reflect Russia's intention to remain a regional geopolitical force, largely in its former territories. President Putin's 18 March 2014 speech announcing the annexation of the Crimea suggested he was fed up with Russia being ignored, stating, 'Russia strived to engage in dialogue with our colleagues in the West . . . but saw no reciprocal steps.' The Ukraine crisis has also raised the fear that buffer states that border Russia and which are not members of NATO – and hence not safeguarded by Article 5 of the NATO Treaty that states any attack on one NATO member is an attack on them all – could be vulnerable.

Perhaps the lesson is to ensure economic engagement in order to minimise future problems. Germany has seen increased economic ties with Russia, but the crisis highlighted a deficit of strategic trust between the EU and Russia, particularly a lack of clarity and under-standing about their future relationship. The future economic potential of such a relationship of 650 million people should not be underestimated, particularly if the EU became the key player in the modernisation of Russian industry.

Meanwhile, in Western Europe there is a legacy group that has a strong military presence largely because of the past or demands from NATO to provide capabilities in expensive niche areas: this includes the UK, France, Italy and Germany.

In contrast to Asia's spending, Western Europe is seeing military budgets coming under increasing pressure. The net effect is that in 2012, for the first time, defence spending in Asia overtook spending by NATO's European members. In its annual report the International Institute for Strategic Studies (IISS) pointed out that European defence spending has returned to its 2006 level, in nominal terms, and is falling, and its manpower is down one-quarter from 2000. Some attribute this to Europe's recent economic mess, but it is more than that. In the post-Cold War era, there seems to be a shift in economic thinking across large swathes of Europe. Does the Ukraine change this?

After forty-four years at the centre of the Cold War, from 1945 until the fall of the Berlin Wall in 1989, many of the small and medium-sized European countries do not feel the need to retain a hard-power presence. To justify spending sizeable amounts, there needs to be a perceived or real threat, and that for many of them is no longer there. While defence budgets are being squeezed, it might be premature to suggest this is an actual loss of European hard power. Rather, the level of expenditure is being reduced to what is appropriate for a post-Cold War world.

The issue for the bigger European countries might be slightly different, particularly with Russia being an unpredictable regional power, with Germany, the UK, France and Italy all having significant military capabilities, but for them the question is what their regional as well as global focus is. They do not want to squeeze spending so much that they become a free-rider on the US, happy for it to act as a global policeman. The fact that France and the UK were involved in Libya and that others, such as Germany, also sent peace-keeping troops suggests that this need not be so. Greater concern about Russia might ensure it isn't. There is a strong case for having a defence capability, although perhaps there will be a stronger case in the future for pooling resources across Europe, with near neighbours and allies. The net result, though, is that, despite the political commitment, Europe is, to use the words of the IISS, 'no longer an exporter of security'.

It says something about the way the world economy has changed that it is not seen as essential for countries to spend heavily on their military defences or their armed forces. This has to be a good thing, if it can be sustained.

How things will develop remains to be seen. Economic performance and a country's expectation about its future role are important influences on defence and military spending. Just as it would be wrong to ignore these changing dynamics, it would also be dangerous to draw the wrong conclusions.

In economic terms it might be thought that hard power is a high-income good in that, while a basic amount of military spending is always required, it is only as an economy starts to grow that it might wish to spend more – both because it can afford it and because it sees an increased need for it. The trouble is, in practice, it might not work out like that, as the Cold War showed. Certainly defence is a big global business, with about 2.5 per cent of global GDP spent on it.

The recurring question about hard power is whether there will be new geopolitical tensions and, if so, could they threaten future global growth? There are many regions of the world to focus on, but most think the biggest issues will be in Asia.

The pivot

Is talk of a US pivot more rhetoric than substance? Secretary of State Hillary Clinton first mentioned it in November 2011, emphasising that this was about increasing diplomatic, economic, strategic and also military presence. It was the president's remarks to the Australian parliament in Canberra that same month that got everyone excited.

Obama's message was: 'The United States is a Pacific power, and we are here to stay.' Not, of course, that anyone expected them to leave, but the point was that pressure on its military budget would not impede US focus on the Asia-Pacific region. So what does the pivot mean? The points made by Obama in that Canberra speech were threefold. US presence would be more broadly distributed, remaining strong in Japan and South Korea while increasing in South-East Asia. Second, the US presence would be more flexible, with new capabilities. Third, it would be more sustainable by virtue of working alongside its allies.

There has been a lot of comment on what this means in terms of military clout. One aspect that triggered much media coverage at the time was the US desire to place a full marine task force in Australia by 2016 but, to put this in perspective, Darwin is as close to Beijing as Dubai is, so perhaps the point should not be overstated. Yet it is a reflection of a regional shift.

The question is whether that regional shift, with President Obama saying America is a Pacific power, is because China looks likely to become a regional power but not to threaten the US as a global power. The pivot reflects the growing importance of the Asia-Pacific region. That makes sense given both the likely increased US economic interaction with Asia and China's increased focus on the South and East China Seas. It suggests an increased US focus on both South-East Asia and India, and also, with the positive economic prospects there, a desire for Asian countries to develop their military capability.

The pivot reaffirms the US's intention to engage more with Asia and also to be seen to be a presence there to stand up for its own interests. One likely aspect is a reaction to recent problems in the China Seas.

There is an interesting view – and I think that it is a key part of the story – that this is less about the number of troops and increased hardware and more about ensuring that Asia retains a pro-US bias in its economic thinking and speaks American in its business. As President Obama said in that Canberra speech, 'History teaches us the greatest force the world has ever known for creating wealth and opportunity is free markets.' This makes the pivot more a force for good.

Retaining a free-market approach has to be a win-win for both the US and China, and indeed for other nations. Notwithstanding the importance of the state in the East and of public–private partnerships in the West, keeping to this approach would be positive for Asia's development. It also would allow best practice to be copied in other regions.

That seems to have been reinforced by comments made by then Secretary of State Hillary Clinton and also by US defense secretaries at recent Shangri-La Dialogues in Singapore, an event seen by many as the major defence and military conference in Asia. In 2012 Defense Secretary Panetta said the US would allocate 60 per cent of its naval assets to the region by 2020, and in 2013 Defense Secretary Hagel said it would base 60 per cent of its overseas forces in the Asia-Pacific. Clinton, meanwhile, made the point that treaty alliances with Japan, South Korea, Australia, the Philippines and Thailand were the fulcrum for the US strategic turn towards the region. These comments reinforce the pressure on other countries to increase their spending, instead of the US.

It suggests that Asia will become the new hard-power hot spot, and raises the question of whether we shall see a new Bamboo Curtain. This is a term that never really caught on in the way that 'Iron Curtain' did, in part because the Cold War was played out in Western Europe and while the Iron Curtain was fixed, the Bamboo Curtain across East Asia proved more flexible.

The *Financial Times* in April 2011 described Asia as a 'region riven by disputed terrain'. The analysis began by mentioning that in the wake of the tsunami China sent a rescue team of fifteen people to Japan. As the author of the piece, David Pilling, wrote, 'It was the first time Tokyo had accepted such a mission from China.' That in itself is amazing and perhaps says something about the issue of saving face in Asia and the idea that accepting help from outside is a sign of weakness, but it also reflects more the inbuilt animosity and distrust both countries have for each another. Yet the acceptance of help was a positive signal.

Certainly there is no shortage of issues across Asia. North Korea is one. China has handled the North with maturity, even though the North doesn't appear to listen to or to fear China. It is hard to see how the North's current state can survive. The immediate worry for most is the endgame and the regional instability it might cause. On one trip to South Korea I visited the Demilitarised Zone, the three-mile strip separating the two countries. The most remarkable thing is how close it is to Seoul, as well as how many troops are stationed there.

Yet when we consider how poor and backward the North's economy has been, its military capabilities must surely be limited. But no one really wants to risk finding out. The issue then is what happens to the North's economy. Does it become a poor, less dangerous country under Chinese influence? Or could it unite with the South, which should be all too aware of how much this might cost, given how expensive German unification was for West Germany? That region of North-East Asia has huge potential, not just with a united Korea but also when one considers how much north-eastern China has developed, with cities such as Shenyang and Dalian, the latter now transformed into a major state-of-the-art international port. It has all the makings of an even more prosperous economic region.

Of course, while I am looking at this in terms of economic potential, there is a military argument that China would sooner retain the devil it knows, a difficult North Korea, than a pro-US united Korea as its close neighbour. Perhaps, but as I outline below,

greater economic co-operation might make even that less of a concern in coming decades.

Now the territorial disputes in the South and East China Seas
have displaced worries about North Korea as the issue to focus on
in the region. Perhaps in part this reflects the progress made in
managing the Korean situation. But the China Seas disputes are
dangerous because they are historical grievances in a region where
history, and loss of face, matters.

In days gone by, military might was necessary to protect trade
routes from pirates and enemy nations. Nowadays, an additional
cross-border concern is cyber-attacks. These can take many forms,
being attacks on companies or even on the payments systems within
countries. One consequence is to provoke increased spending across
the whole technology area, with positive commercial spin-offs.

Today, control of trade routes is generally addressed through
trade deals. If one talks about trade in a military context, it sounds
very aggressive. It implies that a country wants to dominate and
coerce others. Yet, from a strategic perspective, it is remarkable how
there are a certain few vital sea channels for trade to flow through.
These are called 'choke points'. In previous centuries it would have
been essential to control them. Now it is crucial to keep them open.

Take Gibraltar. It is a tiny peninsula at the far southern tip of Spain,
ceded to Britain in the Treaty of Utrecht of 1713. It proved strategically
important over the following centuries, as the narrow Gibraltar Strait
controlled access between the Atlantic Ocean and the Mediterranean
Sea. Amazingly, it is still under British control, though the Spanish
would like it back. Indeed, it hit the headlines in August 2013 as these
two European allies had a dispute over it. Now the Strait of Gibraltar
is of less strategic importance in today's peaceful Europe.

Meriting greater future attention is the 'Gibraltar of the East':
Singapore. Few use the phrase any more, but that is how it was seen
by the British until it fell to the Japanese in the Second World War,
in one of the biggest and most embarrassing military defeats ever.

It was of crucial strategic importance then, as it is now, because of the Malacca Strait.

This narrow, shallow strait, only five hundred miles wide, connects the Indian and Pacific Oceans and is one of the busiest and most important trading routes in the world. As China's and India's economies grow, the strait's importance is likely to grow with them. Currently, it accounts for the vast bulk of China's imported oil and one-quarter of global trade – a proportion that is rising. The neighbouring South China Sea, into which the Malacca Strait feeds, accounts for half of global trade.

Perhaps it is no surprise that the US Navy is harboured in Singapore. As with the Strait of Hormuz (through which much oil and gas pass in the Middle East), the Panama Canal and the Suez Canal, the Strait of Malacca is a choke point. Blocking any one of these would be devastating for global trade. Fortunately, the naval presences are aimed at keeping them open.

For China this creates what is sometimes called the Malacca Dilemma – the fear that in the event of a skirmish or conflict with the US the strait could be easily blocked. In recent years, China has tried to circumvent this potential problem by transporting energy overland. This makes sense, and will probably continue, but it does not release China from its Malacca worries. Moving energy overland from Central Asia cements the importance of the Shanghai Cooperation Organisation, potentially deepening China's ties with countries in that group – including Russia. Indeed, as rail and road links develop in coming decades, and if security overland improves, then the time saved will lead to more trade links over land between western China, Central Asia and Europe.

This will take decades, and for now it is hard to see land pipelines replacing China's dependence on transporting energy by sea. What is more, economics suggests pipelines are more expensive. They are also far from safe, given the security risks in some of the countries they run through. Pipelines are vulnerable in times of tension and, while ships can be blocked, it is easier to sabotage pipelines than hundreds of oil tankers of unknown ownership. Pipelines are inflexible and cannot be rerouted if disrupted. So China's dependence on transporting energy by sea remains.

One of the interesting issues is whether the China Sea proves to be a new Persian Gulf, rich in resources, particularly oil and gas. Partly reflecting this, there are many counter-claims for ownership of various islands from countries across the region. While some claims might be linked to resources, others reflect historical positions.

Three hot spots in the South China Sea stand out: to the far south, the Spratlys; to the north, the Paracels, and, to the east, Scarborough Shoal. Since 2010, China has called the South China Sea a core interest, on a par with Tibet and Taiwan. This could become problematic, as core interests have tended to be red lines that China does not expect other countries to cross.

The Spratly Islands are two hundred and thirty resource-rich small islands and atolls disputed by China, Vietnam, Taiwan, the Philippines, Malaysia and Brunei. They have been under Vietnam's control since the seventeenth century and, according to Vietnam, China's interest is recent. The Paracels are disputed by China, Vietnam and also Taiwan. The Scarborough Shoal, to the west of the Philippines, is disputed by the Philippines, Taiwan and China. The dispute in the East China Sea is over a group of islands called the Senkaku in Japan and Diaoyu in China. The *Economist* had a front page at the end of 2012 showing a picture of these islands with the headline: 'Could China and Japan really go to war over these?' It was a valid question. The islands are tiny, although they can be seen as both strategically important and as offering access to resource rights. Another object of periodic tensions is the Southern Kuriles. Russia seized these four sparsely populated islands during the Second World War; Japan refers to them as the Northern Territories.

There is increasing interest in the sea maps China has, and in the number of dashes it places on them. Its nine- and ten-dash-lined maps are much talked about. The dashes, like the island chains, are linked to where China sees its future regional influence.

In 1988, Admiral Liu Huaqing outlined a plan for three island chains. The date for achieving the first phase has already passed without it being reached. By 2010, the idea was to control, largely for defensive reasons, a first island chain with a permanent blue-water presence in the South China Sea.

By 2025 the second chain was to be further away from China's mainland, from the Aleutians through to Papua New Guinea, a country rich in resources. The aim here would be to limit US capabilities and tie countries there closely to China.

The third island chain, by 2050, was to be even further afield, to include Antarctica. All this highlights China's regional ambitions. The aim is to extend its blue-water capabilities – the ability of its ships to exercise power far from home, by operating across deep oceans – as it ventures beyond its immediate maritime periphery.

Freedom of navigation is a crucial issue – and this is where the US and China are at loggerheads. The UN Convention on the Law of the Sea is the international authority. But what is bizarre is that both countries cite the same article, 58, which deals with 'rights and duties of other states in the exclusive economic zone', in support of their own view. The US cites paragraph 1 of that article, while China cites paragraph 3, which says that due regard must be paid to the interests of the coastal state. This shows how complex the situation is, but if only one article is the issue then perhaps there is little reason to worry about sea lanes and trade being affected.

There is general unease in Asia about China's military aims. Perhaps this should not be a surprise. China was winning many friends but in recent years there have been a number of largely maritime disputes that have caused disquiet. Added to this is history; China's approach of not explaining itself, and its aggressive behaviour in some of these recent naval episodes. The US, it seems, is using this to overstate the threat from China. Hence the fear of a new Cold War and the danger that the US is being too hawkish, fighting a proxy war against the Chinese. But the risk of an air–sea battle must be low.

Given all this, worries about the relationship between China and Japan have escalated, with Japan's Prime Minister Abe talking at the beginning of 2014 of building a new Japan, in terms of both reviving its economy and also its own role as the main regional power. The risk of problems between China and Japan cannot be ignored – and one is reminded of Mikhail Gorbachev's remark to Margaret Thatcher when they met for the first time in 1984, citing a Russian proverb, 'Once a year even an unloaded gun can go off', meaning if tensions build up, something can go wrong.

My feeling is that this will evolve into a less contentious environment, particularly as trade and business flows develop, but how it does so depends on the actions of all sides. In hard-power terms, 'actions change outcomes'. When it comes to military power, it is necessary to watch what countries do as well as to listen to what is being said.

The Indo-Pacific

It is not just the future relationship between China and the US or Japan that warrants attention: so too does that between India and China.

In recent decades, the term 'Asia-Pacific' has become increasingly important in economic and trade terms. It is used commonly, even though the vast number of countries in the Asia-Pacific region differ in so many ways, not least in size and scale. Now the new geopolitical and military term is 'Indo-Pacific', used in the Australian Defence White Paper of 2013. The trouble with such documents is that they often overstate the military threat. But in this context it caught the mood of the moment.

In an Indo-Pacific world, India's strategic importance will rise. The US appears to be courting India far more than it has done before. A new trilateral dialogue has been established between India, Japan and the US, and India has been talked of as a linchpin by the Americans. It looks set to build its maritime power. Supported by the US in its desire for a seat on the UN Security Council, it has replaced its non-alignment policy with multi-agreement. Thus, it has expanded the aims of its 'Look East' policy from boosting economic ties with South-East Asia to becoming the 'defence service provider' to South-East Asian countries as well as other states in the Indian Ocean, in turn allowing India access to ports in the region.

India and China have had a tense relationship ever since they went to war in 1962, and in more recent years Chinese support to Pakistan and India's deepening ties with the US – despite a diplomatic row in late 2013 – have ensured such tensions persist. Then there is the inland area, known as the Arunachal Pradesh, disputed by China and India. The Chinese claim this Indian state as South Tibet, whose border is known as the Line of Actual Control and was the scene of the 1962 conflict. Despite that, relationships appear to be improving, helped by the two leaders now meeting regularly. That said, there continues to be speculation about the future maritime policies of both countries. Again, as economic prospects improve, trade could become the unifier, as seems likely.

China's policy in the Indian Ocean has been called a String of Pearls strategy by the perennial critics. The idea is that if one draws the sea route from the Middle East to China, via the Indian Ocean and the Malacca Strait, it would look like a string of pearls. To that end, China has been cementing its ties with countries around the ocean, helping develop deep-water ports. These include Hambantota in Sri Lanka, Gwadar in the Balochistan region of Pakistan, and also one in Bangladesh. It is often said that China would like to build a deep-water port to take the pressure off Chittagong, Bangladesh's second city, which handles the vast bulk of its trade. Sonadia Island, south of Chittagong, is also a possibility. In addition, China is often viewed as courting islands such as Mauritius, the Maldives and the

Seychelles in the Indian Ocean. The decision of the Indian prime minister not to attend the November 2013 Commonwealth Heads of Government Conference held in Sri Lanka received criticism in India for letting the Chinese in, cementing their relation with the hosts.

Too often this is viewed negatively, but one can interpret what is happening in other ways. There is a need to keep some perspective here. Many countries want to develop their own deep-water ports to support their economic development. Furthermore, the South Asia region has one of the lowest fractions of intra-regional trade, and anything that helps build future trade capacity should be viewed as a positive development. So deep-water ports have a positive economic impact, and China is assisting this.

Yet there is a worry as to whether there is an ulterior motive. China has every commercial incentive to develop ties across that region. It is certainly possible for the deep-water ports to serve future dual roles, trade and military, including refuelling and listening posts. But there is no guarantee that this is the way things will go. In reality, it probably depends on a host of different future outcomes. So far the ports seem mainly commercial.

China has defensive, non-alignment and non-interference principles, and so has pursued a policy of not having military bases overseas. But if it was to develop a 'String of Pearls' policy, it is likely it would need bases in those ports. It will be interesting to see if China retains its policy of no overseas bases. At the same time, is it realistic to think that the countries in the Indian Ocean would willingly embrace a Chinese military presence? I doubt it. Most of them appear keen to maintain a balanced relationship with the US and India while developing ties with China. Economics and trade would appear the main drivers.

So why should we worry?

A possible scenario between China and the US has been called the Thucydides Trap, referring to the dramatic rise of Athens in the fifth century BC and the fear it caused in Sparta, then the established power, triggering war and the destruction of both powers. Despite all the various possibilities, I do not think there will be a hot war between China and the US, and it might not even go as far as a Cold War.

I could construct a plausible scenario in which tensions in the Indo-Pacific region rise, adding to geopolitical worries and having an economic impact. But I could also construct a more likely scenario in which military tensions do not escalate. The hot spot increasingly looks as though it will be in South and East Asia. It would be premature to conclude that this will lead to conflict: 'War is remote and dispute management necessary', to quote Patrick Cronin.

There are always issues. Taiwan was the focus two decades ago. Now, economically, Taiwan is becoming more integrated into mainland China. The Taiwan president at the beginning of this century called for a 'Go South' policy, hoping to distance the island from the mainland, but business went north instead: the countries are becoming increasingly interlinked, and rightly so. Economics overcame politics.

In December 2005, I chaired a speech given in London by Zheng Bijian. At that time he was touring the world on behalf of the Chinese leadership, meeting political leaders and giving keynote speeches. His theme was 'China's peaceful rise'. China's development is peaceful, he said, and there is a need to 'look at these issues from the strategic height of bilateral relations'. China's rise is not a threat, and any issues should be viewed in this context.

The Cold War between the USSR and the US had mutually assured destruction – MAD – as the worst-case scenario. Now, as China's and the USA's economic interdependence grows, the fear is of a different type of MAD: mutually assured economic destruction.

China has a market economy that is developing at a rapid pace. It has benefited immensely from the current world economic order, and is likely to want to build on this and strengthen its economic position. China appears to be far away from competing on ideologies in the way the Soviet Union did. Moreover, whereas there was little economic overlap between the USSR and the US, there is much greater economic interdependence between the US and China. This includes large Chinese holdings of US Treasuries, but also sizeable US investment within China. Economic interdependence can be self-feeding, providing more opportunities for engagement and increased communication and a great incentive to work more closely together.

This doesn't mean the two countries will have a love-in. They will compete. But they do not have to fight.

In essence, they have no economic choice but to work together. This should fundamentally change our perception of the outlook, compared with what was encountered through the 1960s, 1970s and 1980s in Europe. If China is indeed as preoccupied with economic development as it appears to be, then its official policy of 'peaceful development' would seem to be its genuine aim, as it serves its interests best. Also, unlike the days of the Cold War, there are many international issues where China and the US could benefit from working more closely together. The risks outlined in Chapter 3, in areas such as pandemics, climate change and trade, are global and require multilateral solutions. The Cold War was about competition and little co-operation; today it is about both competition and co-operation.

The good news is that the politicians and diplomats continue to make progress towards a positive multilateral dialogue. One important example of this was the Asian Defence Ministers Meeting (ADMM) Plus 8 in August 2013, attended by the defence ministers of the ten ASEAN countries plus their counterparts from Australia, China, Japan, India, South Korea, New Zealand, Russia and the US. The communiqués issued at many of these forums can be 'apple pie and motherhood' types of statement where it is hard to disagree with much of what is said, particularly as the emphasis here was on boosting regional co-operation. But at least they are meeting and not disagreeing, and it helps create another forum in which countries are used to speaking at very senior levels should future issues materialise.

Leadership is vital. We should appreciate how strong leadership can defuse most situations, and even move things in a brand-new direction. Take the speech President Kennedy gave on 10 June 1963, only months after the Cuban missile crisis almost triggered war in October 1962. Speaking at the American University, Kennedy moved the world away from a trend towards multiple nuclear states towards a partial nuclear-test-ban treaty.

Such leadership reinforces the importance of political institutions, which will be discussed in Chapter 7. It also links in with energy security and resource nationalism.

The geopolitics of energy supply is always important. This is an important factor in how the crisis in the Ukraine is resolved, given Russia's role as an energy supplier. Also, the possibility of US energy self-sufficiency is particularly significant, both directly in terms of the benefits for the US economy and also indirectly in terms of what it means for energy prices and for US involvement in other parts of the world. The Middle East, including the Gulf economies, is potentially the most vulnerable to change but the likelihood is that the US will retain a strong presence there, even if it is now favouring Asia. This is for a host of reasons, including the fight against terrorism, as a bulwark in the region against Russian influence, and to prevent nuclear proliferation, thereby supporting Israel. Add in unstable, undemocratic regimes and perennial civil unrest and it is easy to envisage future problems there.

It will also be important to follow hard-power developments in nations such as Turkey, Iran and Saudi Arabia, all of which have become more powerful and influential in their region, and yet their greatest challenge is domestic, meeting the economic aspirations of their people and, in the case of Saudi Arabia, potential social unrest. That, too, puts the pressure in all three countries on economic prosperity and growth.

When there has been loss of life and disabilities as a result of wars, talking about the economic cost always seems of secondary importance. Various studies put an actual cost to the US of conflicts in the Middle East region, citing official data, close to $2.2 trillion from 2001 to 2013, including international assistance through USAID. Adding in medical and future, as well as current, disability bills, the total is close to $4 trillion. There are other costs, including the opportunity cost of all this spending – that is the forgone alternatives that this money could have been spent on, plus the damage on the ground.

In 2012 the Middle East accounted for 28.3 million barrels per day of oil, 32.5 per cent of the global total. One other consequence of such wars is that an oil premium that pushes up oil prices tends to result from increased risks attached to crisis in the Middle East. This premium is hard to quantify, and varies depending on the risks.

Given Saudi Arabia's importance as the key swing producer, it is never far from the top of risk assessments. A decade ago, with worries about the succession there, one saw many reports about its future instability. These remain valid, and perhaps help to explain why, in the space of six weeks in the wake of the Arab Spring, Saudi Arabia allocated huge additional funds, equivalent to a third of its GDP, to social spending. Like the rest of the Gulf region, it needs to diversify its economy to create jobs.

Like the Ukraine crisis, the Arab Spring seemed to take almost everyone by surprise, even when it was happening. Just as good economics is good politics, bad economics can be bad politics. But some parts of the world do not allow politics to act as a shock absorber. In India, when the economy is bad the government is voted out, but other countries don't have that luxury, as we saw in North Africa, where the safety valve was not through the ballot box but through domestic unrest.

Saudi Arabia is closely followed by Russia in oil production, a long way ahead of the US. Russia plays a major role in gas production too, just behind the US but well ahead of the other major gas producers such as Iran, Qatar and Canada. Europe became over-dependent on Russian gas – partly a legacy of the German Chancellor Willy Brandt's Ostpolitik rapprochement policy of the Cold War era. Western Europe also came to over-rely on its passage via the Ukraine, which since its Orange Revolution of 2004 has not always had the best of relationships with Russia, as events in 2014 showed. This has led in recent years to alternative pipelines: Nord Stream via the Baltic, and South Stream via the Black Sea.

Energy needs are already resulting in increased inward investment across Africa, providing a further economic stimulus, boosting current and future potential growth there. This also makes Africa more interesting in hard-power terms. And the continent is attracting increased interest, from the private sector as well as other nations.

Water, too, is attracting attention. The UN Food and Agriculture Organization (FAO) has stated that issues over water have often been a source of co-operation, not conflict, between countries. One hopes that remains the case, for as Sanders Research Associates has pointed out, there are 215 international rivers and 300 groundwater basins and aquifers that are shared by two or more countries. The good news is that water has tended to be a unifier, bringing countries together to address issues.

Hard power is an integral part of the consolations of economics. It is one of the four main drivers of the world economy and it is likely to take us in a direction different from that seen in the post-war era. The USSR and the US were at loggerheads, not only wanting to be number one, but with completely opposite economic systems and aims. China and the US are increasingly linked in economic terms. Likewise Russia and the EU could gain from closer future economic ties. Mutually assured economic destruction has replaced the Cold War fear of mutually assured destruction.

Hard power, too, should be seen as a positive for the US and Europe. It keeps the US at the forefront as the world's superpower, a position it looks set to retain for some time. That will allow it to keep open the choke points for global trade mentioned above, such as the Malacca Strait and the Strait of Hormuz. As in the Cold War, the military pre-eminence of the US should help it stay at the forefront of scientific and technological change.

Europe's hard power might appear to be eroded, but it is perhaps more accurate to say it is more focused. The larger Western European nations are likely to retain a hard-power presence, especially after the Ukraine, supporting the idea of a multipolar world, and perhaps pooling their future resources, while the smaller ones will be free to divert spending to other economic areas.

The increased hard-power ties between China, Russia and other energy-producing regions will underpin the growth we spoke about in earlier chapters of new trade corridors and increased trade flows between different regions of the world – Africa, Latin America, Asia and the Middle East.

Asia is modernising, led by China, and this will see defence assuming a bigger share of economies there. Japan's economy is likely to benefit, reinforcing its technological clout.

The US pivot might be as much about ensuring a pro-US attitude across Asia, and it is premature to say there will be a new Cold War or a new Bamboo Curtain. But there is little doubt that hard power will remain a key driver. China appears keen on pushing its aims to be a regional power in Asia, Japan is resurrecting its regional might, matched by President Obama's assessment that he is the first Pacific president. Russia too is keen to remain a regional power. It would be foolish to say that things could not go in the wrong direction, given recent developments in the Ukraine and the China Seas, but it seems far more plausible to say they will not. The story of China's peaceful rise has been a powerful one to date. Perhaps it is the upholding of free markets that will be the most important economic outcome. There is a saying in China, 'Wise people will seek common interests, while the unwise will focus on their differences', and the US and China increasingly share interests in common.

7

Who runs the world economy?

Who runs the world economy? Is it possible for anyone to run something of that size and scale, with so many different countries and peoples? Even if there were groups that did want to run it, what are the levers they could pull in order to achieve a particular outcome and course of action?

These are valid questions. More businesses are starting to see international opportunities outside their home market. Rising food and energy prices have worldwide implications as they take an increasingly large proportion of the disposable incomes of many people, especially of the poor. Globalisation has added to competition, keeping wages down in many Western economies, while at the same time the competition for talent and jobs is intense. Finally, more people around the world are seeing their incomes rise, allowing them to travel, spend and invest internationally. In this environment, we need worldwide institutions with teeth.

One way the world picture is changing is that economies are more interdependent than ever. In the past it used to be said that if America sneezed the rest of the world caught a cold. While what happens in the US is still vitally important, we live in an increasingly multipolar world with more than one key economy. It is no longer only the actions of the US that have a global impact. We can catch colds from all sorts of countries now. Yet it is not only risks that know no bounds; the interdependence of the global economy means more countries can share in the proceeds of growth. Perhaps the analogy to focus on is that smiling, too, and not just sneezing, can be contagious. Perhaps in the future the saying will be: 'When India or Africa smiles, the whole world is embraced by its confidence.'

In any economy, the outlook depends on the interaction between the fundamentals, policy and confidence. All three are important, yet confidence is almost impossible to measure. Confidence by itself can take an economy only so far, yet its importance should not be underestimated. Firms need it before they invest or take a risk; people need it before they spend a lot of money. Although confidence might not be the only factor needed to propel an economy to the upside, its absence will drag it down; its economic impact is asymmetric.

People tend to be more familiar with the way things work in their own country, as this is where their laws are passed, taxes paid and, as long as the country is a democracy, votes cast. What happens at a national level can either influence or be influenced by what happens elsewhere. This is why it matters more than ever before to get a grip on regional and global institutions. After all, they might have even more power and influence over how things work in the future. Let's examine the issue of who runs the global economy.

Show me the money

Some might say it is not institutions but money that makes the world go round, in which case a good starting question should be: who has the money? It is remarkable, and perhaps frightening, how much money is concentrated in the hands of so few.

On the plus side, in recent years, emerging economies have generated more wealth. This is good news and reflects their growing slice of the global economic cake. It is good news because it is helping to bring more people out of poverty and it provides a firmer footing on which to build future global growth, with multiple areas of stronger domestic demand. One trend worth noting is that whereas globalisation and the growing world economy have seen the income divides fall between countries, within some countries they have risen. This offers an interesting economic debate in itself.

Should we take it as a sign that globalisation is working at an international but not at a national level, or instead conclude that it is good news as long as the world economy is doing well, and not be unduly worried about the relative breakdown?

Since the 2008 crisis, the response by governments in the West of bailing out the banking system, and the decision of the US, the UK and European central banks to keep interest rates low, appears to have caused the rich to get richer, as high-valued properties and financial assets have benefited. It is important to say here that the 'rich' in question are not necessarily the middle classes but the super-rich – the 'have yacht' as opposed to mere 'haves'. These post-crisis initiatives also had a profound impact on the pools of money held by institutions and countries. The economist Stephen King in *When the Money Runs Out* points out that since 1990 in the US, 58 per cent of the rise in income has gone to 1 per cent of the population. Professor Joseph Stiglitz explains that he uses the term 'the 1 per cent' to 'refer to the economic and political power of those at the top' as he makes a powerful case for addressing inequality and taking on vested interests.

There are many lists of wealthy individuals, but comparisons of rich institutions are less common. In terms of individuals, according to *Forbes* magazine, in 2000 there were 470 dollar billionaires. By 2014 there were 1,645 billionaires.

It is hard to picture a billion, but perhaps it is easier to conceive of it in terms of time. There are sixty seconds in one minute; 3,600 seconds in one hour. To reach one million seconds would take twelve days; to reach one billion seconds takes thirty-two years! That is how big one billion is, using the commonly accepted American billion of a thousand million. The obsolescent English billion (a million million) would take far longer.

This stokes the global policy debate about income disparities and tax. Globalisation makes it harder to tax areas that are mobile, such as multinationals or high-skilled workers, unless all countries buy into a common policy approach to global tax. It is an example of how the effectiveness of national policies – in this case on tax – can be influenced by global developments.

A rich list of the world economy is probably an impossible concept, as it is not a simple matter to compare like with like, but it is possible to see where some of the money lies. According to *Forbes*, the world's richest people are Bill Gates (Microsoft), $76 billion; Carlos Sim Helo (telecoms), $72 billion; and Amancio Ortega (Zara), $64 billion. These fortunes are huge, but it is the institutional and sovereign money that warrants attention.

In terms of foreign-exchange reserves, China has $3.8 trillion, Japan $1.3 trillion and Saudi Arabia $723 billion. Like any of the amounts mentioned here, these are liable to change, according to economic and market conditions, as well as policy. It is natural to think of reserves as being there to fend off speculators and for use in times of currency crisis, but when amounts grow large they can be used for other purposes, and indeed some of China's reserves were used as seed money to set up their sovereign-wealth fund, which invests in and buys assets across the globe. In recent years more countries have established such funds, and these are a potential source for development and other spending within countries, both now and in the future.

The biggest sovereign-wealth fund is Norway's, now $838 billion in size, while Abu Dhabi's, which is more secret and harder to measure, amounts to around $773 billion, and the China Investment Corporation is $575 billion. These large amounts give each of these countries considerable financial muscle.

The private-sector asset managers also wield considerable power: Blackrock, $4.1 trillion; Allianz, $2.5 trillion; Vanguard, $2.1 trillion; UBS, $1.9 trillion; State Street, $1.9 trillion; and PIMCO, $1.9 trillion. In terms of hedge funds, which were the biggest worry ahead of the crisis but proved to be the dog that did not bark, the large funds are Bridgewater, $83.3 billion; Man Group, $64.5 billion; and Brevan Howard, $36.6 billion.

This list is not meant to be comprehensive; it simply illustrates some of the names, amounts and types of funds. One could add to it with state pension funds, corporate pension funds and private equity. Largely as a result of the policy of cheap money, the years since the financial crisis have brought little change. In some areas, such as currency reserves or asset management, information is transparent and public, although that is not the case everywhere.

The figure I find remarkable is the size of the holdings of the Norwegian sovereign fund, as its wealth has been built up over only the last half-century. In recent years this fund has diversified its investments more into emerging economies, as well as into countries with which Norway now does more trade.

So where can this global money go? A look at the size of capital markets shows the scale they assume in many Western economies and highlights the need for these economies to come to grips with the lessons of their banking crisis. It also displays the potential for emerging economies to scale up their capital markets in order to benefit fully in future growth. Efficient and properly regulated capital markets help growth.

In October 2013 the IMF reported the size of global capital markets as 372 per cent of global GDP, including stock-market capitalisation of $53 trillion, debt securities of $99 trillion and bank assets of $117 trillion. Bonds, equities and bank assets amounted to $269 trillion. Valuations can vary significantly over time, but debt markets are significantly bigger than stock markets, both being dominated by the US. One legacy of the crisis has been a regime of financial repression in which the combination of low interest rates and a dysfunctional banking system has failed to perform the role of channelling savings and funds to where they are needed.

The scale of financial markets varies, with the largest rated at 3,097 per cent of GDP in Luxembourg, 1,224 per cent in Ireland and 804 per cent in the UK. No wonder these countries benefit from good financial times but are left vulnerable in bad times. In Europe and Japan capital markets are more than five times bigger than their domestic economies, in North America over four times bigger, but in Asia only two and a half times bigger. In Latin America and the Caribbean they are less than twice as large; in Africa and Eastern Europe about the same size, and slightly less than this in the Middle East. There is no ideal size for capital markets. One of the lessons of the 1997–8 Asian economic crisis was the need to open up capital markets and to develop a financial system at a speed best suited to domestic economic needs. What is particularly interesting is the potential for future capital market development across a host of regions. The challenge is to get it right and not to grow too big, or too quickly.

The Group of Thirty is a private-sector body of respected international experts and former policymakers and has nothing to do with other similar-sounding but official government groups such as the G7 and G20. This influential Group of Thirty, which meets and produces reports to inform policy, pointed out in a 2013 report on *Long-term Finance and Economic Growth* that the average maturity of bank loans is 4.2 years in the developed world, and 2.8 years in emerging economies. This may be too long, not too short, as banks are not best placed to finance long-term projects. What is really needed is developed capital markets. These can preserve us from having to bail out banks again, the way taxpayers did before. Deeper and broader capital markets would allow 'disintermediation', a shift away from a reliance on bank finance, which would permit new markets to develop and permit new opportunities such as the ability to attract more funds into longer-term infrastructure investment.

The need then will be to build bridges connecting those who need capital with those who can supply it. The suppliers include sovereign-wealth funds, pension funds and insurance companies. They have no shortage of instruments they can buy in the West but, increasingly, the opportunities are across the emerging world, and it is there that countries need to have domestic capital markets that are big enough to absorb inflows, which would lessen the incentive to resort to controls on the movement of money. An overriding theme has to be the prime need to use finance as a force for good, as a source of investment.

A firm's decision on where to invest clearly has an impact outside its home market. How multinational companies operate their supply chains can affect many countries and the course of international trade, with parts produced in different locations. The same is true in the service sector, with people and experts in multiple locations contributing to a project.

One of the earliest and most famous economists, Alfred Marshall, writing in his *Principles of Economics*, first published in 1890, said that, like trees in the forest, there might be large and small firms, but 'sooner or later age tells on all of them'. There is a life cycle for firms, as there is for people. Firms need to reinvent themselves to remain relevant and competitive in changing economic conditions, and those that don't will die. The same is true for institutions.

Yet that is only part of the story, and even Marshall had revised his thinking within a few years after seeing substantial data from America, Britain and Germany. As early as 1910 he had observed 'Giant Redwoods' in these economies. The economist Leslie Hannah summed these up as firms that had 'built significant technical, organisational, and marketing capabilities, thus acquiring often unassailable first-mover advantages, so that they generally still dominate'. Even a century ago, global companies had emerged.

Nowadays, there are industries, firms and brands that are very international, but firms need to be seen in a different context from countries. With occasional exceptions such as the break-up of Yugoslavia or the collapse of the Berlin Wall, countries rarely change in modern times, and when they do it happens in response to a major event – either war or the collapse of artificial barriers. In contrast, as secure as firms might sometimes seem, over time they come and go remarkably often. When I started work in 1985, Manufacturers Hanover and PanAm were two companies with a global image, but they had disappeared only a few years later. Even now, firms that are household names can collapse or shrink, such as MySpace, the most visited social networking site in the world between 2005 and 2008, but now way down the list.

In the course of globalisation big international firms have become more mobile, able to shift their operations around, creating jobs in multiple locations. Their national ties are often loose. Countries across the world court global companies hoping to attract their investment and jobs. A consequence of this is a greater disconnect between a company's place of origin and where it bases its operations. Many of the biggest companies listed on the major stock exchanges carry out a large amount of their business overseas. Manufacturers or call centres might shift their operations to where costs are low, while service-sector firms go to where they see demand. The jobs they create are mobile.

Who pulls the levers?

There is another way to look at global influence, apart from money, and that is in terms of powerful policy groups around the world. Let's look at the principal global institutions. There are many of these, ranging from the International Monetary Fund and Group of Twenty to the World Trade Organization – the IMF, the G20 and the WTO, as they are increasingly known. In addition, in the wake of the financial crisis, the Bank for International Settlements (BIS), the so-called central bankers' bank, has assumed a global role, as has the Financial Stability Board (FSB). Meanwhile, the Paris-based Organisation for Economic Co-Operation and Development (OECD) continues to sway the global debate, although the tools at its disposal are limited. That said, in a global economy where knowledge as well as power is important, the ability to influence the economic and political debate can be crucial. Now, knowledge and access to people are seen as fundamental sources of value, as is perhaps demonstrated by the prices paid for internet firms. Likewise, the importance of global institutions and groups might not be based solely on how they settle issues and allocate funds, but also on how they influence thinking, attitudes and behaviours.

The more we think about these groups the more we are likely to wonder if they work in the way they should, and how likely they are to work well in the future. How, for instance, will they interact with national governments? Given that there are major changes under way in the world economy and the financial system, we need to be asking ourselves: are the global institutions we have in place fit for purpose, or do they need to change? If they are not keeping up with the economic and financial changes of the twenty-first century, should that not concern us? And how can we ensure that these institutions do a good job to help the world economy continue to grow and prosper? All of these questions should be at the back of our minds when we think about the world economy and about these global groups that try to run it.

The big challenge with both regional and global groups is that there appears to be a natural desire always to expand, never to slim down. This makes a revamp all the more necessary. The danger is that the more groups you have, the less effective they become. The good news is there have been great successes, and effective global governance is a worthwhile goal. Perhaps it is worth reflecting on some of the times when global groups have worked.

Global successes

Global policy co-ordination focuses on the drivers of the economy in many countries. It requires an awareness of the damage that one country's actions might cause to another, and of the times when it makes sense to act together to maximise opportunities and achieve successful outcomes.

Bringing leaders together forces different countries to look at issues in more detail, taking account of other countries' perspectives and the stances they are likely to adopt. It calls for comprehensive conversations and consultations among officials ahead of any meetings of country leaders. Summits among world leaders are preceded by months of dialogues and meetings between officials who are often referred to as sherpas. They meet below the radar, iron out issues and decide on where progress is possible. Good sherpas are unsung heroes. They have the ability, it seems, to ensure a constructive outcome, without any major loss of face.

There have been success stories, such as the Millennium Development Goals (MDG), outlined in 2000 and covering eight areas: poverty, primary education, empowering women and gender equality, child mortality, maternity and health, HIV and AIDS, the environment, and a global partnership for development. The MDG are still work in progress, with some encouraging successes to date.

I think there have been two heydays of global policy co-ordination. In view of the times when they occurred, there is every reason to think that they can be repeated, if needed, in the future. One was in the mid- to late 1980s with the Plaza and Louvre Accords; the other came during the recent crisis with the London Summit.

In August 1985 the big international economic problem was the strength of the dollar. At that time most things were priced in dollars and many currencies around the world were tied to the dollar. Finance ministers and central bank governors from the major economies of the Group of Seven (G7) met at the Plaza Hotel in New York and agreed the 'Plaza Accord', which was designed to weaken the dollar. The aim succeeded. In spring 1987 they met again, this time in Paris, and the 'Louvre Accord' was agreed; this time to stabilise the dollar. It was a sign of global policy success, although some in Japan felt that it led their country to adopt policies such as the artificially low interest rates that contributed to the economic bubble of the late 1980s.

Despite Japan's reservations, the Plaza Accord and the Louvre Accord were viewed as successes. And rightly so. One additional impact is that, ever since then, global financial markets have always been on their guard ahead of meetings of the G7, the G8 or the G20. Markets, in particular, have always waited for the communiqué released at the conclusion of these meetings that makes the outcome known to the waiting media. The big focus was usually on what was said on currency policy – often on the yen in the 1990s, or the Chinese yuan in more recent years – or on overall economic conditions. It also gave the major policymakers the ability to influence the financial markets. This was a lasting legacy.

It wasn't until the London Summit of April 2009, over two decades later, that the next milestone in global policy co-ordination was put in place. Intervening meetings, at various locations, invariably led to communiqués that sent signals to the markets that all was well and the collective brains representing the politicians and the central banks were comfortably on top of the situation. That was the common subtext of communiqués. Let's be frank, it would be hard for politicians to own up and say we haven't got a clue what to do. Their communiqués often had an element of spin, guiding the financial markets in a particular direction.

The London Summit of 2009 was different. Seen later as a success, ahead of it politicians genuinely didn't know what to do. That is also what many people feared, but it was not something that they wanted to be told. They knew something needed to be done. It is here that I am reminded of one of Ronald Reagan's classic quotes, when he told his officials: 'Don't just do something, stand there!' His point was that officials intervening can often make matters worse, not better, and perhaps it makes more sense to let the market, or nature, take its course. Often that is the right thing to do, but in a crisis, when confidence is low, uncertainty high and there might have been a failure by the markets to reach solutions, firm leadership is needed.

The financial crisis of the preceding months had triggered fear across the globe. People were worried. Policymakers and politicians needed to take action. But what action? Young children left on their own in a big house might feel scared without adults around. The presence of the grown-ups eases their fears. The financial markets were the young children; the politicians had assumed the role of the adults. The fact that there wasn't much that they could do was not the point. Sometimes restoring confidence is the best outcome such global meetings can hope for, and that often means saying the right thing.

The G20 had met the previous autumn in October 2008 in Pittsburgh, under President George W. Bush, and in the words of the UK Treasury, the G20 had agreed to 'a new and decisive systemic international approach to handle the challenges to the world economy and financial markets'. Dominique Strauss-Kahn, then heading the IMF, appeared to play a prominent role in ensuring that the Fund focused on avoiding economic Armageddon. UK Prime Minister Gordon Brown hosted the London meeting in April 2009 and had built a global alliance ahead of the summit. After all, he had headed the key decision-making group at the IMF for many years and was thus in a good position to make his personal contacts count. The UK and the US led the case for a fiscal expansion, which they saw as necessary to prevent a depression in which spending and output would slump and unemployment soar. Others, led by Germany, France and the Czech Republic, opposed a fiscal boost.

Although Gordon Brown takes a lot of flak for his period in office and his handling of fiscal policy, when it came to two of the big calls of his time as UK chancellor and prime minister – not joining the euro and the London Summit – he got it right. In the event, the London Summit boosted confidence. It was in the run-up to London that the details were ironed out, when the G20 finance ministers and central bank governors met in Horsham in Sussex in March 2009 and agreed to pump liquidity into the system. In addition, the London meeting agreed to provide funds for trade finance and also to give more money to the International Monetary Fund. The success of the London Summit was that there was coordination of macroeconomic policy, agreement on a common agenda to reform international financial regulation, and a consensus on governance reform of international financial institutions. Appearing strong and united in the face of adversity helped confidence.

US President Barack Obama described London as historic 'because of the size and the scope of the challenges' faced as well as the 'timeliness and magnitude of our response'. Although the Americans and the British did not get the unanimous agreement on fiscal policy that they wanted, I think Obama was right. The London Summit helped prevent depression. It is hard to imagine, but without it the financial chaos and loss of confidence of the preceding few months would probably have continued and then deteriorated.

Global policy tends to work only when it is in everyone's best interest to act anyway. And it has been suggested that the participants at the London Summit would probably have acted the way they did in any case, summit or not. Perhaps.

There seems little doubt that global policy was taken to a different level. Ahead of the London Summit, policy invoked the three Ts: it was Timely, Targeted and Temporary.

The London Summit transformed this into the three Ss: Synchronised, Sizeable and Successful. That worked well.

Since then not everything has worked so smoothly. In the West, monetary policy has evolved into the three Us: Unlimited, Unclear and Unknown. *Unlimited* in terms of the amounts being played with, as interest rates hovered close to zero for many years in the West and the central banks pumped in large amounts of money. *Unclear* as to how successful this policy has been, because success in this respect is hard to measure. The counterfactual is always difficult to argue. It is next to impossible to say what would have happened if nothing had been done, and part of the focus of policy was to stop things getting worse, as well to ensure recovery. *Unknown* in terms of the longer-term repercussions of keeping interest rates so low for so long, and in exit strategies.

Despite the uncertainty that has been triggered, the way global policy has been co-ordinated should imbue us with confidence about the way crises can be handled in the future.

The IMF

To understand and appreciate the important role that global economic institutions play in the world today, we have to look back to the Second World War. The most significant aspect of the post-war global economy was the emergence of Japan and West Germany as economic powers. For Germany, the global response after the war had a big bearing on this outcome. For Japan, the Korean War was the catalyst.

The Potsdam Conference of July 1945, held on the outskirts of Berlin, brought about the division of Europe as the 'Big Three' of the US, the Soviet Union and the UK carved up the post-war map.

I mentioned in Chapter 1 how the Marshall Plan of April 1948, which pumped US money into Europe to help it to recover and build a bulwark against communism, played its part in the West German renaissance. It was named after General George C. Marshall, the then US Secretary of State, who launched the Plan in his address to the graduating class at Harvard University on 5 June 1947. Known officially as the European Recovery Plan, it was not only effective at the time but still has some relevance for Europe. It was based on two key principles: one, that one country's imports were another's country's exports, so sustaining a recovery in imports by one European country would help another. At that time countries feared unsustainable trade deficits if they imported too much.

Hence, when imports rose, they tightened policy, kept growth weak, and the US feared that the European voting public would turn to the communists. The other principle was free trade among European countries, to help confidence and investment. During the four years of the Plan, America transferred about 2.5 per cent per year of its GDP to Europe, a huge amount, and that in turn contributed to a period of rapid European recovery.

In some ways, the debate over the pros and cons of that Plan was a minor version of the current debate about austerity, and subsidies to help demand but at the expense of supporting economies that might need to shed state influence in order to succeed. The key aim of the Marshall Plan was to revitalise the German industrial base, seen by the Americans as essential to the recovery of Western Europe, and as necessary to keep Soviet influence at bay. The replacement of the Reichsmark with the Deutsche Mark (DM) in 1948, which helped keep inflation in check and encouraged the *Wirtschaftswunder*, economic miracle, of the 1950s, made a big difference. Germany recovered. It was even able to end food rationing after the end of the war sooner than Britain.

The Marshall Plan was implemented by the Organisation for European Economic Co-operation (OEEC), which was the forerunner of the modern-day Organisation for Economic Co-Operation and Development (OECD) formed in 1961. Whereas the challenge for many groups such as the G20 is to make themselves relevant and effective in stable times as well as during crises, the OECD in contrast has already shown itself effective through stable as well as turbulent times. To maintain its influence the OECD will have to expand its membership. For instance, by 2030 the five largest economies in the world could be China, the US, India, Indonesia and Brazil, but of these none apart from the US is currently a member of the OECD. In recent years there have been encouraging developments as the OECD opened discussions for membership with a broad range of countries.

As a group the OECD has played a major role in embedding the acceptance of the free flows of investment, capital and services across a large part of the global economy, and its mission to improve the economic and social well-being of people around the globe seems particularly useful. It doesn't itself have levers to pull, but can exert influence over those who do.

Notwithstanding the rise of West Germany and Japan into economic powers, it was the 1944 Bretton Woods Agreement that proved to be the most pivotal economic development. It shaped the post-war economy. Anticipating victory in the war, in 1944 the Allies needed to review the future of the world economy after the conflict.

The agreement was named after Bretton Woods, in New Hampshire, where, in July 1944, twenty-nine countries met and decided to establish the IMF and the International Bank for Reconstruction and Development, otherwise known as the World Bank. These 'Bretton Woods twins', as they became known, set the post-war economic agenda. The Fund, a non-profit-making organisation, renowned for its orthodox economic approach, presided over economic thinking and helped out countries in balance-of-payments crisis or in economic difficulty. It was an economic backstop. But help came at a price, which was the so-called IMF 'conditionality'. If the IMF helped a country, it would also tell that country how to get its economy back into shape. This was not to every country's liking, not just because it put an outside body in charge, but because orthodox programmes usually meant tightening the national purse strings and imposing a more austere way of life. The World Bank, however, was profit-making and financed countries that needed to develop, and it also lent to poorer countries.

Ahead of the Bretton Woods meeting, it was not clear what would be decided: there was a battle between the British economist John Maynard Keynes and the US technocrat Harry Dexter White over the proposed International Monetary Fund, outlined in Benn Steil's book *The Battle of Bretton Woods*. The UK wanted flexible exchange rates, individual countries to have more power relative to the Fund, a bigger Fund and a longer transition period before it was formed. The Americans opposed all of these views. Even though the UK and the US were allies during the war, Bretton Woods was a clear and successful attempt by the US administration to squeeze the UK's post-war economic influence. It worked, and created a global system with the US economy and the dollar at the core. Currencies were linked to gold and tied to the dollar. Britain won the war but lost the peace.

From a US perspective the new dispensation made sense; for the rest of the world it brought stability, and it worked for a long time. When, in 2008, after the financial crisis, Gordon Brown and French President Nicolas Sarkozy called for a fundamental rethink of the global financial system, it was reform of the post-war Bretton Woods system that lay at the heart of their thinking.

Changing with the times

There is little doubt that both the IMF and World Bank need to reform, and this is now happening. Both are run based on the past with their power base still dominated by the US and Europe: the US chooses the head of the Bank, while a European gets to run the Fund. Since its inception, the Fund has had eleven heads: one Belgian, two Swedish, one Dutch, one German, one Spanish and five French. The head of the World Bank is always an American. This needs to change, as too should the voting structure, to become more representative of the world economy.

There has been a strong desire to change the voting structure to give more say to emerging economies at the expense of Western countries. The pressure for this has soared in recent years. The World Trade Organization works on a 'one country, one vote' principle. While that sounds good, it still resulted in countries blocking a free-trade agreement that would have been good for the world economy, under the Doha Round; I discuss this later. In contrast to the WTO, the IMF has a quota-based voting system, which means that a small number of countries dominate and can block change.

The US has 16.75 per cent of the total voting power. Given that an 85 per cent majority is needed on some key decisions, such as changing the quotas, this effectively gives the US a veto. Some other key votes need a 70 per cent majority. Japan has 6.23 per cent, Germany 5.71 per cent, and both France and the UK 4.29 per cent. Quotas are reviewed every five years, and on request. In 2008 there was a minor change to quotas: 6 per cent was reallocated to emerging economies. But there is still a long way to go.

The US and Europe are reluctant to lose their influence. China has 3.81 per cent of the votes and India 2.34 per cent. This will be resolved only if Europe gives up some of its power, helping the IMF to become more representative. But Europe thinks the US veto should be loosened.

But it is more than voting structures that need to change. The economic focus of the IMF needs to shift. It has a deflationary mentality. As a result the IMF is not universally liked. Questions over the economic impact of the IMF and the World Bank are not new. As long ago as January 1976, the *Economist* magazine ran a piece entitled 'Do we need an IMF?' When the IMF is asked to help a country, it always says much the same thing, regardless of the circumstances: cut government spending, raise taxes, remove subsidies, repay international borrowers. Markets first, people second.

The aftermath of the Asian economic and financial crisis of 1997–8 was probably the low point for the IMF. The IMF was the global organisation that countries turned to for help, but it wasn't very helpful.

The crux of the problem was that the IMF's analysis was wrong. At the time, various Asian economies faced a shortage of demand and a collapse in activity and investment. The fear was deflation, with prices falling. The IMF's prognosis was based on its fear that inflation was the overriding problem. Countries were told to adopt policies that would squeeze demand further. In Indonesia, which was badly hit, I remember a placard held aloft in one demonstration reading: 'IMF = I'M Fired'. That hit the mark. The American economist Jeffrey Sachs once observed that the IMF always tells people to tighten their belts, even the poor, who can't afford belts. That was the feeling conveyed in Asia then. When the Asian countries recovered from that crisis, as practically all countries recover from whatever crisis they are in, they retained a lasting image – one that still prevails today – of an IMF that was Western-focused, biased and unhelpful.

Since then Asian countries have relied less on the IMF. In particular, countries across the globe have built up their own defences. Currency reserves are higher; indeed, whereas a decade ago Asia held one-third of global currency reserves, now it holds two-thirds. Foreign-exchange reserves are the amount of other countries' currencies that a country holds and that it can call on or use in the event of a problem. As reserves rise now, there is what I call 'passive diversification' taking place: the dollar is still the dominant currency in which reserves are held, but while countries are still putting a majority of their additional reserves into it, the amount is noticeably less than before. They are not actively selling the dollar or moving existing reserves out of it, just holding a smaller proportion of their reserves in dollars.

There is a cost to holding foreign-exchange reserves. For instance, it might mean that a country keeps its own currency cheap in the first place by selling it to buy other currencies in order to build up reserves, but for many countries these costs are secondary to the fact that the reserves are there to be called on if needed and are visible. This visibility might act as a deterrent, like a burglar alarm, particularly if the reserves are high enough. It signals potential resilience in the event of a crisis.

One legacy of the latest Western financial crisis was that countries across the world with high reserves were seen by speculators in the foreign-exchange markets as being better able to defend themselves, and hence were less prone to speculative attack. The trend since then is that even more countries now want to build up reserves. This suggests that fewer countries across the globe want to rely on the IMF.

The irony is that while emerging economies everywhere are less keen on turning to the IMF for help, in recent years it has been the wealthy European economy that has looked most in need of its assistance.

The headquarters of the IMF are in Washington, across the road from the World Bank. The World Bank has a better image than the IMF, as it does good work, but it too is not without criticism about its effectiveness. I remember one visit to the World Bank headquarters when huge posters proclaiming 'Make Poverty History' hung in the marble concourse and entrance hall. I was reflecting on how removed this seemed from the whole ambience of the building, as I sat in the coffee area on the mezzanine level overlooking the ground floor, while a pianist played Brahms and we drank cappuccinos.

The Bretton Woods system worked well. It lasted from the end of the Second World War until the early 1970s and it provided the backdrop against which the world economy boomed. If ever one needed an example of why stability in financial markets is important, this period was it.

The 'Nixon Shock'

During the late 1960s tensions began to build, not helped in the US by the inflationary consequences of the Vietnam War, which had started in 1961. In 1971 the world economy was hit by the 'Nixon Shock'. This was probably the most crucial economic decision of the last fifty years.

US President Richard Nixon changed the rules of the game, unilaterally deciding to end the Bretton Woods system. The dollar was no longer going to be held fixed against the price of gold, but instead would be allowed to float, able to move up and down. It was the start of the global foreign-exchange markets as we know them. It also launched an age of uncertainty. But if the rules of the game have changed before, why can't they change again, if needed? That, in many respects, is what the Chinese have been asking in recent years, questioning whether there is a need for a multilateral currency system to replace the one dominated by the dollar and, in their mind, by US interests.

Nixon announced his decision in a television address in 1971. His explanation was straightforward: he was making changes because they were in the best interests of the US. The rest of the world didn't figure in his thinking. Indeed one of the apocryphal stories is that, ahead of his decision, he was told by advisers that other countries would not like it, particularly the French. His reply was to tell the French where to go – in blunt terms. In some respects, it reflected the legacy of pressures building up on the US economy, just as they would build up at the centre of any currency system that had been in place for a long time. He had to act.

The president said he was protecting the position of the dollar; that there had been one crisis a year for each of the preceding seven years; there was an 'all-out war on the American dollar', and he had to 'defend the dollar against the speculators'. The aim was to stabilise the dollar.

Nixon asserted in his television address that the US was a 'forward-looking and trustworthy trading partner'. No one would have thought otherwise if he hadn't said it. The statement recalls his address to the nation over Watergate, when he said there would be no whitewash at the White House: it was the mention of the word whitewash that raised suspicions. Likewise, the Nixon Shock left a sense of unease in other countries, particularly when the US backed its policy with a wage–price freeze and a 10 per cent tax on goods imported into the US.

The legacy of the 1971 Nixon Shock was seen in subsequent years, with the oil crisis and the inflationary 1970s. But in terms of global-policy co-ordination it led to a system that is still in place, albeit after many evolutions. Out of the chaos that followed, countries needed to restore stability and set some new ground rules.

In the early 1970s the Organisation of Petroleum Exporting Countries (OPEC), founded in 1961, flexed its muscles. Oil prices had been raised in response to the dollar devaluations of both 1971 and 1973, and then were raised sharply by OPEC in response to the Yom Kippur War of October 1973. As oil prices soared, economies ground to a halt. Oil and currency turmoil showed that problems were global in their impact. The G8 owes its origins to the aftermath of the crisis situation of the early 1970s, and highlighted how important it was for a shared agenda. Nowadays we might need to keep our eyes on the gas equivalent of OPEC, the Gas Exporting Countries Forum, with eleven members, including Russia, Iran and Qatar, who collectively hold almost three-fifths of global gas reserves.

The early days of G7 and G20

From 1973, in response to the difficult economic times, the Group of Six (G6) met informally for the first time. The G6 comprised the biggest six economies in the world at that time: US, Japan, Germany, the UK, France and Italy. In 1975 the G6 took formal shape, at a summit in France, and it was agreed that the leaders would meet each year. The aim was fireside chats to talk about key issues. In 1976 Canada was added, some say to give the US support, and the G7 was formed. By 1997 it had become the G8 when Russia joined in the wake of the ending of the Cold War.

When it was the G7, it was a coalition of the like-minded, liberal democracies of the West, who faced similar challenges but also had a similar view of what the world should look like. The addition of Russia was at odds with this, even after the Cold War, but the G7 wanted to remain relevant and not see its power diluted, so Russia was admitted.

Whereas the G7 and G8 worked well, now the world has the G20. It is debatable whether this too can work well. The G20 grew out of the 2007–8 crisis just as the G7 emerged from the early 1970s crisis, in an arbitrary way. It is supposed to be the new governing group that influences the global agenda. But no one is quite sure whether it works, and indeed, as if to reflect this concern, the G8 still exists and meets, so we have both a G8 and a G20. It is not clear why the G8 should meet; its efforts could be better focused on making the G20 work effectively.

The trouble is that the G20 is not a group of twenty: it consists of twenty-nine global organisations and countries, sometimes more! With maths like this, perhaps it is no surprise that there was a financial crisis. The twenty consist of Argentina, Brazil and Mexico from Latin America; Australia, China, India, Indonesia, Japan and South Korea from the Asia-Pacific region; Canada and the US from North America; and seven members from Europe, though in fact eight attend: France, Germany, Italy, Russia, Turkey, the UK and both the European Council and the European Commission. Then come Saudi Arabia from the Middle East and only South Africa from Africa. So with the European Council and Commission, the twenty is really a twenty-one. But it gets even more complicated.

In addition, the Netherlands and Spain often attend, as do the following organisations: Financial Stability Board, IMF, Association of Southeast Asian Nations (ASEAN), the New Partnership for African Development, the UN, the World Bank and the World Trade Organization. So twenty-nine in total. In addition, some countries become members for a year – as Chile did in 2012, perhaps wondering why Argentina was a full-time member and it was not. This reflects the arbitrary membership and highlights the need to drop some countries. Little wonder that it is said that the G20 is more like a discussion chamber and a talking shop than a new decision-making authority to replace the G8.

Perhaps patience is needed. Even though the G20 met at head-of-state level (presidents or prime ministers) for the first time in 2007, it had existed at finance-minister level since December 1999, when they met in Berlin. That was in reaction to the Asian financial crisis of 1997–8, but it was not given much power beyond consultation to begin with. It was in 2007–8 that the G20 came of age.

It was already clear before the 2008 crisis that global policy needed to evolve. In 2002 UK Prime Minister Tony Blair invited five leading emerging economies to the G8 Summit at Gleneagles in Scotland. This was the G8 plus the Outreach 5 of Brazil, China, India, Mexico and South Africa. It was hailed as the 'new paradigm for international co-operation'.

By 2008 things had moved on, and the Heiligendamm Process strengthened the dialogue between the G8 and the important emerging market economies, aimed at dealing with the biggest challenges facing the global economy. The action was necessary because the G8 could not meet the challenges alone. Alongside this, Germany launched its own GIBSA initiative, of regular, informal, high-level meetings between Germany, India, Brazil and South Africa, also sometimes referred to as the Quadrilogue.

A couple of years ago, after the Arab Spring uprising across North Africa, a UK minister explained to me that if the Arab Spring had happened only a few years earlier it would have been the US and the UK who were active behind the scenes and exerting influence, but now they were playing second fiddle. Instead it was Saudi Arabia, Turkey and Iran who were pulling the strings. In some respects that captures how, at a regional level, the old ties are changing and new power brokers are emerging. Given all this, there are some key issues to consider.

The issues

Is the Group of Twenty the best number to have or should it be a smaller number? It seems that G20 is not working as well as it should and that G8 is too unrepresentative of the realities of the world economy. Perhaps a smaller and more effective group than G20 but bigger than G8 is needed, perhaps a G14. The difficulty is that we would probably end up with yet another new group, without getting rid of the others.

Some say that a G2 might be better – the US and China alone. I disagree, and so too I suspect would many other countries, including China, given its focus on a multipolar world with a number of different power bases, including a powerful Europe as well as a strong China to counteract the US. While the G2 currently talked about is China and the US, the G2 that was talked about after the fall of the Berlin Wall was the US and Europe. How times change.

Will the future be a bipolar world dominated by the US and China or a multipolar world with many centres of influence? At its most basic it would be the US, Europe and China. But one could easily envisage more centres: Brazil, India, even Nigeria or Turkey. Certainly the Chinese would want to avoid a unipolar world, or Pax Americana, where the US dominates. In soft-power terms one might see this in terms of the Washington consensus versus the Beijing consensus.

Should the focus be on non-economic as well as on economic issues? Just as the G7 evolved from focusing mainly on economic issues to addressing all the key problems of the day – economic or not – then that too might become the natural template for the G20 or even a G14 were it to emerge.

Can these groups of countries take systematic ownership of global issues, given all the uncertainty as to who should be included and over their effective size? How to enforce decisions and implement them is both a challenge and an opportunity, as is the question of which levers to pull or push, and how to ensure that they will stay put once in operation.

How do you bind the different groups together? There is a strong case for establishing complementary groups that link well with one another and that try to deal in different ways with regional and international political, economic, finance, trade and investment issues. But while there are benefits from diversity in membership, it should not mean that policies are watered down to appeal to everyone. The unintended consequence is that people 'talk their own book', pushing only what is in their best interests, the agenda gets diluted and countries do their own thing anyway.

Don't forget Bandung

If we are to really see global groupings work properly it will be important to appreciate that some countries approach things from a different perspective. Let me give you two examples from China.

One thing I have always found interesting is the Chinese insistence that no country should interfere in the internal affairs of another country. This is a legacy of the Bandung Conference, which took place in Indonesia in April 1955, and which eventually led to the Belgrade Conference of 1961 and the creation of the Nonaligned Movement. The Bandung Conference was hosted by the Indonesians and was aimed at promoting Asian–African ties and opposing colonialism and neocolonialism. The conference produced a ten-point declaration whose fourth point was 'Abstention from intervention or interference in the internal affairs of another country'. This was focusing on political and non-economic issues and has since been adopted by the Chinese, almost as their mantra.

The second example relates to the importance of strategy, theoretical thinking and dogma in China. In March 2012 I took part in a two-day conference at the Party School in Beijing, a behind-the-doors session between the UK and China on the new global architecture in an interdependent world. I was asked to speak as part of the UK group. The conference was a great success and proved how these two countries could work together.

The difference is that while strategic thinking is very evident in China, it seems to matter less in many Western democracies where winning the next election is the focus. The Party School has a university-style campus in Beijing, with top professors, and it brings together Party members at all stages of their careers, who spend time, sometimes weeks or months on end, at the School to be taught about dogma and how it relates to current issues. In short, it is about ensuring that the Party stays relevant. We were told the sessions might be attended by a small number of students – some were, but these were not the eighteen-to-twenty-five-year-olds that I think of as students; they proved to be fifty- and sixty-year-old policymakers and business people, all senior and on courses at the school, some, I later learned, had reading lists, others projects to do. It was impressive. The US is pretty good at this too, and I saw this at first hand when the National Intelligence Council held a two-day closed-door meeting in Washington to discuss different scenarios for the Middle East. In contrast, the UK doesn't have such a strategic focus, although since 1994 it has had an excellent Foresight Group, in the Office of Science, that carries out deep, insightful research on particular areas. Long-term strategic thinking is a big plus.

Trade matters

After the Second World War, the General Agreement on Tariffs and Trade (GATT) was created, aiming to boost world trade by reducing barriers to trade including tariffs placed on many goods, preventing dumping and protecting intellectual property. GATT was replaced by the World Trade Organization in 1995, and along the way a series of trade rounds have occurred – usually named after a location, sometimes after a person. These trade rounds include Geneva 1947,

Annecy 1949, Torquay, Geneva 2, Dillon (after the US Treasury Secretary, because they met in Geneva again and clearly didn't want to call it Geneva 3), Kennedy, Tokyo, Uruguay and Doha.

The Uruguay Trade Round lasted from 1986 to 1994. Then came the Doha Round, which was an attempt to remove all the barriers to global free trade. In 1996 four key areas were identified as part of the Doha Round. These became known as the Singapore Issues and covered trade and competitiveness, trade and investment, government procurement and trade facilitation. Then in 2003 the Cancun Talks moved into the hot political area of farm subsidies.

Despite all these meetings there was a collective failure. Larry Elliott, writing in the *Guardian*, described the failure of Doha as 'Murder on the Orient Express': everyone playing a part in its death. Ironically, the biggest stumbling blocks were areas that are likely to see strong future growth in trade, such as services and agriculture. If ever one could think of a step that would really help the world economy this was it. Of course, there are so many vested-interest groups around the world, so many places where subsidies and tariffs prevail, that too many countries jibbed at the ideas behind Doha. Perhaps, also, it showed that some issues might be too complicated to settle at the global level.

One of the remarkable features of recent years is how many world leaders reaffirm their commitment to the Doha Round and then do nothing about it. Perhaps if these meetings took their name from what is at stake rather than the location there might be a better chance of some success. If Doha had been thought of as an 'agreement on trade, otherwise jobs will not be created', then perhaps the public would have been more aware of what was at stake and there would have been greater pressure and political agreement to get a deal done.

The alternative to free-trade agreements and being bound by global rules is a second-best outcome where countries or regions work out bilateral trade deals with one another, or 'plurilaterals', where a handful of countries reach deals on a narrow set of issues. These are usually portrayed in a positive light, but the downside is that whereas a multilateral deal would ensure common rules across the globe that benefit everyone, bilateral and regional deals do not always achieve this. This lack of clarity can make it costly and competitive for some businesses.

Smaller countries find it both harder and more expensive to negotiate deals, and in some respects can be vulnerable to bullying or manipulation by the much bigger economies with which they are negotiating. Also, countries might have a bias to protect certain sectors that could otherwise suffer – and when this happens, it usually turns out that people end up paying a higher price, either as consumers or as taxpayers, or as both.

Although the current trend towards mega regional trade deals should help growth – such as the Trans Pacific Partnership involving the US and many Pacific countries, and the Transatlantic Trade and Investment Partnership between the EU and US – there have been suggestions that these mega deals might become charters for multinational firms to have the upper hand over governments in matters deemed to infringe the freedom of companies to operate. It is an area that warrants future attention.

The World Trade Organization needs to ensure that these issues are addressed, as there will be greater future financial flows as well as trade flows. There is a need to ensure level playing fields between countries, so that the West and the East do not feel in future that they face added barriers when they buy, sell, invest or trade with each other. In December 2013 the WTO was able to claim some success, with a global deal at its ministerial meeting in Bali, aimed at simplifying cross-border trade. This was its first comprehensive agreement, ever.

Think global, act regional

In a changing global economy, many countries might find that regional unity provides strength. There are four regional groups likely to play significant future roles: the Shanghai Cooperation Organisation, ASEAN, the Arctic Council and the European Union.

The Shanghai Cooperation Organisation is particularly interesting because it includes China and Russia, could include India in the future, and covers a strategically important region of the world – Central Asia. Either the Chinese were – even by their high standards of strategic planning – thinking remarkably far ahead when this group was established or perhaps it emerged more by accident than design. Whatever its origins, it has the potential to become more important.

Founded in 1996 to consider security and military issues, it comprised China and Russia and the three Central Asian republics of Kazakhstan, Kyrgyzstan and Tajikistan. It expanded to include Uzbekistan in 2001 and since then has grown further to include a group of countries who aren't yet members but who have observer status, namely India, Iran, Mongolia, Pakistan and Afghanistan. The importance of energy and of the future relationship between Russia and China makes Central Asia a strategically important region, and one worth watching.

Another significant regional grouping is the Association of Southeast Asian Nations. ASEAN was formed in 1967 by the Philippines, Indonesia, Thailand, Singapore and Malaysia. It now has ten members, and also includes Myanmar, Brunei, Cambodia, Vietnam and Laos. Its combined population is 600 million and the size of its economy $2 trillion, bigger than either India or Russia.

ASEAN was founded originally as a foreign-policy organ, aiming to stop the spread of communism in the region and to focus on nation-building. Over time the focus has changed, and it now places greater emphasis on the economy. ASEAN plus 3 was an informal grouping with China, South Korea and Japan to cover currency and financial issues. There is now a free-trade agreement to reduce internal tariffs in the region and to establish an East Asian Community. It also has fed into the East Asia Summit, which additionally includes India, Australia and New Zealand. ASEAN used to talk regionally and act nationally. Now it is moving towards an environment where the whole is greater than the sum of the parts. As a single economic region, ASEAN is creating new trade ties across the globe.

The Arctic Council, established in 1996, is one group that could grow in importance over time and in probably unexpected ways. The success of the Arctic Council is too early to judge, but it has continued to evolve. It has eight permanent members, five of which have territorial claims over some of the Arctic Ocean. These five are Russia, Canada, the US (whose claim is via Alaska), Denmark (whose claim is via Greenland) and Norway. The other three permanent, and non-coastal, members are Finland, Iceland and Sweden. Initially the Council was seen as having an important environmental role, and it still does, but the opening up of sea lanes, plus the potential resources in the Arctic, have given it a new dimension. As a result, a host of countries have joined the Arctic Council as observers, and it is now sometimes referred to as the Coldrush Club.

Finally, there is the European Union, which has continued to be dragged down by the euro, a currency system which is fundamentally flawed, but to which all EU members apart from Denmark and Britain are committed to join. In recent years, there has been a self-propelled downward spiral in which political problems have fed economic ones, and the resulting debt problems have fed banking problems. The European Central Bank stepped in during 2012, acting as an effective block between the economic and debt problems and between the debt and banking problems. This worked, and bought some time.

When Ireland joined the EMS – the European Monetary System – it was known in Dublin as 'Easy Money Soon'. That was a sign of trouble in store. In the good times the money flowed from the centre of the euro area to where yields and returns were highest, feeding property booms in the periphery of Europe. Then during the bad times – as in recent years – the money flows back to the centre, feeding future inflation there. In terms of monetary policy, one size does not fit all. The UK saw these problems and opted not to join the euro. Just as Ireland saw the EMS as 'Easy Money Soon', London saw the ERM or Exchange Rate Machanism as 'Europe's Recession Mechanism'. Now the EMU or European Monetary Union could easily be referred to across Europe as 'Even More Unemployment'.

Europe needs to restructure and reform, making its single market work properly, embracing innovation in the way that the US does, and confronting its welfare bill. The modern welfare state is a European phenomenon, and while in many ways it is admirable, looking at it from afar raises questions. For example, at the annual Asian Development Bank meeting in Hanoi in 2011 I was struck by how many speakers were amused that Europe paid people not to work. They simply couldn't understand it. This issue came to centre stage in late 2012 when Chancellor Merkel pointed out that Europe had 7 per cent of the world's population, 25 per cent of its income and a massive 50 per cent of its welfare spending. In 1997 I wrote a column in the *Financial Times* pointing out that history showed that large monetary unions could not survive unless they became political unions and that is the direction in which Europe Union may need to go.

Summary

Although the IMF, the World Bank, the G20 and WTO dominate the global economy, the most important global group is a non-economic one, the United Nations, but that too is badly in need of reform. Given its geopolitical status its actions can clearly have a global economic impact. The UN Security Council is trusted with overseeing peace and security. Its five permanent members are the victorious Second World War powers of the US, Russia, the UK, France and China, each of which has a veto, and the Council is then made up to fifteen with ten rotating members, each of which serves for a period of two years.

Countries pressing for reform include those who want to become permanent members, such as Japan and Germany, who are now the second- and third-largest funders of the UN, and India and Brazil, who provide large numbers of peacekeepers. Not everyone is so keen, even though the US supports Brazil's and India's case. It is hard to see an easy solution, given that the existing permanent members have a veto, but just as the number of non-permanent members rose from six to ten in 1965, another rise is always possible. But the reality is that this is another group that needs to change in order to move with the times.

So what does all this mean for the world economy? Global policy institutions are evolving. The process is slow, but now that the momentum is there, we should expect to see further change. In economic terms an ideal world might be one in which politicians and policymakers always act together in order to achieve the best global outcome – a type of economic common good. Unfortunately this does not happen too often. Such global policy co-ordination makes sense on paper but is hard to achieve in practice. But there are some specific examples that stand out and give grounds for optimism, particularly when one thinks of common challenges ahead.

Wealth and spending power are heavily concentrated. That in itself reinforces the case for the right institutional framework across the globe. Whether it is rich or poor countries, or internationally mobile firms, there is a need for everyone to abide by the same rules. We need the right institutional framework more than ever, now that so many concerns seem to know no bounds. But while there is a need for global institutions, they need to be the right ones, address-ing the key global issues. Global policy co-ordination can work and make a difference, so the more such institutions are credible, the more effective they can be. They must also be set up in the right way, so that they reflect how the world economy is changing and have legitimacy in the eyes of most, if not all, countries across the globe. They must be the right size: the G20 is too big, G2 too small.

The IMF is seeing change in its voting rights and needs to move further. The World Bank should evolve from being headed up only by a European. The policies they advocate should reflect the needs of the countries they deal with, not an inbuilt policy bias and rigid mantra. The IMF has been too deflationary in its thinking. The World Bank, perhaps alongside regional development banks such as the African Development Bank or the Asian Development Bank, should continue to help countries address longer-term needs, including infrastructure, where it can be hard to attract private-sector finance.

If countries decide to work together on policy – whether at a regional or a global level – they have to accept some trade-offs and compromises in terms of their own domestic policy. Given that good economics means good politics, alliances in regional or global groups should make sense in economic and not just political terms.

Regional groups look set to grow more powerful and important. If there are to be global and regional economic institutions, then they should have clear goals to focus on, with firm levers to pull. They should either have direct access to these levers or strong influence on the national governments that do. This leads us on to the topic of policy.

8

Focusing on the issues that matter

In the future, successful economies will be those that observe the following guidelines: adapt and change; play to strengths; and position effectively, either by making themselves an attractive place in which to invest or creating an enabling environment that makes them a hotbed for entrepreneurs. Given the global macroeconomic outlook, the successful countries will have at least one of the three Cs: Cash, Commodities or Creativity. That is, the financial resources, the natural resources, or the human ingenuity and skill to thrive, all aided by sensible economic policies.

Within many countries, there are clusters that allow a certain location to excel in a particular field. The best scientists want to be with the other best scientists. The best Formula One mechanics and engineers want to be with the other Formula One specialists. Once a critical point has been reached, a location starts to have a magnetic pull, attracting other like-minded people or firms. In some cases this can be planned for; in others it just happens. We can't always know what the trigger will be, but we can often say what will prevent it, whether it is a hostile anti-business environment, poor transport or excessive personal tax rates.

The previous chapter focused on who runs the world. Here we look at the big policy issues confronting economies. If the institutions that govern the world economy are changing, should policies change too?

The answer will be influenced by the type of economy desired. One would hardly expect to find many people in possession of all one's ideal personal characteristics. The same goes for economies, but what might a good one look like? Research by the economists

Blanchflower and Oswald shows: 'Happy countries are dispro-portionately rich, educated, democratic, trusting, and [have] low unemployment.'

The end-goal for an economy might be strong sustainable growth with rising living standards and a high degree of happiness, and once this stage has been reached, self-reinforcing features that keep things that way. Reaching this end-goal requires a number of features:

Right balance:
- the right mix between an efficient, focused public sector and a profitable private sector, allowing the public sector and the market to work together
- a welfare system that is affordable and targeted at those in most need
- a tax system that works and fosters enterprise, including low and simple taxes
- an environment where the private sector thrives, and does so backed by a reliable legal system, protection of intellectual property rights and safe working environment

Investing:
- a supply side of the economy that delivers access to technical, sporting, creative and academic education (all too often it is only the latter, and not for all, that is delivered)
- an environment that encourages innovation and rewards entrepreneurs
- high but not excessive domestic investment and high rates of productivity

Proceeds of growth:
- a good quality of life, with ample affordable housing, low crime, environmentally friendly policies, effective and cheap mass transport systems and access to affordable health care

- full employment, and although it is always said that economies want high-skilled jobs, the reality is that they need the right mix of low-, medium- and high-skilled jobs – not everyone can be a scientist or corporate finance expert, or needs to study at university to contribute to an economy, although access to skills training needs to be available
- breaking down the vested-interest groups and oligopolies that can sometimes dominate key industries (this latter point argues for more openness, transparency and accountability in economic policies)

Policy:
- a credible macroeconomic policy framework that keeps a lid on inflation and ensures there is sufficient demand in the economy
- policy shock absorbers, so that the economy can cope with unexpected problems (these might include a good fiscal position or high currency reserves and certainly a credible monetary policy)
- or a variation on this last approach, some countries opt for a flexible exchange rate as well as an interest-rate policy that allows both to move freely, acting as shock absorbers when economic conditions change
- the right hard, soft and institutional infrastructure

The list is long, but none of it amounts to wishful thinking: many economies already meet several of these guidelines. Yet the length of the list reflects how complex economic management can be. The lesson is not to micro-manage and plan too much; as the Soviet system showed, that approach is doomed to failure. Planners in rooms can't legislate for the drive, skill, ambitions and motives of people. Yet, as we currently see in China and Singapore, clear longer-term planning can work in an economy just as an overall strategy can succeed in a company. When there are clear and deliverable goals, the public and private sector can collaborate in an economy – the London Olympics was a classic example. But, the main focus should be about creating the enabling environment to allow the private sector to deliver, free from government interference, ideally to encourage innovation and entrepreneurs and allow people to do their own thing, whether it is to start a new business, to work in a bar or to be a porter in a hospital.

In economics, allowing the market mechanism to work is the right way to proceed, as it allows the price to clear, sends the right signals and allows outcomes freed of prejudice. On occasions, the market will not work, or produces outcomes that are far from equal and not always seen as desirable, in which case there is a role for the public sector. But not every market failure justifies state intervention, as many if not most times it may just be part of an evolutionary process that takes time and which the market mechanism will solve without the need for public involvement or money. Of course, there are times when the role for the public sector need not be secondary, such as in driving research or long-term investment, or in defence.

Policy issues

Before examining today's key policy issues, consider what global leaders and policymakers focused their attention on over the last forty years. The best way to do this is to consider the G7 and G20 meetings.

One lesson from re-examining policy issues is that there are many things that do not change over time. The communiqué issued by the G7 on 17 November 1975 after its first three-day meeting, the *Declaration of Rambouillet*, bears this out. Its fifteen points are as relevant now as they were then, in the wake of the energy-price shock. Jobs and inflation figured prominently, as did shared beliefs and responsibilities. Also, in a world of growing interdependence, each country needed to play its full part, with closer international co-operation and constructive dialogue. Hard to disagree, isn't it?

Indeed, point nine of that 1975 communiqué could have been written now, not four decades ago. It read: 'We believe that the multilateral trade negotiations should be accelerated . . . [should] aim at substantial tariff cuts . . . [and] at significantly expanding agricultural trade and at reducing non-tariff measures.' Trade continues to figure prominently as an important policy area, and rightly so. It is a win-win situation, in which advances are positive for the vast majority. One has to ask: if the heads of the biggest economies in the world have talked about this for forty years, why have they not made more progress? Perhaps the lesson is to observe what they do, and not simply listen to what they say. Sometimes they can agree to things at a global level only to find that domestic politics do not permit them to enact decisions they have subscribed to. French and Japanese farmers, for instance, can block their politicians.

In recent years, the main worries of global leaders and policy-makers are reflected in the communiqués from the G20 summits.

The first meeting in Washington in 2008 focused on the financial system – that was no surprise given that the financial crisis was the reason the group was meeting. But it wasn't just about sorting out problems; it included the need for access to finance to aid development.

The second G20, the successful London Summit of April 2009, had specifics, such as trebling the resources available to the IMF to $750 billion, additional lending, finding $250 billion for trade finance, and all proposed in the context of rescuing the world economy. The green economy received a push, too.

The third G20 at Pittsburgh in 2009 stressed ways for the members to work together, a focus on the regulatory system and the need to ensure that all countries had access to food, fuel and finance. It is hard to fault any of these. They reflect longer-term hopes and desires, as well as the mood of the time.

The fourth G20, held at Toronto in June 2010, focused on financial inclusion and the large numbers without access to banks or finance, completing the Doha Development Round, and also an Anti-Corruption Action Plan. Again, hard to disagree.

The G20 meeting in Seoul, in November 2010, gave prominence to 'fiscal consolidation where necessary'. It is easy to agree with anything that bears the qualifier 'where necessary', but getting the balance right on fiscal policy is a key concern both now and in the future. Modernising the IMF also received a mention in Seoul, perhaps reflecting the fact that South Korea was the first emerging economy to chair such a meeting.

The Cannes G20 meeting the following year included an Action Plan for Growth and Jobs, including addressing youth unemployment and promoting core conventions ensuring fundamental principles and rights at work. This clearly had echoes of that first G7 meeting in Rambouillet, and not just because the meeting was in France.

The Los Cabos G20 in Mexico in 2012 also had an Action Plan for Growth and Jobs but, like the London Summit of 2009, it provided specifics and not just generalities, outlining an increase in the IMF's credit capabilities of $456 billion. It also mentioned some of the key areas where one might expect there to be progress across countries, including infrastructure, as well as structural and regulatory reform.

Judging by the central themes of such communiqués, as well as the progression seen over the years, there are many reasons to be positive about agreement in the future on matters of policy. But the more controversial issues must not be overlooked, although with some of them – say currency policy, which was discussed by G20 finance ministers and central bank governors in Moscow in February 2013 – it is not always possible to anticipate when they will come to the fore. In fact the Russian-hosted G20 meeting in St Petersburg in 2013 was dominated by Syria and geopolitical issues, not by economics, thus mirroring how G7 evolved decades earlier from economic to political issues. At the World Economic Forum meeting in Davos in 2014, Australia outlined a focus on global economic issues for its G20 agenda in 2014, with free trade, fair tax, digitalisation and infrastructure all on the agenda.

While any international organisation needs to establish its credibility and show its relevance, this is a bigger challenge for the G20 than for most. It can achieve it by how it operates and behaves, and by what it does.

There is a strong case to be made for multi-stakeholder participation to address global issues by getting all the key people involved. But then once that happens and in order to move matters along and actually achieve things, there needs to be a co-ordinated and multi-disciplinary approach. In an instantly connected world, the speed of communication and the way in which expectations can mobilise and be influenced by pressure groups can sometimes give leaders only a limited time in which to react. This creates a need to be pro-active rather than reactive in engaging with the public mood.

Even though the G20 has legitimacy in scale and size, its diversity can mean reaching agreement only on the small number of aspects where views are truly shared. It goes to show why global groups make progress on easy issues and not on hard ones such as the Doha Round. It also helps explain why the G20 works well in a crisis, when participants are fearful of the future. Perhaps we should change our expectation of G20, accept that it might for some of the time be a global discussion group and not always a decision-maker, and therefore use it as such, to map clear paths to collective thinking. Perhaps it should be interacting with other international organisations to help solve global problems that way. What are the main economic policy issues we should focus on today?

The paradoxes

The first key issue is the need to ensure that policy is geared towards the promised land of global macroeconomic stability. It is not straightforward, as there are some paradoxes that follow from this.

We have already remarked on the 'policy paradox' in the wake of the recent crisis, as the policies we might need to take in the short term are not the same – sometimes are even the opposite – of what we need to do in the long term.

Just as there is a policy paradox, there is a 'balanced economy paradox': a policy that might be necessary and make sense to enable an individual economy to achieve domestic balance might not be the best policy from a global perspective. Imagine a group of friends going to a bar and each deciding not to spend any money: no one would have a drink. Someone has to put their hand in their pocket and spend. This paradox is that we talk about the need to save and invest, and that current-account surpluses are preferable to deficits. Yet for global demand to be strong and to avoid the world economy being at a suboptimal level, not all countries can be savers; some have to borrow and run current-account deficits. This is often the hardest point to grasp.

If Americans had not been spending heavily in the decade before the 2008 crisis, other countries would not have been able to export to the US. Likewise, in the euro area, although countries on the periphery were running unsustainable deficits, if they had not been spending then the countries with surpluses in northern Europe would not have been able to export so much to them. If it is only the countries with deficits that correct and spend less, then aggregate demand will decline. In the future, the new global middle class will live and work in so many places that enough countries will be in a position to boost domestic demand.

There is also a 'regulatory paradox', although it could be called a regulatory burden. Whereas individual regulations might make sense, collectively too many regulations create so heavy a burden that they start to stifle business. Once again, the balance needs to be right.

Balance

Of all these paradoxes, it is the need for balance that can cause most friction, as economists agree that imbalance should be avoided but don't agree on how!

An imbalanced world economy meant that some countries saved too much while others spent too much. The savers being the countries with large current-account surpluses, which effectively means that the country is in surplus with the rest of the world. Meanwhile, the countries with large current-account deficits before the crisis, like the US, the UK, and Spain, were spending too much, and so had to attract savings from elsewhere.

To achieve future balance and global stability requires three things: that countries with large savings spend more; that those with large deficits save more, and that some currencies should adjust, appreciating in the case of countries with surpluses. The challenge is that all three need to happen at the same time.

In the good times, growth must be prevented from relying too much on deficit countries, otherwise unsustainable deficits build up and will be corrected only by a painful adjustment or recession. Then, when there needs to be a shift away from imbalanced towards balanced growth, we have to ensure that it is not just the deficit countries that adjust by cutting demand, but that increased spending by surplus countries counteracts this. If not, demand will suffer and a deflationary bias will be built into the system. The problem is that it is hard to force surplus countries to spend unless they want to; in the eyes of some it means that the 'good economies' could become like the 'bad ones'. There are many countries with large current-account surpluses, including a number of energy-rich economies and a few in northern Europe, including Germany. Arguing that current-account-surplus countries should boost their domestic demand can never be a substitute for current-account-deficit countries getting their economies back into shape, by tightening their belts, but just as with driving a car, if you slam your foot on the brake instead of braking gradually, accidents can follow. This is what has happened in Europe. High current-account-deficit countries, such as Spain, have braked too hard. The accident here was a slump in demand, higher unemployment and what is known as an 'internal devaluation'. Unable to let their currency weaken because they are tied to the euro, these countries have tried to improve competitiveness by squeezing the economy. The adjustment is painful but is working. Indeed, Latin American economies, some of whom are now in good shape, have shown that austerity can work. But it does come at a price, leaving many scars.

Normally these adjustments should be gradual but, as we have seen over the last decade, pre- and post-crisis, they can also be harsh. The argument is that in the severe part of the adjustment phase, the tensions in the system can be eased only if the economies at the core boost demand, to balance the adjustments in the system. Of course, in bad times, uncertainty rises, confidence falls, and even in the 'sound' economies, businesses and people grow anxious and more cautious about spending. Thankfully the European Central Bank stepped in to save the day, but while it can limit the downside, this requires a recovery in demand to deliver on the upside. Demand is key.

One of the strange features in economics is how imbalances or trends that are out of line with reality such as speculative bubbles can persist for so long. Some countries are able to sustain trade or current-account imbalances for a long time – an example is the US in the 2000s. In 2000 there was much coverage given to an academic paper presented at the annual summer gathering of central bankers at Jackson Hole, which asked whether the US could sustain a huge trade deficit. It was a question non-American economists had already been asking, hence their wariness over the dollar's long-term prospects. But in economics, as in life, sometimes situations that look imbalanced prove more sustainable than imagined.

In a yoga class, it is amazing how balanced and poised some people can look as they stand on one leg. They look as if they're about to fall over, but they don't. They are able to sustain the pose, much as the US and some other economies appear able to sustain what appears an imbalanced situation. In contrast, those of us who can't stand on one leg find relief in the fact that someone else can help make it happen. Two people can link arms and stand on their outer legs; each can hold up the other until one gets tired. One imbalanced economy, with a large external deficit, can be offset by one with a surplus. The deficit and surplus economies need one another, and so need to co-operate.

In the wake of the financial crisis, I spoke at the annual Asian Development Bank meeting that took place in Bali. Given the plight of the world economy, picturesque Bali probably wasn't the most tactful place for bankers to be seen. But one outcome of that meeting was that the then ADB president Haruhiko Kuroda, who is now governor of the Bank of Japan, outlined what Asia needed to do to move from export-led to domestic-driven growth.

It included the need to have social safety nets to discourage excessive domestic savings; to provide finance to small and medium-sized enterprises because they were key for job creation; and to have deeper and broader bond markets so that firms could raise finance to invest. In fact, one could expand the latter point to the need to have deeper and broader capital markets across the region, both to help economies develop and grow – allowing firms to raise finance, and people to save and borrow against future income – and also to help mitigate potential inflation pressures from capital inflows.

For Asia to have domestic-driven growth was seen as a necessary part of the world economy moving towards future economic balance, and the good news is that there is every reason to expect this to happen at a steady pace as the middle class grows. It is also being seen across other continents, as the global economy of the future takes shape. While that meeting in Bali was focused on Asian economies, the same policy prescription could be applied elsewhere.

Excessive trade or current-account deficits are not ideal, but sometimes they can be justified by the factors driving them, which in turn influence the ease with which they can be financed. Deficits incurred to fund investment, and which in turn are funded by longer-term capital flows that will not reverse overnight, are manageable.

Eddie George, the former governor of the Bank of England, used to say that imbalanced growth is better than no growth. You can understand where he was coming from, but growth that is too imbalanced might not be desirable for too long. Monetary, currency, fiscal and regulatory policies are all essential here, and usually overlap.

Within this whole story, fiscal policy poses one of the most important challenges, not only for the general public but also in the eyes of the financial markets and international investors. Fiscal policy relates to government spending and taxation, and what to do about the deficits and debts that build up. It often determines the success of politicians, even in non-democracies. As mentioned, Saudi Arabia increased social spending after the Arab Spring. China boosted official spending after the financial crisis, as migrant unemployment soared. In democracies, taxes and spending plans dictate the course of public affairs.

International investors and financial markets can be spooked or reassured by fiscal plans. The downgrading of the US from its triple-A status by one of the rating agencies in August 2011 because of its fiscal outlook hit global headlines.

Government spending and revenue determines whether a country runs a budget surplus or deficit, which then affects overall national debt and hence the number of bonds that need to be issued to raise funds from international investors. A country's budget deficit and national debt are different, but easily mixed up. A deficit or surplus is what happens each year. A budget deficit adds to a country's debt, and it is only when a country is running a surplus that it can start to reduce its national debt. It might sound obvious, but only when you think about it. There are big intergenerational issues here, as the high debts of one generation might have to be repaid by a future one.

As fiscal policy is one of the key issues of this crisis, it is worth spelling out what the rules should be. Economists often talk of high government spending crowding out the private sector, with the public sector doing things private firms could do. In avoiding crowding out the private sector, they should reduce the risk of crises and, when future shocks do hit, they will be better prepared to respond and rebound. The encouraging news for the future is that many emerging economies look set to be following these rules, and this should promote future growth.

There are ten rules of fiscal policy that will matter in the future and are worth enumerating.

Rule 1

First, and foremost, governments should run budget surpluses in good times. This is the most important rule of all. Tax revenue should exceed government spending. When it does, the government can view the surplus as money set aside for a rainy day, or use it to pay down the national debt, thereby reducing future interest payments on it. Strictly speaking, if growth is strong and interest payable is low, then a government can afford to run small deficits. But as there are so many variables, some of them beyond a country's control, it makes more sense to aim for budget surpluses and hope at worst to minimise any deficit.

This is not the usual way that things are done. Instead, the temptation pulls in the other direction, and governments spend when they can. Whereas the budget-surplus rule requires a government to think long-term, too often the habitat of politics is the short term.

When an economy is doing well, tax revenues rise, and spending on discretionary areas such as benefits and the unemployed will fall. In fact the goal of running a primary surplus – which means having a surplus after paying off the interest on the debt – would be an even more effective outcome to aim for.

In life, as in economics, the best time to fix things is when they are going well, not when they are ailing. The trouble is that when things are going well, it is easy to assume that they always will, and to put off confronting the difficult longer-term issues. In terms of fiscal policy, this is reflected in government spending. In Western Europe before the crisis, the governments in many countries spent their way from famine to feast and seemed to assume they could easily go on a diet to get back into shape. What was really required was a change in lifestyle, in the shape of fundamental reform.

Rule 2

Fiscal policy is an effective counter-cyclical policy tool. Here lies the biggest challenge. If governments ignore Rule 1, and fail to run budget surpluses in good times, it means that they are already at a disadvantage if an economy either slips into recession or weakens. As an economy enters recession, people and firms avoid spending, which then puts further pressure on governments to act in a counter-cyclical way – spending when both the economy and demand are weak.

Of course, if governments have behaved badly in the good times, this limits the room for fiscal manoeuvre in the bad times. This has been the challenge in recent years. It can be summed up as two wrongs don't make a right: if the first wrong is spending too much in the good economic times, the second is failing to spend when the downturn arrives. A government budget is not exactly the same as a household budget and has a lot more flexibility. Clearly fiscal policy is not immune from overall economic conditions, and a fiscal expansion works best if there is weak demand, high unemployment, low inflation and low interest rates.

Rule 3

It is not just how much a government spends that should claim its attention, but also what it spends on. Quality matters as well as quantity. This is a rule too frequently ignored. Governments can take long-term decisions and in recessionary times can often raise money relatively cheaply from international investors. Current consumption comes second to infrastructure investment. Even if a country has a budget deficit, it could make sense to boost spending on longer-term needs such as housing and highways, just as a person might borrow through a mortgage to fund a house purchase. Countries need to find a way to fast-track sensible infrastructure projects for this to be taken more seriously as a counter-cyclical tool. No one gets this right, with some taking too long while others rush ahead with projects that are not well thought through.

Rule 4

It is wise to stop before crashing. It is essential to know what lies ahead and to demonstrate that in the way the economy is driven. When budgets need restoring into shape, it is difficult to do this overnight: the call is for a credible medium-term plan to get a fiscal position back into shape, keep financial markets onside and borrowing costs down. Put the foot on the brake gradually.

Rule 5

If you are in a fiscal hole, stop digging. A pro-cyclical policy that tightens when the economy is in recession is credible neither in political nor in economic terms. It amounts to digging deeper into the hole, yet it has been the preferred policy choice across parts of Europe in recent years.

Some politicians might argue that it is only in hard economic times that the public might put up with painful reforms, but all too often there may be no vision or context applied to what is happening. This puts all the pressure on monetary policy, which therefore needs to square with fiscal policy. Ideally they should work in the same direction, although often it might not be desirable to loosen or to tighten fiscal and monetary policy at the same time.

Rule 6

The speed and scale of tightening is a judgement call. It is only with hindsight that it can be said to have been either right or wrong. The phrase 'expansionary fiscal contraction' has been used in recent years, meaning that a contraction in government spending can allow the economy to expand by crowding in private-sector spending. This has happened before, such as in Denmark and Ireland in the 1980s, but it is not the norm, and requires the rest of the world to be growing, and there also needs to be an accommodating monetary policy to offset the tight fiscal policy. Sometimes a country will have no choice but to tighten its belt – because its debt is high and creditors demand action – and in those circumstances my view is that the right type of austerity is to curb government spending and the wrong type of austerity is to raise taxes.

Rule 7

Debts should always be considered alongside assets when a country's balance sheet is being drawn up. We tend not to consider these properly, and probably we should. In the banking crisis, the debts were socialised, which is not how it should have been, as the taxpayer was used to bail out the banks. A government should leave its fiscal position in good shape, both to cope with shocks, and so as to not to place burdens on future generations.

Rule 8

Avoid a debt trap. This is familiar to anyone who has run up debts on a credit card. A debt trap provides less room for manoeuvre. It happens when two factors are in place: a country's debt outstrips its economy, which means that debt is more than 100 per cent of

GDP; and the interest rate paid on debt is higher than the rate of economic growth. It is like maxing out on a credit card and not being able to pay the monthly interest bill. Just as an individual in that position has little room for manoeuvre and has to cut discretionary spending on other areas, so too a country that gets into a debt trap ends up having to curb spending.

Rule 9

Fiscal policy cannot be seen in isolation from monetary policy. Ideally there should be consistency between fiscal and monetary policy, working together when necessary. Fiscal policy should not impose unnecessary strains on monetary policy. One danger with high deficits and debts is this can lead to calls for the debt to be inflated away, through a tolerance of higher inflation. This is a dangerous path to go down. Likewise, in recent years, the strain has been seen with pressure on central banks in the West to pursue ultra-loose monetary policies.

In the UK during Chancellor Nigel Lawson's late-1980s boom and bust there was a misconception that a healthy fiscal position was bound to mean economic stability and that promoted a relaxed attitude about what lay ahead, with monetary policy then allowing a credit boom reflected in rising private-sector debt. The thinking then – which I disagreed with at the time – was that the government should not worry about what the private sector did, as it was based on individual decisions. This has a certain political logic to it, but in economic policy it is necessary to take greater responsibility for the collective actions of the private sector. After all, they can push the economy into trouble, and in a worst-case scenario private-sector liabilities can end up as liabilities of the taxpayer.

Rule 10

Finally, one size does not fit all. This is true for fiscal policy as it is for monetary policy. It means the rules outlined above still hold, but their effectiveness can vary across countries, depending not just on current economic conditions, but also being heavily influenced by the past and by what people think is the right thing to do. An interesting piece of research* showed that given a choice between receiving $3,400 this month and $3,800 next month, equivalent to an implied interest rate of 12 per cent per month from waiting, around 90 per cent of respondents in Germany and Austria would opt to wait, while under 50 per cent of respondents in Italy and Spain were patient. Of course, in some places people are cash strapped and don't have the luxury of waiting, or they may be just short-term in their thinking. The research suggested in countries where people have a lower rate of time preference – they are more patient and prepared to wait – then fiscal multipliers tend to be lower and the cost of fiscal consolidation and the benefit of fiscal expansion are both lower. Northern Europe, such as the Nordic countries and Germany, fit into this category.

In the future I would expect to see greater pressure to run better fiscal positions, largely because that is how the economic debate has progressed. This, in turn, will add to pressure to get monetary policy right, and goes to the heart of the next issue: inflation.

Inflation

If avoiding future global imbalances and learning the right lessons to sustain global demand constitutes the first key economic policy in the coming years, the second will be to keep inflation in check. Alongside high unemployment, high inflation is the perennial economic fear.

Perhaps, first, a word on deflation, where prices fall. This might not be seen as a bad thing by many people, after all we like the idea

---

* See research paper by Marcheggiano and Miles.

of buying things for less. It is not that uncommon to see computers and mobile phones fall in price as new versions are released. Such relative price changes are not the problem, but when there is an absolute fall in prices across the economy we become worried. If people and firms expect prices to fall there is an incentive to wait before they spend, further depressing demand and compounding the problem. In recent years the combination of weak demand and ample spare capacity, alongside intense global competition, has led to deflation fears in Europe, and some other economies, including South Korea. Such deflation worries should ease, as demand recovers, and in a number of Western economies, including Europe and the US, attention should turn to exit strategies from ultra-loose monetary policies, and curbing any inflationary consequences. But as Japan has highlighted over the recent decades, if demand remains weak, deflation is a real threat and this in turn dampens activity. This argues in favour of current accommodative monetary policies in economies where weak demand threatens deflation and reinforces the need for economies with large current account surpluses to do more to boost demand.

In contrast, it is likely that inflation will trend higher in the next few years across a number of emerging economies, as we saw in India during 2012–13. This reflects where some countries are in the business cycle. There is always the need for policymakers to be vigilant to ensure that deflation is avoided and that inflation does not start to creep upwards. There are enough warning signs to suggest that, across the emerging world, inflation could become a bigger concern because of credit growth, rising wages, and stubborn food and commodity prices. Central banks need to be vigilant.

This prospect aside, one of the encouraging stories of our time has been low inflation, and the medium-term policy aim is to sustain the trend. But it hasn't always been like this.

The oil-price shock of the early 1970s – combined with the aftermath of the collapse of the Bretton Woods currency system – led to a tough economic climate. And this manifested itself in high inflation. It dominated the economic debate everywhere throughout the 1970s, particularly in the UK, which was hit badly. So much so that in July–August 1975, Prime Minister Harold Wilson enlisted one of the leading industrial journalists of the day, Geoffrey Goodman, to move from the *Daily Mirror* to Downing Street to write a fourteen-page tabloid pamphlet that was then delivered to every household in the UK. I still have a copy.

The aim of the pamphlet was to explain the government's anti-inflationary policy. This had just been outlined in the White Paper *The Attack on Inflation*, but the pamphlet had to convey the policy to the ordinary person. Inflation had hit 26 per cent in June and the plan was to reduce it to below 10 per cent by the end of 1976. The last page of the pamphlet contained just one quote, in big letters, from the prime minister: 'One man's pay rise is not only another man's price rise: it might also cost him his own job – or his neighbour's job.' It is a pamphlet that has stood the test of time. I wonder whether it is a policy approach that could be used more often when governments face severe economic challenges and need to reach out directly to the people, explaining in layperson's terms the issues and why near-term difficulties are necessary and unavoidable.

Back in Britain in the mid-1970s, as Goodman's pamphlet made clear to the public, 'Inflation, if not brought under control, means industrial collapse and national bankruptcy . . . Pay restraint is the basis of the present battle against inflation . . . A great many people will have to suffer some cuts in living standards.'

Many of these issues are relevant now. There is a tendency to think of the UK as a high-inflation economy and Germany as a low-inflation one. But this is a recent phenomenon. It shows how successful Germany has been in laying the ghosts of its economic past, and if Germany can do that then so too can others in the future. It also highlights how countries are heavily tainted by the crises they have endured. Germany suffered hyperinflation in 1923 and has never forgotten it.

The US, in contrast, suffered severe unemployment during the Great Depression, and this is so etched on its thinking that the US Federal Reserve Board has in its mandate achieving low unemployment as well as low inflation. Other countries have different bogeymen. For the UK the banking crisis will be the future demon to be avoided. India, meanwhile, appears to have to face a crisis every ten years, often linked to problems on its balance of payments and sometimes on inflation, and that is the bogeyman it has to confront.

On 15 February 1971, the UK and Ireland decimalised their currencies. The pound was to be made up of 100 pennies, as it is now. This replaced the old system where the pound was made up of 240 pennies, with 12 pennies in a shilling and 20 shillings in a pound. I was at primary school at that time, and I still find it remarkable that I was able to pay my bus fare with pennies that had a year from the nineteenth century on them, having been minted and first used in the time of Queen Victoria. That such old coins were still legal tender was testimony to how well Britain had kept inflation under control. Apart from the First World War, when annual inflation averaged 15.3 per cent in the UK, only the 1970s saw high inflation, which averaged an annual 12.5 per cent during that decade. In some years there had been deflation, with prices falling.

'The index of retail prices tripled between 1694 and 1948 but has risen almost twentyfold since.' So said the Bank of England in its *Quarterly Bulletin* in 1994 in an article reflecting on the 300th anniversary of the bank. Compare this with the position in Germany. The 1919 Treaty of Versailles imposed tough war repatriations on Germany, but it was the policy Germany adopted to make the payments that caused subsequent economic problems, borrowing to buy foreign currency followed by devaluation, as opposed to loans and taxes.

Whereas the UK retail price index in the UK had only tripled over the 254 years to 1948, in Germany it increased fifteenfold in the second half of 1922 alone. Whereas the Mark stood at 6.7 to the dollar at the time of the 1919 Versailles treaty, by November 1923, when inflation peaked, it was 4,210,500,000,000 to the dollar. At its inflationary peak, prices were doubling every two days. Almost as remarkable as the way inflation soared was the way Germany stabilised prices, with a revaluation and new currency, killing its economic bogeyman.

South America too is haunted by its hyperinflation experience. Through this century, the inflation performance across emerging market economies has been impressive, largely because of macro-economic stability. Argentina and Zimbabwe are notable exceptions.

At the beginning of this century, inflation was in single digits across many emerging economies, the lowest since the Second World War – a dramatic improvement on the triple-digit rates of inflation seen in the late 1980s. That period had witnessed four hyperinflations, which happens when inflation reaches at least 50 per cent per month: in Argentina, Brazil and Peru between 1989 and 1990, and in Russia between 1991 and 1992. South America was as impressive as Germany when it came to curing itself.

In Peru, inflation averaged 1,224 per cent in the 1980s and 113.3 per cent in the first half of the 1990s, slowing to only 6.9 per cent in the second half of the 1990s. In Brazil it rose over the same period from 614 per cent to 1,114 per cent in the first half of the 1990s before slowing to only 7.6 per cent. In one year alone, 1994, Brazilian infla-tion averaged 2,123.7 per cent. Africa too has impressively checked its inflation over recent decades, although some countries there face some near-term inflation risks. But as a sign of how much things have moved on, the inflation rates that count as a problem today would have been viewed as acceptable only a few decades ago.

Competitive pressure is high in the world economy. In China there are 920 million people between the ages of sixteen and fifty-nine, accounting for 67.6 per cent of its population. This Chinese workforce is now part of the global labour force. They have com-peted hard in recent years, and in coming years it will be India's huge labour force that makes its presence felt, and after that Africa's. Moreover, in many Western economies there is a lack of demand and spare capacity. This may keep headline rates of inflation contained. Analysis from the US Bureau of Labor Statistics shows how manufacturing labour costs vary across the globe. One thing that stands out is that despite significantly higher wages in China in recent years, pay is still relatively low there. In fact the BLS data shows that the highest compensation costs are in North and Western Europe, while the lowest are in South and Eastern Europe, Asia and Latin America.

Manufacturing wage costs per hour rise at the highest end to $63.36 in Norway, $57.79 in Switzerland, $52.19 in Belgium, $48.47 in Denmark and $49.80 in Sweden. The figure in Germany is $45.79, in the US $35.67 and in the UK $31.23. The lowest hourly wage costs were seen in the Philippines, $2.10; Mexico, $6.36; Poland, $8.25; Hungary, $8.95; and Taiwan, $9.46. The emergence of China over the last twenty years has helped restrain inflation. Now that wages are rising in China and across many economies, the question is whether this means that China will no longer be exporting deflation and instead might feed inflation elsewhere. Interestingly, the combination of rising wages in Asia, and low energy costs in the US is leading to 'reshoring' as some production returns home.

While globalisation has helped to keep inflation low, the danger would be to miss any domestic signs of inflation that might emerge. One of the lessons of the 1970s is that even though there were many external inflation shocks to trigger cost-push inflation as rising oil prices were followed by wages edging up in response, it was those economies that kept the firmest grip on domestic monetary policy that found it easier to curb inflation. Germany is the star performer here and that is why when it worries about monetary policy we should always listen.

Perhaps current inflation worries, slight as they are when compared with those of the past, suggest that low inflation is not yet fully embedded across all economies – particularly across the emerging world. But if they can keep inflation under control, then this will be a key factor in maintaining future economic growth. As well as the traditional domestic drivers of inflation, there are some issues that stand out – again, more so in emerging economies, but we should not overlook them in the West. These include the strength of expectations. If people and firms expect inflation to stay low, they are less inclined to press for wage increases or to push prices higher to boost margins.

Other issues include how to handle commodity-price swings; gauging the slack that prevails in order to judge how much head-room there is in an economy before bottlenecks are hit and inflation pressures build; the impact of globalisation on inflation dynamics and financial globalisation; and how exchange-rate swings feed through to inflation. With macroeconomic policymaking gaining credibility, so too should the inflation-fighting credentials, particularly as demand starts to recover.

In coming years there will be greater focus on central banks on what has been referred to as: MIP, MAP and MOP, namely micro prudential policy, macro prudential policy and monetary policy. Micro and macro prudential polices are aimed at curbing excessive personal borrowing and asset-price inflation, and will need to be used closely alongside monetary policy. If successful, deflation should be avoided and inflation kept at bay.

Proceeds of growth

In addition to balanced growth and low inflation, the final key policy area is sharing the proceeds of growth. It relates to taxes, welfare and jobs.

One policy area where global as well as national action might be needed is tax. It was as long ago as the eighteenth century that Adam Smith became the first economist to mention tax rules. He had four:

tax should reflect the extent to which people participate in an economy, and thus their respective ability to pay; it should be certain; it should be convenient, and it should take as little out of the people's pockets as possible.

His analysis still resonates today. Taxes should be fair; as predictable as possible; convenient to pay; cost little to collect; be simple to assess and work out, and progressive in that the more that is earned the more that is paid. This does not mean that tax rates should be prohibitively high. Tax should not be there to achieve political aims of arbitrary redistribution, as the economic efficiency of tax would then be diluted, but it should be used to enable an economy to operate efficiently and fairly. It should not discourage work. Nowadays, in too many economies taxation is complex, and certainly not neutral in that it affects economic behaviour either at the individual or at the corporate level.

But across many emerging economies, personal and corporate tax rates are simpler and low. In some economies – such as Singapore or Hong Kong – taxes are relatively low and in return the system appears to work well. In contrast, in many Western economies people feel that taxes are too high. In some of these economies taxes are high and public services good – such as northern Europe, including Scandinavia, Norway and Germany – whereas in others, such as the UK and the US, taxes are high but public sector productivity needs to improve.

A number of Eastern European economies introduced a flat tax after the fall of communism. It is simple and effective. The idea is one low rate on everything: income, capital gains, corporation tax. So simple. So clear. So efficient. Flat tax has much to recommend it, but is easier to implement in economies setting up tax regimes from scratch. In economies with older and more complex systems, a flat tax could create more losers at first than winners through the change, although over time if it helped improve efficiency in the economy and growth rebounded, most people would gain.

Unfortunately, all too often policy decisions are not based on what will produce the best economic outcome over time but on whether there are more winners than losers at the time of any policy change. In Western economies, it would likely need very high tax-free income allowances alongside a flat tax to make the numbers acceptable. But, even without a flat tax, high allowances make sense, to reduce the tax burden on the low-paid.

Another issue is that tax is now international. Tax was one of the main areas of attention at the G8 summit in Northern Ireland in 2013, when sharing information across tax havens and offshore centres was identified as an achievable policy. Those who sidestep the system not only end up reducing their tax burden but also consequently forcing law-abiding taxpayers to pay more. This is no different from shoplifting – shops build the price of stolen goods into their margins – although with tax avoidance and evasion, it is hard to be precise about how much is being lost. Avoidance is legal; evasion is not. The way ahead is to have zero tolerance for evasion and reform tax systems so as to make avoidance unnecessary.

There is another element that is perfectly acceptable, and that is tax competition. Areas of economic activity that are mobile have the option to gravitate to where taxes are lower. That means that companies that are multinational or mobile are able to avoid high-tax jurisdictions. Likewise, skilled workers can be mobile. This would suggest that globalisation exerts downward pressure on the tax on big companies or skilled workers. In contrast, activities or things that are less mobile are liable to be taxed more – housing and spending are likely targets. In the future, globalisation will probably change the parameters of tax.

From an economic perspective, tax should be seen in its own context, but too often taxation is driven less by economic thinking and more by its function of paying for government expenditure. So government spending is seen as the main driver – and then the issue becomes how to raise as much taxation as possible to meet this requirement. One key hope for the future is that emerging economies learn from the mistakes in the West, while Western countries address these matters. In particular there is a need for a twenty-first-century social-welfare system and the need for a new social contract across much of the world.

Economics would suggest there will be a greater acceptance of some key features of a viable social system across the globe, but there is no reason to expect the same system to evolve everywhere. The need in the West is for a new social contract that it can afford; in the East it is for one that will work.

Some of the best parts of welfare systems derive from developments at the end of the nineteenth century. A remarkable feature of the late nineteenth century and early twentieth century was the high number of immigrants. One hundred million Europeans migrated, 60 million of them to the New World. The sharp fall in transport costs, the perceived opportunities in the countries they were travelling to, and the dismal conditions at home, help to explain this. Guillermo de la Dehesa quotes some interesting figures. In the 1880s, for every 1,000 inhabitants, the number of immigrants was 292 in Argentina, 168 in Canada, 118 in Cuba and 102 in the US. Likewise for every 1,000 inhabitants, the number who left their country was 142 from Ireland, 198 from Italy, 95 from Norway. The majority went from the poorest countries in Europe to the richest in the New World. All this contributed to reducing inequality between the two worlds.

Now the concern is that globalisation has helped reduce inequality between countries, but is adding to inequality within countries, as high-skilled workers benefit from new markets opening up, while the low- and medium-skilled workers in the West compete with cheaper workers in emerging economies, or with immigrants at home. The important thing is to ensure that this relative loss does not become an absolute loss. That puts the stress on ensuring healthy economic growth to generate jobs; on wages and taxes that yield sufficient take-home pay, and on welfare systems suitable for the twenty-first century. Western economies have made a rod for their own backs, creating generous benefits during good economic times that will grow expensive to sustain as their populations age. The stronger global growth turns out to be, the less is the pressure on Europe and on the US to reform, although they cannot escape it completely. Also, the stronger growth prospects appear, the more likely it is that countries across other regions fall into the trap of creating a social system that is too generous and so places too great a burden on future generations.

The position of many Western countries was reflected in an OECD report* that stated:

> Accounting for both the tax system and the role of private social benefits reveals that social spending levels are similar in countries often thought to have very different gross public social expenditure levels. For example, total net social spending in Austria, Canada, Denmark, Finland, Italy, Japan, the Netherlands, Portugal, the United Kingdom and the United States are within a few percentage points of each other.

In terms of net total social expenditure the rankings are:

1   France
2   Belgium (from the 4th it would have ranked based on gross spending)
3   Germany (from 7th)
4   Sweden (from 2nd)
5   US (from 23rd)
6   UK (from 12th)
7   Italy (from 6th)
8   Austria (from 5th)

* See reference in the bibliography.

Across the OECD, public social spending rose as a percentage of GDP from 15.6 per cent in 1980 to 19.2 per cent in 2007; then following the crisis it rose to 22.5 per cent in 2009 and stayed around 22 per cent in 2012. It is often easy to blame the unemployed, immigrants or 'benefit scroungers', but the sums expended on these groups are dwarfed by spending in other areas. Although the picture varies from country to country, social spending can effectively cover health, education, pensions and benefits. Of these, health and pensions are often the chief recipients, and in coming decades that seems unlikely to change.

The biggest future problem could be pensions, as people have often not contributed enough during their working life; the payouts are generous, and life expectancy is continuing to rise. So, if people are living longer, receiving generous public-sector or state-pension payouts that they didn't contribute much towards but which the state either pays or tops up, then there will be problems.

When Bismarck introduced the pension in Germany at the end of the nineteenth century it was a forward-thinking step that Germany has continued to honour, despite the inflationary horrors of the 1920s, and one that others have sought to follow. But when it was introduced, the pensionable age was set at seventy. Life expectancy was fifty-nine. The pensionable age was lowered to sixty-five during the First World War, but still stood way above life expectancy.

When the US introduced its pension system a few years later, it too set the pensionable age at sixty-five, when life expectancy was sixty-two. Now in the West the pensionable age has hardly moved while life expectancy has continued to rise.

Some people might even be retired, and receiving a pension, for longer than they were working. In some public-sector occupations the retirement age can be lower than in the private sector – an issue highlighted by Greece during its strikes over austerity in 2011 and 2012. All of these issues reflect the inability of Western politicians – over many decades – to heed sensible economic advice and make tough, painful, but necessary decisions.

What should countries outside Europe do? The world economy has already seen more people brought out of poverty than could have been imagined over the last few decades. China is the clearest example of this, but it still contains huge numbers on low incomes. There are further huge numbers that need to be brought out of poverty elsewhere, not least in India and across large tracts of sub-Saharan Africa.

The middle-income trap becomes the next issue, as living standards rise. For a country to move from middle to high income is far harder than to progress from low to middle. This is the issue currently confronting China, as it soon will confront many others, but with the right policies it is manageable.

The changing global economy throws up an immediate challenge and an exciting opportunity in the area of social welfare. If a social-welfare system were to be created from scratch, which model should it follow? The role of the state has been seen as justified in providing old age, disability and survivor benefits. This is because of the absence of fully developed markets, lack of planning by an economically active population, and income-distribution inequalities that do not enable part of the population to deal with these contingencies.

A pay-as-you-go system, where current workers pay for those who have grown old, has been the preferred route in many places. But the system lacks long-term viability, and this realisation is sending shock waves, as the number of those in work declines in relation to those who are not working – both the young and the old. The dependency ratio is the number of younger people who are in education plus the number of older people in retirement, as a proportion of those who are in the productive part of the population, who are usually in work.

As with any measure that tries to capture large-scale trends and developments, this one is not exact. For instance, many older people can look after themselves and are not dependent on anyone. But, just to complicate it further, the old might cost more than the young to support. Even so, the dependency ratio helps to convey an idea of how things are changing and also of possible problems if nothing is done. The higher the dependency ratio, the greater the potential problem.

There are clear divergences here across the globe. To reduce the ratio, there is a requirement to have fewer people being supported, more in work, or the ratio of those in work rising faster than that of those needing support. Then there is the question of how much people in work contribute and how much those who are young or old receive.

The dependency ratio is 50 in the US, 52 for Germany and 53 for the UK, and in all three countries it is rising, which means there are about fifty people being supported by every hundred in work, so two workers to each non-worker. The lower the dependency rate means fewer non-workers to be supported. In Nigeria the ratio is 88 and falling; in India 53 and falling. China's fell from a peak of 81 in 1965 to 36 in 2010 but started to edge up in 2012 as the workforce declined. To examine pensions in isolation consider the old-age dependency ratio, which takes only those over sixty-five as a proportion of those in work. The old-age dependency ratio has risen from 15 in the US in 1950 and is set to rise steadily to 50 by the end of this century, while in India it is below ten and is rising gradually this century.

The alternative to a pay-as-you-go system is for people to contribute personally. In some respects this is the equivalent of an insurance system, where people take responsibility for their own needs. Even then not everyone will be able to manage – and there will always be some who take the view that they do not need to contribute and that the state will look after them rather than letting them fall into poverty.

The more rigorous alternative would mean each individual paying for him- or herself; this would need to be a regulated system with mandatory contributions. Chile and Singapore both have insurance models that force the burden onto individuals in terms of contributions during their working lives, with the government taking some of the responsibility for ensuring that the fund grows.

In other countries, high domestic savings will play their part. High savings help fund high domestic investment. But if all these savings are sitting around in the bank accounts or under the mattresses of lots of individuals, then they can't be used in another way. If it was possible to channel them into pension funds or some sort of savings schemes, where people can have access to their money when they need to, then the collective amount, centrally managed, would not be sitting idle and could be used in effective ways. There is a need for a relatively cheap way of ensuring that the financial system helps channel domestic savings into domestic managed funds, as this would allow these collective funds to play a more positive part in domestic long-term investment needs.

I like the Chilean model, as it is based on individual contributions, and so puts the onus on the individual to make his or her own contributions and thus take responsibility. It does not involve tax breaks that favour the wealthy, as has happened in some Western countries, and the system has evolved to provide better safeguards for those who are poor.

The Chilean scheme is simple, yet it has also been possible to evolve it to make it more effective. The system was introduced in 1980, but in 2006 it was found that a significant part of the population lacked sufficient funds to support themselves during old age. In 2008 President Michelle Bachelet introduced important reforms that improved coverage and introduced greater flexibility. The three basic pillars of the scheme are: a poverty-prevention element to ensure that everyone has a basic pension to live on; a mandatory contribution based on people contributing and receiving benefits based on a formula linked to contributions; and a voluntary option that allows people to increase the amount they contribute if they want to have greater choice later.

This is why it is good to see what other countries have done: to survey the successes and failures.

Allowing best practice in pension provision is one thing. Saving money on global subsidies is another, and is likely to be one area where future progress can be made. Although often these subsidies are not counted directly as part of the social bill, they can effectively be seen as part of it. The world spends $1.9 trillion on subsidies. That is 2.5 per cent of global GDP and 8 cent of government revenues.

Subsidies are often established in good faith, say to help a strategic or politically important group – often farmers. Energy subsidies, to protect customers, are another popular kind. The countries paying the largest energy subsidies in total are the US ($502 billion), China ($279 billion) and Russia ($116 billion).* These are colossal sums. Reducing subsidies would not only relieve pressure on budgets in these and other countries, but more importantly it would allow the price mechanism to work properly. Prices are not just what we pay for things, they also convey information – and in an environment freed of excessive intervention, regulation and subsidies, prices would work better in conveying information and in allowing the private sector to respond, directing investment into necessary areas.

The other component of the proceeds of growth is jobs. Today, despite worries about globalisation, scores of jobs are being created across the globe. From 2007 to 2012, those employed in industry across the globe rose from 653.8 million to 703.2 million and in services from 1,251.3 million to 1,375.4 million. In agriculture the figure was virtually unchanged at 1,048.8 million in 2012. In 2000 the respective figures were 533.6 million, 1,020.3 million and 1,057.3 million. More people are being brought into work.

* See the paper by the IMF in January 2013 mentioned in the bibliography on energy subsidy reform.

Despite this, there are over 200 million people unemployed worldwide, and in Europe and Africa youth unemployment is high. It is instructive to look at the economics of this. The lack of aggregate demand in those regions has a part to play, as does the tendency for firms to retain existing workers. As demand recovers the jobs picture will improve. But what is also worth noting is the way that supply-side issues are often identified, and how progress is being made on these. For instance, the 2012 International Labour Conference identified three pillars in the action plan for youth as: a knowledge-sharing platform with a virtual network; advocacy, focused on partnership and campaigns; and technical assistance. What stands out here is that these were not the grand plans of G20 but measures that were quite specific and micro in nature.

According to Jose Harris, the word 'unemployment' was coined almost accidentally by the economist Alfred Marshall in 1888 and then seeped rapidly into popular use. The first English work devoted to unemployment during the period of strong growth in 1870–1914 was that of A. C. Pigou in 1913, and it took the then popular view that unemployment was the result of wages not being flexible enough. The Poor Law of that time held that work was always available; people simply needed to look harder in order to find it. Nowadays, rightly, it is widely accepted that there are many more factors to contend with but, as in the nineteenth century, pricing an individual's work is important, as there is a need to be competitive.

Could there be a renewed role for unions in this global economy? As their power declines, because of the squeeze on labour, the case for their existence grows. There is a wider issue here, which is how the balance of power between labour and capital is shifting – and in turn the relationship between workers and firms has changed in recent decades with workers receiving a smaller share of economic success. In the West, the wage share fell from 73.4 per cent of national income in 1980 to 64 per cent in 2007, reversing the previous post-war trend and adding to worries about inequality. It is not just how wealth is split between countries but how income is divided within them that influences people's feeling of well-being. This fall in the share of wages has tended to be attributed to four areas: globalisation, new technology, 'financialisation' and a change in bargaining power away from workers. Financialisation reflects the growth of finance and the fact that more of national income goes to profits, interest payments and dividends instead of wages, and that the pay of those at the very top has not only risen but is aligned more with the share price and so more with shareholders than with workers' wages. But not all these areas need be negative for future wage share, as globalisation should bring more opportunities in terms of growth and trade, while technology helps productivity. The challenge is that real wages have fallen behind the growth in productivity. There might be an innovation lag as it takes time for workers to adjust to new technology and be able to benefit from it. There also needs to be more focus on financialisation as discussed in earlier chapters and on bargaining-power issues.

Many forget the reason unions were formed in the first place: to protect artisan employment, later evolving into safeguarding workers' rights. In the future these roles should be central. In good firms there should not be conflict between the wishes of shareholders, managers and workers but, in competitive markets, too often there is. There must not be a race to the bottom on workers' rights and pay, but greater acceptance on common standards. It is hard to force through minimum wages, especially for small firms working under tight margins, but acceptable working conditions, a focus on living wages and holiday entitlements are areas where progress is due.

So policy issues can be addressed at a national, regional or global level. I've outlined three broad policy issues relevant across the global economy, and where there is likely to be progress. One, there is the need for balanced global growth, both within and between countries. Fiscal positions matter within economies, current accounts across them. Two, there has been tremendous progress on inflation and there is a renewed need to keep inflation low. Three, the final key policy issue is to share the proceeds of growth, with an emphasis on taxes, welfare and employment.

In coming decades we are likely to see further progress on achieving a welfare system suited to the twenty-first century. The key is to learn the lessons from across the globe, and to enable the market mechanism to work, and if there is market failure then for the government to step in. All of these are vital aspects of building a strong and stable path to future growth. They contribute towards an enabling environment in which people and firms are free to spend, save, invest and trade.

9

Positioning for the future

A couple of years ago, I was invited to Cambridge to attend King's College annual dinner. There were two loyal toasts, one to the existing monarch and one to Henry VI who had founded the college six centuries earlier. Celebrating the old and the new. As a guest, I sat among members of the economics faculty. The conversation was fascinating and fitted with my perception of how the subject of economics was shifting.

To my left were people younger than me, whose conversation was dominated by talk of game theory and mathematical economics. To my right, older people, who spoke about political economy, jobs and growth. It was as if the two groups were speaking different languages. Admittedly there are many branches in any subject, but even so it reflected the changes in the discipline: the old and the new, like the loyal toasts. The challenge is how to pull them both together, so the net impact of economics is at its most powerful.

Rebuilding the subject

The years since the financial crisis have been testing for the economics profession. It has fed a common perception that economists always get it wrong. Often, economic forecasts prove accurate but turning points are always a problem. In terms of the crisis, despite the perception, there were a fair few who either predicted it or were not surprised by it, although they didn't get every aspect right. Despite this, to the bulk of economists it was a bolt out of the blue. Too many bought into the idea of the 'Great Moderation', the belief that the good times would continue.

There is nothing wrong with making a mistake in forecasting – people should not be penalised for putting their necks on the line – but one lesson is that the consensus should be challenged. Paul Ormerod notes in *Positive Linking* how Olivier Blanchard, now the IMF's chief economist, gave a speech extolling the virtues of global policymaking, saying that global macro was in good shape, the same month the crisis hit! There is often an implicit assumption in forecasts – the 'policy anticipation effect' – that policymakers, usually smart and on top of their game, will do the right thing. Before the crisis the short-term mood of the financial markets was captured by the comment made by the head of a US bank that 'as long as the music is playing you've got to get up and dance'.* In the face of such short-termism it is vital for economists to retain their independence and call it as it is, and not be swayed by near-term pressures.

Economics is a social science. Unlike a natural science, it cannot carry out experiments in labs and then say that, in practice, the results will always be the same. People don't behave the way that chemicals or atoms do in scientific experiments. In a complex system such as an economy where so many variables can impact, it is often not until events are actually unfolding that it is possible to say what the outcome will be. Because humans are involved, we couldn't even be sure that if we were able to repeat an economic event in exactly the same circumstances that we would get the same outcome.

The consolations for economics include both an increased recognition of the challenges with the subject's current mathematical approach and a renewed interest in other branches of the subject, each of which should help us understand better the current and future drivers of growth: economic history, a global view, behavioural economics and networks. But, as the saying goes, we mustn't throw the baby out with the bathwater.

---

* This comment was made by Chuck Prince, the chief executive of Citibank, to the *Financial Times* in July 2007.

Making the maths count

There is so much in the subject that works – we first need to tighten up the mathematical analysis, or to use it in the right way. In recent decades economics has tried to become more scientific, making econometric modelling and mathematical models more central to the subject and in turn more important for policy.

There are occasions when one can have strong, accurate convictions about what will happen, but the reality is that economics is not geared to pinpoint forecasts of near-term events, such as the next trade or public debt figures. Such high-frequency weekly or monthly data are difficult to forecast. It is, of course, possible to make correct forecasts, but economics is better suited to providing scenarios, based on assumptions about what could happen and how people might react. This used to lead to the image of a two-handed economist, saying, 'On the one hand . . . or on the other hand.' I have always tried to avoid saying this, instead preferring to take a view. The reality is that we don't know what will happen, particularly in the near-term. There are occasions when one can have a strong, accurate conviction about the near-term outlook as opposed to a view, but often economics allows one to have more confidence about what the outcomes will be in a few years' time.

Economic models also tend to assume things return to the previous norm, and can often miss the big turning points and changes when they hit. How many models in 1978 predicted the emergence of China over the following thirty years? None. How many in 2007 or 2008 predicted the financial crisis? Very few.

Mathematical or econometric models can work and add value in certain specific areas, but when they become too big and are applied to the whole economy, they have a huge margin of error. They are useful as a guide to the potential impact of a future event or to demonstrate how a change in an important variable such as the price of oil might work its way through an economy.

There is the matter of how information is used. Questions are often about the bottom line. Are you bullish or bearish? Will the dollar go up or down? This can make the use of scenarios problematic, particularly in the financial industry. Let me give an example. A number of years ago, I was asked to give some scenarios about an outlook. The probabilities I attached to these scenarios were 50, 35 and 15 per cent. The bulk of the listeners wanted to focus only on the main scenario, without regard to the others. One person in the room had previously been in the oil industry, where scenario-planning is more common, and only he understood that the scenario with a 35 per cent probability needed to be taken very seriously, particularly as it was a scenario that would normally have only a 2 per cent probability. Imagine if you were told that there is usually a one-in-fifty chance of being knocked down crossing a particular road, but today there is a one-in-three chance as the cars are driving too fast. Unless you were stupid, you would alter your behaviour to reflect the risk. Too often that does not happen when scenario-planning is used, particularly in the financial sector.

Perhaps the solution is not to attach probabilities to scenarios, but to talk through them so that the issues can be fully understood. But people have to want to listen. Too often there is a tendency to put all the eggs in one basket, focusing on the main scenario and not taking the others seriously.

Exciting times

There is still a long way to go for the subject and the teaching of it to understand better how an economy works, and the 2008 crisis demonstrated this clearly. There are still too many widely divergent views on how monetary policy works, for example. But some of the issues are even more fundamental than that, such as the operations of the financial system itself and the creation of credit need to be fully reflected in realistic models of the modern-day economy.

Indeed, much of the national-accounts analysis of the subject was established in the days when manufacturing dominated, and so today economic models don't reflect properly how economies are changing in terms of the service sector. Consequently the economic models on which analysis and forecasts are made need to improve.

Economic history merits greater focus in the teaching of the subject. Combining rigorous analysis with economic history is a potentially powerful combination. There are many areas where lessons from the past would be invaluable, particularly in macro-economics, financial analysis and public-policy decisions.

Having a global view is more important than ever, as the world economy becomes increasingly interlinked. Also, we can learn from international comparisons that indicate which country has the best practice in addressing economic challenges.

Perhaps the economics mainstream is too dominated by the West. Just take the number of Nobel Prize winners in economics. Since the Prize was first awarded in 1969, only one winner has come from outside Europe and the US, Amartya Sen of India in 1998, although two of the European winners were from the Soviet Union and twice it has been shared by economists with joint US–Israeli nationality.

Behavioural economics, too, is now seen as a more important area, as this helps explain how people act and shows that they do not always behave in the way that rational economic models might expect. It means outcomes are more unpredictable, and that there is a clear role for the government, regulators and policymakers in driving or influencing outcomes. The interaction between the public and private sectors is part of the story. Perhaps this might lead on to a better idea of how to measure economic success. Currently success is measured by looking at the growth rate of gross domestic product, which adds up an economy's output. We could take it one step further and look at average living standards in terms of per capita income.

The Soviet countries looked at different measures from GDP, partly because on that basis they scored poorly. Although their economic model was terrible, perhaps they were right about the need for a different way to measure success. In recent years, measuring happiness has become an economic issue. For instance, in GDP terms, how should one account for leisure time increasing, poverty declining or longevity increasing? These are not measured directly in terms of an economy's worth, but for most people they would be seen as better guides to how well a country might be doing. By way of illustration, one group of economists has calculated a well-being index called the Genuine Progress Indicator that takes into account social and environmental issues, such as resource depletion and waste generation.

Economics also needs to work more with other disciplines to try to get a grip on future events. If it has taken a crisis for us to understand how complex the world economy has become, then we should take note that science suggests that in complex adaptive systems the following happens: crises occur regularly and the frequency of a crisis happening might be inverse to its magnitude; predicting individual crises is impossible; there is no relationship between the size of the triggering event and the magnitude of the subsequent crisis. In economics it is more complex, as the expectations and actions of people can influence the outcome. The lesson I take from this is that we need to use economic analysis to lessen the possibility of imbalances and problems emerging, that we should not be surprised by anything, and that we need to see good economic times as the period to build up ammunition for the future – high reserves, budget surpluses, high interest rates, ample savings, effective social safety nets. Then we need to use these appropriately when shocks hit and crises occur.

Being prepared for the upside and for strong growth is just as much of a challenge as protecting against the downside. In life we don't go through each day, month or year thinking only about what could go wrong. We plan ahead for success, more education, holidays, work. We need to ensure that we use economics constructively and positively, particularly as many economic drivers, as I have outlined, offer cause for encouragement.

Following from that, it is perhaps only natural that another new, or revitalised, branch of economics to emerge in the wake of the crisis is the study of networks. This is particularly interesting in a whole host of areas. A significant implication is the importance of cities, particularly large ones. These are nodes in a network, with the size, scale and location of the city influencing how important a node it is. Cities can apply economies of scale to provide services, jobs and accommodation efficiently and cheaply. They also become the first line of defence in the event of a global crisis or epidemic. Urbanisation will be one of the key drivers in the next few decades, as cities become the main means of provision of health care, education, services and jobs. Middleweight cities that we have paid little attention to might become places we wish to visit or even household names: Chongqing or Fushan in China, Curitiba and Florianópolis in Brazil, or the vast metropolitan area of Randstad in the Netherlands.

So the discipline of economics is itself learning, and this should strengthen the way it is taught and used.

Consolations for people

Which is the best economy in the world and is it even possible to judge such a thing? Certainly the US could lay claim to that title if it were measured by economic size, but also for the way it has allowed generations of people to realise the American Dream. Based on GDP per head, it would be between Qatar, the gas-rich Gulf state; Singapore, which has made the most of its strategic location; or one of the smaller European favourable tax regimes such as Monaco or Luxembourg. China is the second biggest in terms of economic size but low down, around ninetieth, in terms of income per person. Or we could look at countries with the lowest income disparities as measured by Gini coefficients, and these include a number in Europe, such as Denmark, Norway and Slovenia.

Or we might consider economies that position themselves in the best way to play to their strengths, by pulling ahead of others in the areas they are good at, investing, innovating and reinventing themselves constantly. It is just as necessary to create an environment for both sustained growth and potential future growth. Achieving success is one thing, sharing its spoils is another.

When I was growing up in Kilburn, an area of London full of Irish immigrants, it was not uncommon to hear people say that Britain was the best country in the world. There was no evidence, in economic terms, for these claims. But the fact that so many people, including my parents, would say this, and think it, showed that when people look at economies they take more than current economic well-being into account. Perhaps it is also a reflection of immigration and of expectations. For my first eleven years, until we moved into a council flat, my experience was of six of us living in two rooms and having a tin bathtub that had to be brought in from the backyard to the scullery and then filled up by repeatedly boiling the kettle for water for a bath. So clearly immigrants place a different measure on how they assess success. Aspirations and opportunities for their children, particularly in education, might be seen as the key measure as opposed to current economic wealth. And what Kilburn lacked in wealth, it made up for in terms of access to a good education and health system. When one looks at successful economies around the world, that is a big part of their success.

Immigrants can fall into many categories, often a combination of cheap, skilled and hard-working, but there are many variations, from qualified doctors, recent graduates, to those starting from scratch or seeking a new life. In Japan in the 1990s, at a time of great economic debate about its population, it was said that immigrants should do the three Ds: Dirty, Dangerous and Demeaning jobs. I have never liked, anywhere, the idea of a demeaning job, and I would say that no job should be demeaning. When I was growing up that was very much the case in the UK: most people had respect for the jobs that others did and had pride in the jobs they did themselves. I wonder whether this is a far more important part of an economy's success than people or indeed economists realise, as it helps social cohesion, as well as managing economic expectations.

Generally speaking, immigration is good, and the contribution of immigrants needs to be evident and valued. Sometimes a country might want large numbers of immigrants, at other times fewer. After all, more houses, schools or hospitals might be needed. Immigration can prove a demographic dividend if planned for, a demographic disaster if not. Benefit migrants should be avoided, and one way to do this is to limit the available benefits. At the height of its empire, Rome swelled to a population of one million, huge by the standards of the time, as people received free bread and constant entertainment. It wasn't until seventeen centuries later that another European city was to grow this big. It is a salutary lesson. There are pull factors that attract, as well as push factors that force people to leave.

The opening up of China thirty years ago, and more recently of Vietnam and now of Myanmar, show how their previous policies of closing the shutters and resisting the world didn't help in the long run.

Consolations for business

What are the wider economic implications for business?

Embrace change, by planning strategically. We need to see through near-term uncertainty, potential downside risks and likely financial market volatility, in order to identify the underlying economic drivers.

Think global. Perhaps this should be called the Paradox of Size. As the world economy grows, it appears to shrink. Despite a growing global economy, different regions of the world appear to be affected by events elsewhere as never before. The world is more interconnected in terms of communications, transport and awareness of issues, and hence more joined together in economic terms. It is reasonable to expect this to continue, as people's tastes and thinking become more shaped by global developments. Businesses still need to take this into account, as new markets open up, new competitors emerge and as global supply chains are heavily interlinked. In a global economy, investing in the brand – whether it is a business or an individual – matters more than ever, especially as new markets grow and new competitors emerge from them.

Yet it is important to put such global influences alongside the domestic and regional factors, cultural and economic, that clearly influence the outlook. In some respects we need to see the world both from 36,000 feet and from six feet, as domestic demand will be the biggest driver in most economies, but more of the ideas will be global.

Another lesson is to appreciate the scale of the opportunity that lies ahead.

Competition is vital. It is possible to compete on cost or quality, and while there is always the need to be competitive there will always be someone somewhere who can do it more cheaply. Quality of the product and service becomes key. This fits with the desire of countries to move up the value curve; it means firms investing and innovating and it implies people increasing their skills. In the global economy of the future there will be many things that are still much the same, but there will be change in many areas, too, with new technology, new acceptance of the way things should be done and a focus on knowledge-driven growth.

There is a need for a standard of morals and ethics. The crisis highlighted huge issues in the West in terms of how economies operate and are run, and there are similar governance issues in other economies, too.

Changing demographics mean businesses need to change how they think about age. In any role it should be one's ability, not one's age that matters. Younger people might want both the security of tenure of employment and the flexibility of being part of global networks. As people live longer, younger people might have a different approach to work. Likewise, the concept of what it means to be old could change, and working practices will need to reflect this. Career changes will become desirable, and allow people to bring experience as well as new skill sets into different industries.

It is not just age, but gender, too. The World Economic Forum is playing a lead role to take on the issue of gender disparity, working on a data-driven approach in three countries, Mexico, Turkey and Japan, with the hope of rolling out best practice elsewhere. As the Forum states, 'At the macro level, countries that invest in girls and integrate women into the workforce tend to be more competitive.' It is up to business to embrace this, across the globe.

Globalisation favours mobile firms and high earners. In many areas, greater transparency should be the answer, as it also favours the customer if he or she knows all the tariffs and charges, and can make informed choices about moving his or her custom. In other areas mobility is the key. So don't just think global, think mobile too.

Consolations for investors

Where should investors place their money? In the near-term, they need to ask whether markets are pricing properly for risk, and, within that investment environment, what constitutes a risk-free asset. Over the next few years there is likely to be a normalisation of real bond yields in Western economies, perhaps rising towards 3 per cent, overshooting on the upside as they rise. That might set a good benchmark for the return on other investments, subject to risk. Low interest rates can not only result in a mispricing of risk but they can also contribute to a misallocation of capital in an economy, so when interest rates rise, in an economic recovery phase, this can result in a shake-out in the economy, and so provide opportunities for cash-rich investors.

There should be ample opportunities. In many countries, although not all, investment ratios are rising as firms start to plan for the future; replacement ratios are rising as people finally trade in their old cars and other durables for newer ones; new consumers are buying products for the first time; there is an infrastructure boom, and environmental concerns point to a new green investment boom, with technology playing a central role.

Investors can anticipate longer-term trends linked to the main macroeconomic drivers such as increased domestic demand, higher trade, a rush for resources or urbanisation and how cities can operate in smarter ways. Take people. The younger middle class across the globe will buy similar items, being very brand-aware and technology-savvy. With older people being the fastest-growing part of the world's population, they will be spending more of their own money on looking after their own needs and perhaps those of their children or grandchildren.

Japan has been at the cutting edge in developing commercial items for older people, so much so that even something as mundane as a toilet has become spectacular. Marcel Duchamp might turn in his grave to see how practical this is. A button is pressed to lift the lid, another to warm the seat, another to rinse the toilet and then another to transform it into a bidet. The Japanese are innovating in so many areas of technology from labour-saving robotics to new green buildings that are more efficient in energy use.

One exciting example of this is the Japanese architect Nikken Sekkei's impressive evaporative-cooling bioskin building, aimed at offsetting the urban heat-island effect that warms up Tokyo in the summer. By collecting rainwater on the roof and passing it through pipes that run tastefully around the outside of the building, it cools the building and the surrounding streets, the pipes acting in the same way as the bamboo shields that used to cool the Japanese houses of the past. It is another sign of how creativity and technology can recycle old ideas, making them relevant for the present. Sekkei didn't patent the design, preferring the open-universe approach of sharing, which helps maximise information sets, as I discussed earlier.

Investors can also follow the money, in the sense of looking at what the countries that have the cash need. Many fast-growing emerging economies will want to buy the things that they need but don't yet have. As their growth has been based on low-cost labour, they need to become efficiency-seeking by buying technology to transfer back home; quality-seeking to help move up the value curve; strategic-asset-seeking by buying brands, and resource-seeking if they want access to energy supplies.

Investors can look to buy into regions and countries that offer the best potential. Some countries appear oversold such as the US, the UK and Germany offer solid future potential, and then there are future growth economies, such as the 7-per-cent club in Africa, or big emerging economies across the globe.

Investor groups are changing, and with increased opportunities across multiple regions we are likely to see different groups working together more often. This could be state capitalism in the form of sovereign-wealth funds, or the growing group of wealthy private capital led by mega-rich people, and perhaps, as technology and regulation develops, increased participation by many others with smaller savings. Capital markets need to evolve to reflect this.

Consolations as an arc of growth takes shape

Rather than cover the whole globe, let me outline just a few of the potential interesting stories to come. We might see an arc of growth stretching from China through India into Africa, through the three main populous regions of the world. In part this might reflect a migration of manufacturing to where labour costs are low, as well as, in the case of Africa, the availability of commodities and water.

This would necessitate increased infrastructure spending for India. I am very positive about India, but sometimes when I arrive there I have to take a deep breath as I see at first hand the difficulties the country faces.

South Asia, including India, Pakistan and Bangladesh, holds about one-fifth of the world's population but accounts for tiny proportions of both the world economy and global trade. It has been a relatively insular region in economic terms – although very open in others. At the turn of this century it was not uncommon in East Asia for countries to see China only as a competitive threat, and barely a few years later those attitudes had changed, as they viewed it as a growth opportunity and a market to sell into. In the same way that China transformed East Asia, it would not be a surprise to see India open up and have a transformational impact on growth across South Asia, and also between that region and others, such as ASEAN, the Middle East and the east coast of Africa.

One example is the planned $90 billion Delhi–Mumbai Industrial Corridor, covering seven states with plans for a six-lane highway, high-speed freight rail, nine industrial zones and twenty-four new cities. Even delivering on part of this would be transformational, and it is a sign of the ambition that exists over large parts of the globe.

On many economic measures India lags behind China, but that should not be a surprise. Whereas China opened up in 1978 and quickly made headway, India opened up much later, in the early 1990s, and then proceeded to do very little for much of the rest of that decade. India can grow strongly, and probably at double-digit growth rates, but it is some way from achieving that at the moment. Its financial markets are already open; its currency floats, and its central bank, the highly credible and independent Reserve Bank of India, sets interest rates and allows the market to operate – a lesson some other emerging economies need to follow. And a final plus is its democracy, although sometimes this can be seen as slowing the pace of change.

India is a complex economy, with a prosperous west and south and a backward hinterland. At the time of India's independence, it was uncertain whether the country could remain as a single entity and it was marked by serious unrest. That is no longer an issue, and just as the political divide was overcome, so too could the huge economic divisions be addressed. To deliver on its growth potential, India needs to overcome its infrastructure, regulation and corruption issues. India has a huge potential domestic market, which is not only likely to foster the growth of many successful domestic firms but is also a huge market for international companies to sell into. Income standards are rising. Its working-age population is expected to rise close to 120 million this decade and by 98 million in the 2020s, a decade during which China's working population is expected to decline by 51 million. So India will have a young and cheap working-age population. Its urban population is expected to rise from 340 million in 2008 to 590 million by 2030, with Mumbai and Delhi then expected to be two of the world's largest cities.

Often overlooked, one of the main economic stories in coming decades is likely to be Africa's growing importance. The trouble with Africa is that most people will not believe change until they see it, but that risks missing what is already happening there. The other challenge is that investors, while right to be positive, might discount too much good news too soon, and it might take far longer for rewards to be realised. Africa has been described, often, as a continent that inspires, surprises and disappoints, all at the same time. It is possible to be both hugely optimistic and equally pessimistic about Africa.

Africa has been characterised by economic underperformance, as it accounts for 20 per cent of the world's land mass, 15 per cent of the population but just 2 per cent of global trade and only 1 per cent of the world economy. Like South Asia, it has a long way to go to catch up. Populous and poor, it is a collection of largely small, fragile economies, a number of which have suffered conflict in recent generations.

Although Africa was less financially integrated than other regions, it was still harmed by the financial crisis, but in a more indirect way, as trade slumped and capital flows dried up, the latter delaying investment inflows into the region.

The future story, though, is how the continent is likely to become globalised at a fast pace. Already it has 650 million mobile-phone users, allowing greater connectivity within countries and across the continent, and keeping it in touch with the rest of the world in a way that it wasn't previously. It is not only becoming more integrated but the more the region does well, the less possible it is for international firms to turn a blind eye to it. While there are many firms that invest in Africa, making high returns, the vast majority cite reasons not to go there, some valid, but many a legacy of the past. It will take time for such perceptions to change, but in the meantime Africa is likely to make steady progress.

'Pan-Africanism' might become a more common future term, capturing the mood of the time. There are already ambitious infrastructure plans in place, particularly aimed at providing much needed access to power across the continent. There is sizeable international investment in solar-energy plants across northern Africa, to provide energy to Europe. There are also plans to create the Trans-African Highway network. Increased intra-African trade will be one future feature. A world green revolution is possible, too, as a result of both higher demand for food and increased investment and technological advance in its production. If so, Africa, along with Latin America, would benefit most. But it requires infrastructure and financial support.

There are a handful of dominant African economies, led by South Africa, Nigeria and Egypt, respectively the 29th, 37th and 40th biggest in the world. The region was often viewed as having to grow around 2.5 per cent per year just to match population growth and so stand still in economic terms. Yet Africa has seen economies enjoy strong growth and, in the first decade of this century, six of the fastest-growing ten economies in the world were there: Angola, Chad, Ethiopia, Mozambique, Nigeria and Rwanda. For a time, 6 per cent was regularly viewed as the growth rate Africa needed in order to make genuine progress. I like the idea of a 7-per-cent club, as economies that grow at this pace each year double in size over a decade. Africa looks set to have a number of such economies: Angola, Botswana, Ethiopia, Ghana, Mozambique, Nigeria, Sierra Leone, Tanzania, Uganda and Zambia.

These join a number of such high-growth economies outside Africa, including some in the —stans and Eastern Europe, including Azerbaijan, Belarus, Kazakhstan and Tajikistan. And in Asia there are Bangladesh, Cambodia, India, Indonesia, Myanmar and Vietnam. Thus we see the strong picture globally. Of course, many of these 7-per-cent economies are relatively small, though growing strongly, so their growth needs to be seen alongside that of the major countries in Europe, China, Japan and the US.

Expect increased investment into the commodity-producing regions of the world, whether it be energy, metals, food or water. Some of the commodity stars will be in South America. The Latin American region can be divided into subgroups. Mexico has continued to do well, despite a big drugs problem, and is increasingly linked with the US, so ought to do well. Brazil, the potential star of the region, needs to address its infrastructure gap, and will over time, but three countries that have played to their strengths as commodity producers are Peru, Chile and Colombia, and they also have the ability to benefit from future growth in the Asia-Pacific region.

The way these South American economies have transformed themselves from past economic problems to solid growth now offers hope for some of the economies that have gone through very painful adjustment in the last few years, particularly on the periphery of Europe, such as Ireland, Portugal or Spain.

Consolations for reform

This leads on to the next issue: embracing reform.

China needs to reform to avoid the middle-income trap. India needs to reform to benefit from its democracy and realise its demographic dividend. Europe needs to reform, or else it will not be able to afford its generous welfare system. The US needs to reform to address inequality and rising obesity. The financial sector needs to be reformed so that it better serves economic needs around the world. Reform is also needed to address and head off energy concerns and inequality. Reform is both about economies realising their upside potential and addressing downside risks.

Many emerging economies need to be like giraffes. Having benefited from picking off the low-hanging fruit, they now need to adapt to pick the fruit that is much higher and potentially more rewarding, which could mean addressing labour productivity in the Gulf, reversing financial repression by paying savings and dividends in China, tax reform and infrastructure spending in Brazil, or resource-rich economies such as Nigeria continuing to move away from being a rentier economy living off its oil to becoming more production based.

India is one place where the upside is huge. It has all the potential to become more successful by moving up the value curve, with a pool of English speakers, good links with the US and Europe, free-trade agreements with other parts of Asia, increasing ties with Africa, a head start in IT and software, good technical education, and enabling legislation that will allow it to make headway in business and professional services. It does have to reform other areas, including health and education, to address widespread poverty, corruption, the role of women in society, as well as excessive regulation and insufficient infrastructure.

Embedding institutions is crucial. Infrastructure plays an important future role, in all its guises: hard, soft and institutional. It is institutional infrastructure that many emerging economies need to develop in coming decades. Refining property rights in the nineteenth century was central to economies such as the US prospering and to capitalism realising its potential. Some factors that are not easy to measure in economic terms, such as intellectual property rights and confidence in contracts and the legal system, are vital. These should become more embedded across a wider array of economies, as a natural consequence of development. It should be a positive both for Western economies such as the UK that can export best practice and for the recipient countries themselves.

One region that needs to reform is the Middle East. It might find it hard to escape the uncertain near-term regional politics, but a reform agenda can help. In the Gulf and the Middle East, the focus should be on the three Ds: Demographics, Diversification and the Dollar.

The Middle East is becoming like Janus, the Roman god with two heads, looking in opposite directions. In the past the Gulf economies looked to the West, their economic cycle heavily influenced by events there. Now the region is increasingly linked with the East as well as the West, and needs to look both ways.

The Arab Spring impacted North Africa but exposed many things, particularly the need to provide jobs. Demographics point to a very young Middle Eastern as well as North African population, and as a result there is a strong need for economies there to diversify. Energy is capital-intensive and by its nature will not create enough jobs for the region's young population. Diversification provides the opportunity. Dubai has diversified, creating a vibrant economy few could have imagined decades ago and one that has rebounded from a significant setback during the financial crisis. Expo 2020 will add to its creative appeal. We are now seeing diversification across the region, but it needs to happen in North Africa too.

The link of Middle Eastern currencies to the dollar might also eventually have to change. Future economic policy might become less linked with the US, both if the Middle East is successful in seeing diversification at home and as exports into Asia and elsewhere increase. The same currency issues will be seen across Asia, and reinforce the likelihood of a stronger future global currency system, with a number of major currencies. This is likely to mirror changing future trade flows, but also will necessitate continued development and deepening of well-regulated capital markets, a trend that is under way but still has a considerable distance to go.

Consolations for Europe

Venice once dominated sea trade. Then, in the space of less than a century, its importance declined dramatically. Venice seemed to have it all, perfectly placed at the head of the Adriatic to connect the two worlds of Europe in the west and the Islamic and Byzantine empires in the east. Its power continued to expand, driven by trade. By the late thirteenth century it was Europe's most prosperous city and in 1482 it was the printing capital of the world. But things changed. Venice did suffer a military defeat, but the significant changes were outside its control, namely Columbus discovering America and Portugal finding new trade routes to India. Venice lost what it thought was its monopoly on trade.

It is often easier to embrace change if it can be anticipated. It doesn't mean the outcome always has to be visible, but at the least some idea about future direction should be present. The world economy, now, is changing. No one wants to be like Venice, overtaken by events.

Can Europe learn from Venice? Europe faces the biggest challenges. As an economic region it is the largest in the world, and a potential source of strength and stability in a multipolar future. But nothing is guaranteed, as Venice showed.

Europe needs more demand now, and it needs more supply-side economic reform to ensure the economy competes.

The European Central Bank has halted Europe's self-feeding downward spiral, but there is a fundamental problem. Within any economy there are local divergences in performance, reflected in differences in living standards and addressed by fiscal transfers and labour mobility. This happens within Europe, but the variations in competitiveness are seen in large regional differences, in living standards and unemployment.

Imagine a runner, who is not really that fit, in a long race. She sprints with all her might to make up lost ground on the leader. But once alongside, she is in for another shock as she realises just how fast the leader is going and that she will have to run at a speed she is not used to just to match the leader and keep up with her from now on. She can't do it on her own. She needs the leader to hold her hand and pull her along. That in a nutshell is Europe.

The periphery is being asked to catch up to the leader – through competitive internal devaluation, squeezing wages. Supply-side changes are being made to help close competitiveness and productivity gaps. They are doing it, and becoming fitter as a result, and this is good news, but for it to be sustainable, they also need a helping hand from the front-runners, led by Germany.

I think it makes far more sense for Europe to go at two speeds, with a fast-speed and a slower-speed group. History shows that currency unions of large sovereign nations have to become political unions in order to survive. In economic terms, for Europe, that means greater future help from the centre to the periphery, and also greater influence over the policies that can be pursued there. Chancellor Merkel has managed to balance these challenging political and economic issues. Europe has already taken tough economic medicine. Stronger global growth should make this painful economic adjustment, which is already under way, all the more worthwhile. Europe needs to continue to restructure and reform, not only to confront its welfare bill, but to make its single market work properly – particularly in services – and also embrace innovation in a way that the US does.

Consolations for the US and the West

Economics is known as the dismal science but when one considers what lies ahead, economics should be able to dispel this image. One way to do this is to address some of the main current concerns occupying people's minds, particularly in the West. A number of fears prevail there about the outlook. Not least is the misplaced worry that Western economies are now locked into a period of weak growth, so-called secular stagnation, with living standards no longer rising. Mirroring this worry is the fear that the current generation will not be as well off as their parents. In America this would be viewed as the end of the American Dream.

Throughout history there must have been countless times when people feared change, the worry being that it would threaten their livelihoods – the classic example being the Luddites, textile workers in the early nineteenth century who opposed industrialisation. Although their sector suffered, the economy overall gained. Economic growth and advance rarely occurs in a straight line, and such advances, whether in agriculture, industry or technology, result in change whereby some groups gain more than others. Despite change – or because of it – the world economy has continued to grow, often with setbacks along the way. Moreover, it has continued to create jobs, and over the last half-century the numbers in manufacturing and services have trebled to around 2.1 billion people.

Central to some of the current pessimism in the West is a combination of concerns about the overhang of debt, inequality and jobs, and worries about future innovation. The challenges that persist in the West are not new, although the scale of them might be greater than before. As with any issues that build up over time, they also need time to be addressed fully. Yet, for each, there is the need for economic growth.

I find it interesting that the general consensus in favour of the good times continuing before the 2008 crisis has been almost completely replaced by a prevailing pessimism, particularly in the West. It is almost as if economics – and the general mood – suffers from a status-quo bias that the prevailing conditions will persist, whether good or bad. And that the current trend – whatever it is – is expected to prevail. But recessions do end, policy usually works, people want to spend, and recoveries tend to happen.

The challenge of the debt overhang remains a Western worry. Economists Reinhart and Rogoff point out that the way out of a debt overhang is no different in the West from in the East, with options including growth, default, restructuring, inflation or austerity, plus some financial repression that hurts savers, either as interest rates are kept low or pension funds are encouraged to buy low-yielding government debt. Growth is the best way, hence the vigorous use of counter-cyclical policies in the West and the reliance on ultra-loose monetary policy. A return to growth would make major inroads into the debt mountain.

Then there is inequality. If one looks at the US, the top one-fifth takes 51 per cent of income, the next fifth 23 per cent, then 14 per cent, 8 per cent and 3 per cent. Given such income disparities the issue is to ensure that those on low incomes can do well, and that there is future opportunity for them, or their children, to succeed. This requires a combination of factors such as: access to good education, minimum wages rising in line with productivity growth, and low taxes.

On the jobs front the biggest challenge is for young people. While this concerns me, I am encouraged at the focus it is now receiving.

The International Labour Organisation report, *Global Employment Trends for Youth*, outlined the challenge but also proposed achievable solutions. The challenge was that youth unemployment was one in eight globally, with large variations, while in Western economies the number of young people not in employment, education or training was one in six. The ILO's fivefold solution comprised: boosting aggregate demand and access to finance; education and training to help the transition from school to work and to address labour-market mismatches; targeting disadvantaged youth; assisting young entrepreneurs; and equal treatment of young people in the labour market. Implementing this would provide a way forward and it is encouraging that workable solutions to even deep-rooted problems have been identified.

But the big fear to overcome is the idea that workers in the West will lose out. Here the vital issue is relative versus absolute change. Imagine if in 1988 everyone in the world was registered on a scale of 0 to 100 with 0 being the poorest person and 100 the richest. A detailed analysis by the World Bank in December 2013 on 'Global Income Distribution' showed that over the twenty years from 1988 until the 2008 crisis, the biggest gainers were those who back in 1988 would have been at 40 on that global income scale and those who gained the least were around 85. The interesting point is that the people who are in the range 81 to 90 were from the advanced economies. They were better off than 81 per cent of the world's population, but when you look at how they compare with others in their own country where they live, such as Australia, Germany and the US, they were in the lower half of the income scale. These low- and middle-income earners in the advanced economies had still gained over this time, but not as much as many in the developing and emerging world. Often we overlook levels in economic comparisons and by global standards, the West is still very rich. In recent years because of the recession these earners in the West have seen their incomes squeezed. What the West needs in order to overcome its fears is to see a sequence of events, beginning with recovery from the recent recession that allows incomes to rise. It then needs to see that the world economy is continuing to grow, because just as a rising tide lifts all ships, rising global growth will benefit all. Then the West needs to position itself to grow. The best way to do this is innovation.

The West remains a key innovator. The Thompson Reuters 2012 Top 100 Global Innovators survey, for instance, included 47 firms from the US, 32 from Asia and the rest from Europe, perhaps unexpectedly dominated by France with its strong position in scientific research. Although there were no Chinese or Indian firms included in this survey they are innovating, as well as buying up technology when possible, and investing.

Encouragingly for the West, it is still well positioned to be both a source of new innovation and to benefit from elsewhere. The economist Robert Gordon fears the US might face too many headwinds that will limit its future innovation, and that the great inventions of the past are unlikely to be repeated. That is possible, but I think it unlikely. Investment, innovation and diffusion of new ideas are essential for future growth. Emerging economies are making strides to boost their universities, invest in their infrastructure and create enabling environments in which general-purpose technologies will be found, as was the case with the computer. This is great. History shows great inventions know no bounds and their success is eventually shared. Whether we are to witness a new breakthrough remains to be seen but there are no reasons why we shouldn't. At the very least we shall have lots of incremental innovations, aiding productivity and efficiency.

I have argued that we could be about to see a fifth industrial revolution.

The speed at which we can travel might not have continued to increase – this is an example sometimes cited that shows innovation is slowing down – but the speed at which an individual can do things has, thanks to the internet and new technology. In fact technology spending in East Asia overtook that in North America in 2013, by $282 billion against $257 billion, and the interesting aspect is not just whether existing technology is sold more widely but also whether things that are technically possible become commercially viable. I have outlined earlier that we could see a new industrial revolution centred on green energy, or even small-scale manufacturing. 3D printing has the ability to revolutionise manufacturing, squeezing supply chains, changing how we meet demand, and keeping costs down for producers and consumers.

There are so many examples of technological advance, such as the combination of advances in data. DNA and stem-cell research is already allowing great advances in an individual's awareness of his or her own likely medical future, and this in turn should create a new market for suppliers. The registration of patents, too, shows few signs of slowing, a sign of ongoing innovation.

What other areas are there where there is already cutting edge, innovative work? In the environmental area there is the use of renewables, green tech and energy storage. In technology there is the use of big data, digital intelligence, cloud technology, presumption which refers to the breaking down of the barriers between consumption and production, and making use of the internet. In health there is biotech and genomics, contributing to rising life expectancy. In industry it is not just 3D but also advanced materials, advanced robotics, self-driven cars and waste management. This impressive list isn't a comprehensive list of existing areas, and think how many new ideas are being worked on in universities across the world as I write?

A vision

We need to understand the world economy, in order to put in context what is happening and embrace the change that has already begun.

The first key driver, outlined in Chapters 1–4, is the changing shape of the world economy, reflected in the shift of economic and financial power from the West to the East. A number of factors are interacting, particularly the rise of China, new technology, demographic trends, urbanisation, the rise of the middle class and new trade corridors. The net effect is stronger global growth, led by a wide range of economies.

There is a need to heed the lessons of the 2008 crisis. A build-up of macroeconomic imbalances must be avoided, with deficit countries saving more, surplus countries spending more and currencies adjusting. The financial sector could have an Apollo 13 moment if it learns the right lessons and the consequences of the four Gs: Glass–Steagall, Greenspan, Governance and Greed.

A second key driver is soft power, discussed in Chapter 5. This is a powerful force and continues to reflect the dominant creative strength of many Western economies. It is also a creative influence on economic development.

Likewise with hard power, the third key driver, addressed in Chapter 6. Although this too is changing, the US dominates as a global power, while China is emerging as a regional power, as too might Japan, and the Indo-Pacific will become an area of great importance. The main result of the US pivot towards Asia might be to help instil free-market trade and thinking across the region. Many smaller European economies, meanwhile, might enjoy a further peace dividend, as defence spending declines.

Who runs the global economy? This was the focus of the fourth key driver, covered in Chapters 7 and 8: the policy and political shift. This is reflected in the changing characteristics of global policy institutions. The G7 has become the G20. The IMF's voting rights are changing. Regional power blocs are emerging. This is still work in progress. In coming years there is the need to see new institutions prove themselves in stable economic conditions, as opposed to during a crisis, and for global institutions to evolve their governance to reflect the new economic order.

What should these global institutions be focusing on? That was the subject of Chapter 8. It identified the consistency of some of the main policy issues over the years, and identified the major ones now: the need for economic balance, to keep inflation in check and to ensure more people have the opportunity to benefit from the proceeds of growth.

Overall, the combination of these four drivers, in economic and financial power, in soft power, in hard power and in political and policy power, points not only to a changing global economy but also to a growing one.

Between 1870 and 1914 annual global growth was 2.8 per cent in real, inflation-adjusted terms. Just growing at this average rate over the next two decades would boost the size of the world economy from around $74 trillion to $129 trillion. At the other extreme, replicating the 5 per cent seen between 1945 and 1973, in the golden age, would allow the world economy to reach $196 trillion. I am not suggesting that 5 per cent is likely, nor 2.8 per cent either. With China's growth rate estimated to slow to 5 per cent over the next twenty years and Europe's growth modest, but stronger than now, I am making a cautious assessment of a global trend rate of 3.5 per cent over the next twenty years, which some might say is not particularly optimistic. It could even reach 4 per cent.

This increase exceeds population growth, including the growing younger populations in South Asia and Africa and rising older populations in North-East Asia and Europe. Living standards will rise.

Over that period, 3.5 per cent annual growth would almost double – in real terms – the size of the global economy to $147 trillion, and average income per head would rise by two-thirds. But if real growth were to reach 4 per cent, helped by technology and creativity and greater awareness of best practice, the global economy would reach $162 trillion, with the average income across the globe up 80 per cent, and while there will be significant relative differences, the point should be that such a rise reflects how the global economic cake will get bigger. There is still significant near-term uncertainty and challenges that should not be dismissed, but at the same time, we should not lose sight of what might lie ahead.

There is a need for a two-handed economic approach to the future. Adam Smith, the founding father of modern economics, highlighted the need for both an invisible and a visible hand. The invisible hand is the importance of the market. The visible hand ensures the right morals and ethics. Get these right and there will be consolations for every economy.

Bibliography

Adams, Timothy D., open letter to Tharman Shanmugaratnam and Marek Belka, 16 April 2013

Adema, Willem, Pauline Fron and Maxime Ladaique, *Is the European Welfare State Really More Expensive?*, OECD Social, Employment and Migration Working Papers No. 124 (Paris, 2011), http://dx.doi.org/10.1787/5kg2d2d4pbf0-en

Bank of England, 'Instruments of Macro Prudential Policy', discussion paper, (London, 2011)

Bank for International Settlements (BIS), *Triennial Central Bank Survey: Foreign Exchange Turnover in April 2013: Preliminary Global Results* (Basle, 2013), http://www.bis.org/publ/rpfx13fx.pdf

— *Derivatives Statistics,* updated 7 November 2013, http://www.bis.org/statistics/derstats.htm

Bean, Charlie, 'Global Aspects of Unconventional Monetary Policies', panel remarks at Jackson Hole, 24 August 2013

Beattie, Alan, *False Economy: A Surprising Economic History of the World* (London, 2009)

Bernanke, Ben, 'The Great Moderation', speech, Eastern Economic Association, Washington, DC, 20 February 2004

Blanchflower, David G., and Andrew J. Oswald, *International Happiness*, NBER Working Paper 16668, National Bureau of Economic Research, January 2011

Booth, Jerome, *Emerging Markets in an Upside Down World* (London, 2014)

Borio, Claudio, and Piti Disyatat, *Global Imbalances and the Financial Crisis: Link or No Link?*, Bank for International Settlements Working Papers No. 346 (Basle, 2011)

Die Bundesregierung, *Shaping Globalization – Expanding Partnerships – Sharing Responsibility: A strategy paper by the German Government* (Berlin, 2012)

Burk, Katheen, and Alec Cairncross, *Goodbye, Great Britain: The 1976 IMF Crisis* (New Haven, CT, and London, 1992)

Byrne, Liam, *Turning to Face the East: How Britain Can Prosper in the Asian Century* (London, 2013)

Carr, Bob, 'Southeast Asia: At the Crossroads of the Asian Century', Fullerton Lecture, 9 July 2013

Crafts, Nicholas, *Britain's Relative Economic Performance 1870–1999* (London, 2002)

Cronin, Patrick M., 'The Strategic Significance of the South China Sea', paper submitted to *Managing Tensions in the South China Sea* conference, 5–6 June 2013

Dchesa, Guillermo de la, *What Do We Know About Globalization?: Issues of Poverty and Income Distribution* (Oxford, 2007)

Deloitte, *London Futures, Globaltown: Winning London's crucial battle for talent* (London, 2013)

Economist Intelligence Unit, 'Best country to be born in 2013 announced', 21 November 2012, http://www.eiumedia.com/index.php/daily-comment/item/851-best-country-to-be-born-in-2013

Elliott, Larry, 'Doha trade talks' killing has no shortage of suspects', *Guardian*, 25 April, 2011, http://www.theguardian.com/business/2011/apr/25/doha-trade-talks-death-suspects?guni=Article:in%20body%20link

Energy Futures Lab and Grantham Institute for Climate Change, *Halving Global CO_2 by 2050: Technologies and Costs* (London, 2013)

Ernst & Young (EY), 'Soft power variables', 2013, http://www.ey.com/GL/en/Issues/Driving-growth/Rapid-growth-markets-soft-power-index-Soft-power-variables

Financial Stability Board, *Strengthening Oversight and Regulation of Shadow Banking*, 29 August 2013

Fouré, Jean, Agnès Bénassy-Quéré, and Lionel Fontagné, *The Great Shift: Macroeconomic Projections for the World Economy at the 2050 Horizon* (Paris, 2006)

George, Eddie, speech, 13 February 2002, http://www.centralbanking.com/central-banking/speech/1431847/speech-eddie-george-bank-england-governor

Global Firepower website, http://www.globalfirepower.com

Gordon, Robert J., *Is U.S. Economic Growth Over? Faltering Innovation*

Confronts the Six Headwinds, National Bureau of Economic Research NBER Working Paper Series 18315, August 2012

Gowing, Nik, 'Skyful of Lies' and Black Swans: The New Tyranny of Shifting Information Power in Crises (Oxford, 2009)

Group of Thirty Working Group on Long-term Finance, Long-term Finance and Economic Growth (Washington, DC, 2013)

Hannah, Leslie, Marshall's 'Trees' and the Global 'Forest': Were 'Giant Redwoods' Different?, Centre for Economic Performance Discussion Paper No. 218 (London, 1997), http://cep.lse.ac.uk/pubs/download/DP0318.pdf

Harris, Jose, 'From sunspots to social welfare: the unemployment problem 1870–1914', in Bernard Corry (ed.), Unemployment and the Economists (Cheltenham, 1996)

HM Government, Attack on Inflation: A Policy for Survival: A Guide to the Government's Programme (London, 1976)

Howell, David, Old Links and New Ties: Power and Persuasion in an Age of Networks (London and New York, 2013)

International Institute for Strategic Studies (IISS), Strategic Survey 2013: The Annual Review of World Affairs (London, 2013)

International Labour Conference, Committee on Youth Unemployment Draft Report, 101st Session, Geneva, May–June 2012

International Labour Organization (ILO), Global Employment Trends 2013: Recovering from a Second Jobs Dip (Geneva, 2013), http://www.ilo.org/global/research/global-reports/global-employment-trends/2013/WCMS_202326/lang—nl/index.htm

— 'Global Employment Trends For Youth 2013', May 2013

— 'World of Work Report 2013: Repairing the economic and social fabric'

International Monetary Fund (IMF), 'The decline of inflation in emerging economies: Can it be maintained?', World Economic Outlook, May 2001 (Washington, DC, 2001)

— Energy Subsidy Reform: Lessons and Implications, January 2013 (Washington, DC, 2013)

— 2013 Spillover Report (Washington, DC, 2013)

— Global Financial Stability Report: Statistical Appendix, October 2013 (Washington, DC, 2013)

— Global Financial Stability Report: Transition Challenges to Stability, October 2013 (Washington, DC, 2013)

— *World Economic Outlook: Transitions and Tensions* (Washington, DC, 2013)

— *World Economic Outlook: Legacies, Clouds, Uncertainties*, October 2014 (Washington, DC, 2014)

International Working Group of Sovereign Wealth Funds, *Sovereign Wealth Funds: Generally Accepted Principles and Practices: 'Santiago Principles'* (Washington, DC, 2008)

Keegan, William, *The Spectre of Capitalism* (London, 1992)

Kelly, Tom, 'Britain ousts the U.S. as world's most influential nation: Country tops rankings for "soft power"', *Mail* Online, 18 November 2012, http://www.dailymail.co.uk/news/article-2234726/Britain-tops-global-soft-power-list.html

Kimmitt, Robert, 'Public Footprints in Private Markets', *Foreign Affairs* (January/February 2008), http://www.foreignaffairs.com/articlesm-kimmitt/public-footprints-in-private-markets

King, Stephen D., *When the Money Runs Out: The End of Western Affluence* (New Haven, CT, and London, 2013)

Kuishuang Feng, Steven Davis, Laixiang Sun, Xin Li, Dabo Guan, Weidong Liu, Zhu Liu and Klaus Hubacek, 'Outsourcing CO_2 within China', *PNAS* 110:28 (9 July 2013), http://www.pnas.org/content/110/28/11654

Kuznets, Simon, 'Modern Economic Growth: Findings and Reflections', Nobel Prize Lecture 1971, 11 December 1971, http://www.nobelprize.org/nobel_prizes/economic-sciences/laureates/1971/kuznets-lecture.html

Lagarde, Christine, 'Stability and Growth for Poverty Reduction', speech to Bretton Woods Committee annual meeting, 15 May 2013, Washington, DC

Lechmanova, Natalia, 'China's strategy in the Indian Ocean', LSE dissertation, 3 September 2012, citing data from SIPRI Military Expenditure Database. Stockholm International Peace Research Institute, 2012, http://milexdata.sipri.org/files/?file=SIPRI+milex+data+1988-2011.xls

Li Lanqing, *Breaking Through: The Birth of China's Opening-Up Policy* (Beijing, 2009)

Llewellyn, John, *The Business of Ageing* (London, 2008)

Lyons, Gerard, 'External deficit overshadows Budget surplus', *The Times*, 21 March 1988

— 'The outlook hinges on domestic credit control', *The Times*, 27 June 1988
— 'Devaluation on the agenda whoever wins', *The Times*, 10 February 1992
— 'UK: Manufacturing matters', *Anglo-Japanese Journal* 6(1) (May–August 1992): 3–6
— 'Why rescues are wrong', *Central Banking* 9:2 (November 1998)
— 'Banking the Unbanked', submission of the Commonwealth Business Council to the Commonwealth Finance Ministers meeting, Commonwealth Secretariat, FMM (05) (INF) 7, 18–20 September 2005
— submission made on behalf of the Hong Kong Association to the Foreign Affairs Committee on 'The emergence of the People's Republic of China as a regional power and its impact on the international system', 27 February 2006
— 'State Capitalism: The Rise of Sovereign Wealth Funds', *Financial Times*, 13 November 2007
— 'Testimony before the Committee on Foreign Affairs, US House of Representatives, regarding The Rise of Sovereign Wealth Funds: Impact on US Foreign Policy and Economic Interests', 21 May 2008
— 'The Future of Banking', speech and paper to the Annual China Bankers Forum, Shanghai, 5 September 2009
— 'The global economic outlook', speech, Cambridge Society for the Application of Research, February 2013
McKinsey Global Institute, *Urban World: Cities and the Rise of the Consuming Class* (London, 2012)
— *Financial globalization: Retreat or reset?*, *Global capital markets 2013*, March 2013 (London, 2013)
Marcheggiano, Gilberto, and David Miles, *Fiscal Multipliers and Time Preference*, Bank of England, External MPC Unit, Discussion Paper 39, London, January 2013
Marsh, Peter, *The New Industrial Revolution* (New Haven, CT, 2012)
Mitchener, Kris James, and Marc D. Weidenmier, 'The Baring Crisis and the Great Latin American Meltdown of the 1890s', *Oxford Economic Papers* 8:2, 128–50
Monocle, 'Soft power survey', *Monocle* 6:59 (December/January 2013), see http://wwwpdic.blogspot.co.uk/2012/12/monocles-soft-power-survey-2012.html
National Institute for Health and Welfare and North Karelia Project

Foundation, *The North Karelia Project: From North Karelia to National Action* (Helsinki, 2009)

Nelson, Edward, 'The Great Inflation of the Seventies: What Really Happened?', Federal Reserve Bank of St Louis Working Paper No. 2004-001A (St Louis, MO, 2004), http://papers.ssrn.com/sol3/papers.cfm?abstract_id=762602

Nelson, John, speech, Lloyd's City Dinner, 4 September 2013, http://www.lloyds.com/lloyds/press-centre/speeches/2013/09/john-nelsons-speech-at-the-lloyds-city-dinner-2013

Nye, Joseph S., Jr, *Soft Power: The Means to Success in World Politics* (New York, 2004)

—testimony to House of Lords Select Committee on Soft Power and the UK's Influence, evidence session 10, 15 October 2013

Obstfeld, Maurice, and Kenneth Rogoff, 'Perspectives on OECD Economic Integration: Implications for U.S. Current Account Adjustment', in Federal Reserve Bank of Kansas City, *Economic Symposium Conference Proceedings 2000* (Kansas City, MO, 2000)

Okonjo-Iweak, Ngozi, 'The 2013 Oppenheimer Lecture: Securing Development: Challenges of Economic Inclusion', International Institute for Strategic Studies, London, 19 June 2013

O'Neill, Jim, *The Growth Map: Economic Opportunity in the BRICs and Beyond* (London, 2011)

Organisation for Economic Co-Operation and Development (OECD), *The Chilean Pension System*, Ageing Working Papers, AWP 5.6 (Paris, 1998), http://www.oecd.org/pensions/public-pensions/2429310.pdf

— *The OECD at 50: Better Policies for Better Lives* (Paris, 2011)

— 'Social spending after the crisis' (Paris, 2012), http://www.npdata.be/BuG/175-Antwerpen-Districten/OECD-2012-Social-spending-after-the-crisis.pdf

Ormerod, Paul, *Positive Linking: How Networks Can Revolutionise the World* (London, 2012)

Owen, Roger, *The Eastern Mediterranean during the First Wave of Globalisation, 1870–1914* (Florence, 2001)

Peden, George, 'The Treasury view in the interwar period: an example of political economy', in Bernard Corry (ed.), *Unemployment and the Economists* (Cheltenham, 1996)

Perlo-Freeman, Sam, Elisabeth Sköns, Carina Solmirano and Helén

Wilandh, 'Trends in World Military Expenditure, 2012', SIPRI Fact Sheet, April 2013

'Population pyramids of the world', http://populationpyramid.net

Reading, Brian, *Japan: The Coming Collapse* (London, 1992)

Reinhart, Carmen, and Kenneth Rogoff, 'Financial and Sovereign Debt Crises: Some Lessons Learned and Those Forgotten', IMF Working Paper WP/13/266, December 2013

Rodríguez, L. Jacobo, 'Economist Estelle James Examines Chile's Pension System', Cato Institute, 25 February 2005, http://www.cato.org/publications/commentary/economist-estelle-james-examines-chiles-pension-system-1

Sachs, Jeffrey, 'JFK and the Future of Global Leadership', speech at Chatham House, 16 July 2013

Sanders, Chris, and Elizabeth Savage, *Blue Planet, Blue Crisis: Water in the Age of Limits*, Sanders Research Associates Limited (Dublin, 2008)

Shambaugh, David L., *Modernizing China's Military: Progress, Problems, and Prospects* (California, 2002)

Sharma, Ruchir, *Breakout Nations: In Pursuit of the Next Economic Miracles* (London, 2012)

Shell, *New Lens Scenarios* (London, 2013)

Smith, Adam, *An Inquiry into the Nature and Causes of the Wealth of Nations* [1776] (Chicago, 1976)

Standard Chartered, *The Super-Cycle Report* (London, 2010)

Steil, Been, *The Battle of Bretton Woods* (Princeton, NJ, and Oxford, 2013)

Stern, Nick, *Stern Review on the Economics of Climate Change* (London, 2006)

— 'The Low Carbon Industrial Revolution', speech, London School of Economics, 17 March 2011

Stiglitz, Joseph E., *The Price of Inequality* (London, 2012)

Stockholm International Peace Research Institute, *SIPRI Yearbook 2013* (Stockholm, 2013)

Superintendence of Pensions, *The Chilean Pension System* (Santiago, 2010), http://www.safp.cl/portal/informes/581/articles-8557_recurso_1.pdf

TaxPayers' Alliance, *The Single Income Tax Final Report of the 2020 Tax Commission* (London, 2012), http://www.2020tax.org/2020tc.pdf

Tierney, William G., and Christopher C. Findlay, 'The Globalisation of Education: The Next Wave' (Singapore, 2009), https://www.pecc.

org/resources/doc_download/646-the-globalisation-of-education-the-next-wave

Times Higher Education, '*Times Higher Education* World University Rankings 2013–14', http://www.timeshighereducation.co.uk/world-university-rankings/2013-14/world-ranking

Transparency International, 'Corruption Perceptions Index 2012', http://transparency.org/cpi2012/results

Turner, Adair, Lord, panel discussion, 'How to tame global finance', *Prospect Magazine*, 27 August 2009, http://www.prospectmagazine.co.uk/magazine/how-to-tame-global-finance/#.Uu7E6rlgGK0

United Nations, United Nations Convention on the Law of the Sea, http://www.un.org/depts/los/convention_agreements/texts/unclos/unclos_e.pdf

— 'World Population Prospects, The 2012 Revision' (Washington, 2013), http://esa.un.org/unpd/wpp/Documentation/pdf/WPP2012_Press_Release.pdf

US Bureau of Labor Statistics, *International Comparisons of Hourly Compensation Costs in Manufacturing Industries, 2012* (Washington, DC, 2013)

US–China Economic and Security Review Commission, annual report to Congress, 21 November 2013

Wen Jiabao, speech to China–Britain Business Council dinner, Natural History Museum, London, 1 February 2009

— speech at the University of Cambridge, 2 February 2009, http://news.xinhuanet.com/english/2009-02/03/content_10753336.htm

White, William R., 'Ultra Easy Monetary Policy and the Law of Unintended Consequences', Federal Reserve Bank of Dallas, Globalization and Monetary Policy Institute Working Paper No. 126 (Dallas, TX, 2012)

World Bank, *The East Asian Miracle: Economic Growth and Public Policy* (Washington, DC, 1993)

— *Migration and Remittances Factbook 2011* (Washington, DC, 2011)

— *Economic Mobility and the Rise of the Latin American Middle Class* (Washington, DC, 2012)

— 'Migration and Development Brief 21', 2 October 2013 (Washington, DC, 2013)

World Bank and Development Research Center of the State Council,

People's Republic of China, *China 2030: Building a Modern, Harmonious and Creative Society* (Washington, DC, 2013)

World Bank, Development Research Group, *Global Income Distribution, From the Fall of the Berlin Wall to the Great Recession*, Policy Research Working Paper 6719, December 2013

World Economic Forum, 'The Rio + 20 Multistakeholder Dialogues: First Reactions from World Economic Forum Global Agenda Council Experts', http://www3.weforum.org/docs/WEF_GAC_Rio20_Recommendations_2012.pdf

— *The Global Competitiveness Report 2013–2014* (Geneva, 2013)

— *Global Risk Report 2013* (Geneva, 2013)

— *Global Risk Report 2014* (Geneva, 2014)

World Intellectual Property Organization, 'Brands – Reputation and Image in the Global Marketplace', WIPO Economics & Statistics Series 2013

World Trade Organization, *International Trade Statistics 2013* (Geneva, 2013)

World Trade Organization, *World Trade Report 2013: Factors shaping the future of world trade* (Geneva, 2013)

Zheng Bijian, 'Ten Views on China's Development Road of Peaceful Rise and Sino European Relations', talk at Foreign Policy Centre, London, 15 December 2005

Zhou Xiaochuan, 'Reform the international monetary system', 23 March 2009, http://www.bis.org/review/r090402c.pdf?frames=0

— 'Changing Pro-cyclicality for Financial and Economic Stability', 26 March 2009, http://www.pbc.gov.cn/publish/english/956/2009/20091229122558020522467/20091229122558020522467_.html

Acknowledgements

There are a number of people I would like to thank.

First, there is the team at Faber & Faber, who have been supportive and responsive throughout the process. In particular, to Julian Loose, with whom I had a number of conversations about the book, before we put pen to paper and signed the contract in spring 2013. Julian also came up with the title. Thanks to Kate Murray-Browne, who has overseen editing and the progress of the book. Thanks, too, to Jill Burrows and Merlin Cox for their help on editing, to Anna Pallai for handling the publicity, and to Lisa Baker and Lizzie Bishop in the rights department.

Many thanks to Professor Paul Ormerod, with whom I had the original discussion about the book over lunch. Paul has been among a number of economists who influenced my thinking, during my days as a university student at Liverpool, Warwick and London, along with Professor Patrick Minford, then at Liverpool; Marcus Miller, at Warwick; Maurice Peston, at Queen Mary; and David Currie, who along with Paul supervised my PhD on, 'Testing the efficiency of financial futures markets'.

A number of people provided comments on different chapters of the book, including Chris and Elizabeth Sanders of Sanders Research, Nicholas Garrott who has worked alongside me at City Hall over the last year, Professor Bob Rowthorn at Cambridge University, Natalia Lechmanova who is now at Goldmans, Jinny Yan, Marios Maratheftis and David Mann, who used to be part of my research team at Standard Chartered, businessman and friend from Liverpool Andy Potter and two non-economists, Arthur King and Elf Lyons.

Thanks to the eight people who kindly provided comments and quotes on the book: Sir Howard Davies, Sir Richard Lambert, Professor Lord Maurice Peston, Dr Jim O'Neill, Lord Adair Turner, Professor Lord Nick Stern, Tim Adams, and Boris Johnson, who has been very supportive throughout the writing of this book.

There were three successful book-launch events to mark the publication of the hardback version in June 2014 and I wish to thank all those involved in ensuring these were a great success. First, to Constantin Cotzias and to Bloomberg who generously hosted a launch party at their London headquarters, and thanks to Lord Karan Bilimoria for providing Cobra beer, to Boris Johnson for speaking and comedian Elf Lyons for performing at that event. Second, thanks to Malcolm Sweeting and to Clifford Chance for hosting a talk and launch at their Canary Wharf headquarters. Third, to Jenny Nicholson, Tim Knox and to the Centre for Policy Studies for hosting a launch at their Westminster office. Thanks to all those who came to these well-attended events, and to the other groups that have asked me to speak about the book.

Thanks to my family, who were fantastic throughout the process, offering support and advice, and who were very relieved when it was finished, and to whom I have dedicated this book: my three children Emily-Anne (Elf), Marie-Louise Kezia (Lulu) and Gerard Benedict and, most importantly of all, my wife Annette.

Please enjoy reading the book. If you want to have a dialogue about any aspects of it my Twitter account is @DrGerardLyons.

Index

Index